Contemporary Security Issues in Africa

Contemporary Security Issues in Africa

WILLIAM A. TAYLOR

Praeger Security International

BLOOMSBURY ACADEMIC
NEW YORK · LONDON · OXFORD · NEW DELHI · SYDNEY

BLOOMSBURY ACADEMIC
Bloomsbury Publishing Inc
1385 Broadway, New York, NY 10018, USA
50 Bedford Square, London, WC1B 3DP, UK
29 Earlsfort Terrace, Dublin 2, Ireland

BLOOMSBURY, BLOOMSBURY ACADEMIC and the Diana logo
are trademarks of Bloomsbury Publishing Plc

First published in the United States of America by ABC-CLIO 2019
Paperback edition published by Bloomsbury Academic 2024

Library of Congress Cataloging-in-Publication Data
Names: Taylor, William A., 1975– author.
Title: Contemporary security issues in Africa / William A. Taylor.
Description: Santa Barbara, California : Praeger, an Imprint of ABC-CLIO, LLC, [2019] |
Series: Praeger security international |
Includes bibliographical references and index.
Identifiers: LCCN 2018035272 (print) | LCCN 2018048065 (ebook) |
ISBN 9781440851919 (ebook) | ISBN 9781440851902 (print)
Subjects: LCSH: Security, International—Africa.
Classification: LCC JZ6009.A35 (ebook) | LCC JZ6009.A35 T39 2019 (print) |
DDC 355/.03306—dc23
LC record available at https://lccn.loc.gov/2018035272

ISBN: HB: 978-1-4408-5190-2
PB: 979-8-7651-2627-1
ePDF: 978-1-4408-5191-9
eBook: 979-8-2160-6575-3

Series: Praeger Security International

To find out more about our authors and books visit www.bloomsbury.com
and sign up for our newsletters.

To my sister and her family
Alison, Bryan, and Sophia

Contents

Acknowledgments

Writing a book is always a journey, along which an author accumulates numerous debts to colleagues, friends, and family. I wish to acknowledge some of those many dues here. The entire team at ABC-CLIO and Praeger provided remarkable support. Our collaboration began in 2010 when they awarded me an ABC-CLIO/Society for Military History research grant for *Every Citizen a Soldier*, which was my first national research grant of 14 that I have received to date. The funding afforded financial backing and furnished sustaining encouragement at an early and formative juncture of my academic career. Padraic (Pat) Carlin skillfully administered the grant and became a gracious advocate and dear friend. He and Steve Catalano, my initial editor at Praeger, originally suggested this work; Pat and Steve were tireless champions of my research and writing, providing inspiration, aid, and assistance throughout the whole process. I feel fortunate to count them both as colleagues. Anthony Chiffolo and Kevin J. Downing approved the project, and Elana Palace provided skillful editorial suggestions.

At Angelo State University, President Brian J. May joined Donald R. Topliff, provost and vice president for academic affairs; Susan E. Keith, dean of the College of Graduate Studies and Research; Carolyn Gascoigne, dean of the College of Arts and Humanities; and Tony R. Mullis, chair of the Department of Security Studies and Criminal Justice, in leading our university through significant growth toward great heights. They have always ensured that the university is, and remains, a great place to work. Angelo State University awarded me a Faculty Research Enhancement Program grant that contributed to this volume and funded research at various archives and libraries. Katie Plum, director of the Office of Sponsored Projects, offered numerous proposals and lucid advice about this endeavor specifically and research grants generally; she is a great asset to the university. At Porter Henderson Library, Maurice G. Fortin, executive director, and Mark A. Allan, assistant director for research and instruction services, delivered extensive library resources, including access to a plethora of international newspapers and rare books commandeered through interlibrary loan. Thomas G. Nurre Jr. widely marketed my accomplishments, and Purnell J. Curtis presented exceptional technology support, including assistance with maps and photos. Colleagues Bruce E. Bechtol Jr. and Anthony N. Celso have bolstered my understanding of contemporary security issues; I am most grateful for their cogent insights. Gregory Fremont-Barnes, Saheed Aderinto, Scott N. Romaniuk, Lawrence J. Korb, Robert Nalbandov, and Nathaniel Cogley reviewed my manuscript, and I am most humbled and honored to have their extremely positive endorsements. My student research assistant for this project, Joseph B. Plachno, inspired me through his continual pursuit of knowledge. He, along with my many other undergraduate and graduate students, constantly reminded me of the vital connection between teaching, research, and service.

My family has always provided a solid foundation upon which to build my work. My parents, Richard A. Taylor and L. Diane Taylor, instilled and modeled lifelong learning that stays with me today. My wife, Renee M. Taylor, has been my steadfast companion and soul mate. She, along with our two amazing kids, Madison G. Taylor and Benjamin A. Taylor, bestowed love that sustained me throughout my extensive research and frequent trips. My sister and her family, Alison, Bryan, and Sophia, to whom I have dedicated this book, furthered my interest in and understanding of Africa. Their work and travels on the continent inspired me to learn on my own and pursue my personal journeys.

Even in the midst of such widespread support, I alone am responsible for any errors that remain.

Abbreviations

AFRICOM	Africa Command
AGOA	African Growth and Opportunity Act
AIAI	Al-Itihaad al-Islamiya
AMISOM	African Union Mission in Somalia
APSA	African Peace and Security Architecture
AQIM	Al-Qaeda in the Islamic Maghreb
ASM	Artisanal and Small-Scale Mining
AU	African Union
BRICS	Brazil, Russia, India, China, and South Africa
CAADP	Comprehensive Africa Agriculture Development Programme
CAR	Central African Republic
CBNRM	Community-Based Natural Resources Management
CHRAJ	Commission for Human Rights and Administrative Justice
CPF	Country Programming Framework
DDR	Disarmament, Demobilization, and Reintegration
DRC	Democratic Republic of the Congo
EARF	East African Response Force
ECCAS	Economic Community of Central African States
ECOWAS	Economic Community of West African States
EEZ	Exclusive Economic Zone

EITI	Extractive Industries Transparency Initiative
EU	European Union
FDLR	Forces Démocratiques de Libération du Rwanda
FGS	Federal Government of Somalia
FOCAC	Forum on China-Africa Cooperation
FPRC	Front Populaire pour la Renaissance de la Centrafrique
GDP	Gross Domestic Product
GSPC	Salafist Group for Preaching and Combat
ICC	International Criminal Court
ICRC	International Committee of the Red Cross
ICTR	International Criminal Tribunal for Rwanda
IDP	Internally Displaced Person
IGAD	Intergovernmental Authority on Development
IMB	International Maritime Bureau
IMF	International Monetary Fund
IMO	International Maritime Organization
IRTC	International Recommended Transit Corridor
ISIL	Islamic State of Iraq and the Levant
ISIS	Islamic State of Iraq and Syria
ISWAP	Islamic State's West Africa Province
JTF	Joint Task Force
KDF	Kenya Defense Forces
KPCS	Kimberly Process Certification Scheme
LRA	Lord's Resistance Army
MDG	Millennium Development Goal
MEND	Movement for the Emancipation of the Niger Delta
MIA	Movement for the Islamic Azawad
MICOPAX	Mission de Consolidation de la Paix en Centrafrique
MINT	Mexico, Indonesia, Nigeria, and Turkey
MISMA	Mission Internationale de Soutien au Mali
MNLA	National Movement for the Liberation of Azawad
MONUSCO	Mission de l'Organization des Nations Unies en République Démocratique du Congo (UN Stabilization Mission in the DRC)
MPLA	Popular Movement for the Liberation of Angola
MUJWA	Jama'at Tawhid Wal Jihad fi Garbi Afriqqiya (Movement for Unity and Jihad in West Africa)

NATO   North Atlantic Treaty Organization
NGO   Nongovernmental Organization
NIMASA   Nigerian Maritime Administration and Safety Agency
NMTPF   National Medium-Term Priority Framework
NPF   Nigeria Police Force
NTC   National Transitional Council
OECD   Organisation for Economic Co-Operation and Development
PIF   Policy and Investment Framework
PLAN   People's Liberation Army Navy
PMSC   Private Military and Security Contractor
REC   Regional Economic Community
RMAC   Regional Maritime Awareness Capability
SEC   Securities and Exchange Commission
SEZ   Special Economic Zone
SGI   Security Governance Initiative
SGR   Standard Gauge Railway
SHADE   Shared Awareness and Deconfliction
SLOC   Sea Line of Communication
SNSF   Somali National Security Forces
SPLA   Sudan People's Liberation Army
SPLM   Sudan People's Liberation Movement
SSA   Sub-Saharan Africa
TFG   Transitional Federal Government
TGONU   Transitional Government of National Unity
UIC   Union of Islamic Courts
UN   United Nations
UNAMID   United Nations–African Union Mission in Darfur
UNCLOS   United Nations Convention on the Law of the Sea
UNITA   National Union for the Total Independence of Angola
USAID   U.S. Agency for International Development
VEO   Violent Extremist Organization
WB   World Bank
WFP   World Food Program
WFS   World Food Summit

CHAPTER 1

Contemporary Security Issues in Africa

It was an emotional ending to a heart-wrenching story. Aisha, abducted as a young woman by the Nigerian militant group Boko Haram, reunited with her parents on January 30, 2018, in Borno State, Nigeria, after six long years as a captive of the merciless rebels. One witness observed, "Onlookers at the camp could not help but to join the father and daughter to shed some more tears of joy." Twenty-seven years old and the mother of six children, Aisha would have a long road of recovery ahead, but at least now she was safe and reconciled with her family. Her ordeal was not isolated: Aisha was only one of 50 such young women unified with their loved ones on that exuberant day. Unfortunately, many others had never returned. At the time of Aisha's poignant reunion, 1,384 agonizing days had passed since Boko Haram had abducted the Chibok schoolgirls. For the tormented families of those kidnapped girls, reunification still awaited.[1]

No event epitomized the dangers of the Boko Haram insurgency more than the violent extremist organization's abduction of 276 schoolgirls from the Government Secondary School in Chibok, Borno State, Nigeria, on the nights of April 14 and 15, 2014. The brazen and heinous act sent shock waves throughout Nigeria and garnered attention around the world. Frustration with the government's inability to rescue the schoolgirls seethed into anger and reinforced perceptions of Nigeria's impotence to quell the raging rebellion. Many critics lambasted federal officials at Abuja, arguing that Boko Haram operated with impunity throughout much of northern Nigeria. Blame mounted. The Northern Elders' Forum, a group of powerful ruling chiefs in that region, demanded that Goodluck Jonathan,

Nigeria's president, and his administration either secure the release of the Chibok schoolgirls by October 2014 and defeat the Boko Haram insurgency quickly thereafter or the influential elders would withdraw their support from Jonathan in the 2015 presidential election.[2] Jonathan failed to deliver on his promises to answer their ultimatum and suffered from the loss of their patronage.

The Boko Haram insurgency in general and the abduction of the Chibok schoolgirls specifically were decisive factors in Jonathan's unprecedented setback in the presidential elections on March 28, 2015, the first-ever such defeat of a sitting president in the nation's history.[3] In the aftermath, Boko Haram conducted atrocities and wreaked havoc throughout northern Nigeria. From June to August 2015, the terrorist group killed nearly 1,000 civilians and wounded another 500 victims, rampaging through many villages and devastating large swaths of six states.[4] In response, the federal government launched frequent military offensives against the insurgents with varying levels of success. Boko Haram still has threatened Nigeria, especially in Borno and Yobe states. Nigeria's efforts against the violent extremist group have achieved some victories in the Lake Chad and Sambisa forest areas, but fighters simply have moved their base of operations to new areas as a result. A recent influx of Boko Haram renegades has left many local villages looking like "a ghost town," inhabited only by "the boys," as local residents colloquially have referred to Boko Haram militants. Yusuf Usama, a village tenant, remarked that numerous hamlets "are still deserted for fear of Boko Haram attack," including Jiri, Gudu, Munjim Gana, Munjim Kura, and Kilbiri.[5] Boko Haram's insurgency against Nigeria, including its odious modus operandi of kidnapping young girls that it demonstrated most tragically at Chibok, has been one of many contemporary security issues in Africa where culture, politics, and security have intersected to have profound impacts on the continent. The scale of Boko Haram's brutality in Nigeria has been massive. Mansur Dan-Ali, Nigeria's minister of defense, estimated that Operation Lafiya Dole (Peace by Force) in Sambisa Forest has saved more than 30,000 women and children from the group's clutches over the past two years.[6] Even so, Boko Haram's capabilities have endured largely intact. On February 19, 2018, a brazen raid by the group on the Government Science and Technical College in Dapchi, Yobe State, in northeastern Nigeria, kidnapped another 110 girls in the largest single attack by Boko Haram since Chibok.[7] On May 7, 2018, soldiers of Nigeria's 22 Brigade, a part of the Multinational Joint Task Force (MNJTF), rescued nearly 1,000 hostages, mostly women and children, from Boko Haram in Borno State.[8] As a result, this contemporary security issue and the many others presented in this book have become more important and relevant than ever.

Before analyzing the various contemporary security issues in Africa today, one must begin by understanding the general context for security in Africa, which is the second-largest and second-most populous continent in the world.[9] Covering in excess of 30 million square kilometers, Africa is home to 54 recognized nations and more than 1.2 billion people. Geographically, there are five major regions on the continent, including northern, western, central, eastern, and southern Africa. This volume focuses on sub-Saharan Africa and therefore concentrates on the last four

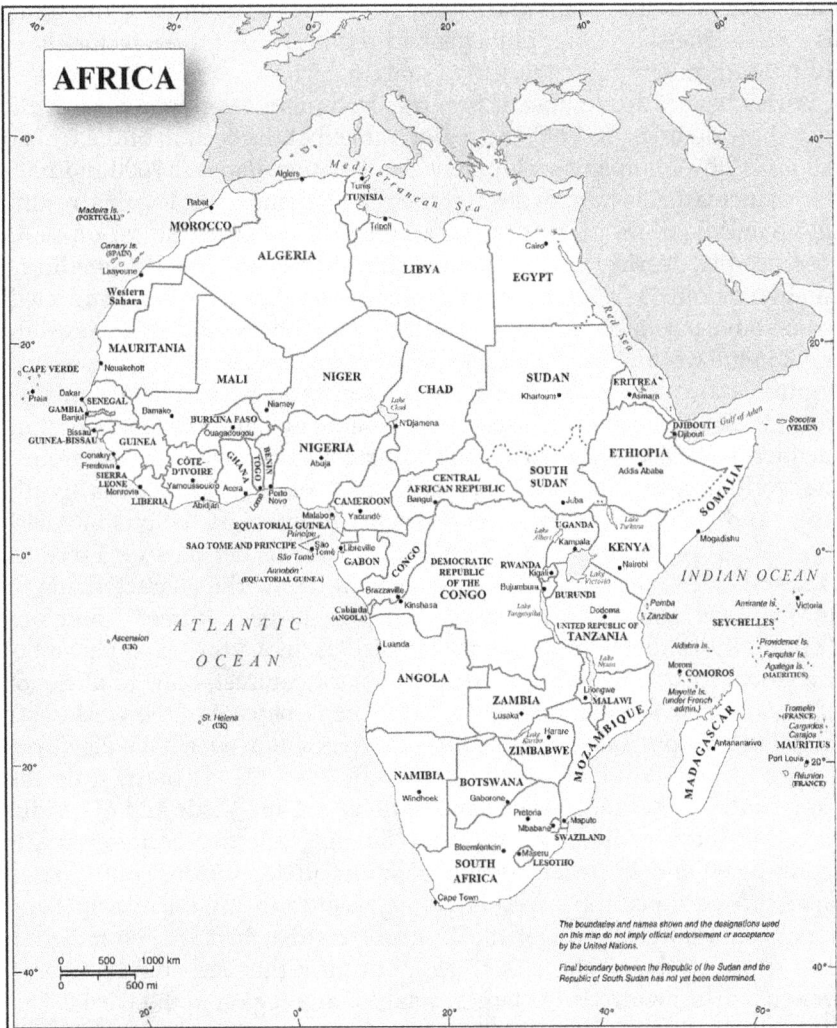

Africa, Map No. 4045 Rev. 7, November 2011. Used by permission of the United Nations Publication Board

areas. In addition, Africa has a cultural diversity that is unmatched anywhere in the world; there are approximately 3,315 ethnic groups in Africa and more than 2,000 different languages spoken throughout the continent. Africa also has a historical legacy of colonialism.[10] More recently, Africa has emerged as an epicenter of rising economic and political power. As a result, it has demonstrated its strategic importance for international actors, including the United States and China, among others. In addition, Africa has the most biodiversity in the world. O. P. Godwin noted, "Africa contains about one-fifth of all known species of plants, mammals, and birds, as well as one-sixth of amphibians and reptiles."[11] All these factors have influenced contemporary security issues in Africa.

Africa has made significant progress in human development over the past three decades. In 1990, the region ranked at the bottom of the United Nation's "low" human development classification. Between 2000 and 2005, Africa increased its human development with demonstrable gains, resting in the middle of the "low" category. From 2005 to 2015, the region again rose steadily, nearing the threshold to transition from "low" to "medium" categorization.[12] While the region has made significant strides, many challenges have persisted. Of the 20 countries with the lowest human development in the world, 19 have been in Africa.[13] As a result of many repressive regimes, Africa has suffered from a palpable and pervasive lack of freedom. In 2018, Freedom House, an independent nongovernmental organization (NGO) committed to political rights and civil liberties around the world, ranked 22 countries in Africa as "not free," 22 more as "partly free," and only 10 as "free." As a result, 44 out of 54 nations in Africa have displayed a dearth of liberty. To put this in perspective, Freedom House in 2018 ranked 195 countries around the world, characterizing 88 as "free," 58 more as "partly free," and only 49 as "not free." Therefore, 22 of the 49 nations worldwide that ranked as "not free," or 45 percent of the global total, have been in Africa. In stark contrast, only 10 of the 88 nations worldwide that ranked as "free," or 11 percent of the worldwide sum, have resided in Africa. Countries in Africa, however, have displayed a wide variation of scores, with many at the lowest levels of the scale and some at the highest end. The island nations of Cape Verde and Mauritius scored at the very high end on the 100-point scale, receiving aggregate scores of 90 and 89, respectively. In glaring juxtaposition, South Sudan and Eritrea scraped the lowest boundary, registering marks of only 2 and 3, correspondingly.[14] Out of the 12 countries that had the worst aggregate scores in the world in 2018 for political rights and civil liberties, 7 were in Africa, which is the largest total for any region in the world. This trend was not just evident in 2018. Over the past decade, many nations in Africa have experienced a significant decrease in their scores, including the Central African Republic (−31), Mali (−28), Burundi (−27), Mauritania (−22), Ethiopia (−21), Gabon (−14), Congo (Brazzaville) (−11), Niger

(–11), Rwanda (–11), Eritrea (–10), Guinea-Bissau (–10), and Kenya (–10). Of the 29 countries with the largest 10-year declines in aggregate tallies, 12 were in Africa. There were exceptions to this general trend, however, as the Gambia evidenced noteworthy improvement, increasing its score by 21 points and transitioning from "not free" to "partly free."[15]

In addition to difficulties related to human development and freedom, security has remained a central predicament for Africa. In fact, improvements in politics, economics, development, stability, and human rights, among others, all are spokes that have revolved around, and fundamentally have required, security. In this regard, Africa has been woefully lacking. Paul D. Williams noticed, "By many indicators, the world judges Africa to be its most insecure region."[16] There have been numerous reasons for this perception. Throughout the 1990s, conflict roiled much of the continent. Violent and prolonged struggles erupted in Burundi, Côte d'Ivoire, Ethiopia, Eritrea, Guinea, Liberia, Rwanda, Sierra Leone, Somalia, Sudan, Uganda, and Zaire/Democratic Republic of the Congo, among others. The Uppsala Conflict Data Program (UCDP) has maintained extensive records on organized violence and civil war, including the number of conflicts around the globe for the past 40 years broken into three categories: state-based aggression, nonstate carnage, and one-sided violence. Several trends have been striking. In 1990, 49 conflicts of state-based aggression, 19 conflicts of nonstate carnage, and 37 conflicts of one-sided violence occurred worldwide, illustrating the prevalence of state-based aggression at that time. In 2000, 39 conflicts of state-based aggression, 46 conflicts of nonstate carnage, and 36 conflicts of one-sided violence transpired, highlighting that nonstate carnage had surged in frequency and prevalence. In 2010, 31 conflicts of state-based aggression, 28 conflicts of nonstate carnage, and 21 conflicts of one-sided violence happened, reaching relative parity between the sources of violence. In 2015, 52 conflicts of state-based aggression, 73 conflicts of nonstate carnage, and 28 conflicts of one-sided violence arose, marking a significant increase across all sources of fighting and achieving a peak for nonstate carnage.[17]

Since 1990, many of these struggles have taken place in Africa. From 1990 to 2010, the region was second only to Asia in the prevalence of violence. In 2016, however, more of these struggles occurred in Africa than in any other region of the world. As a result, Africa has been one of the most conflict-prone regions in the world since 1990, and violence in Africa has risen ominously since 2010, both in terms of the number of conflicts and regarding the continent's share of the global total.[18] Therefore, contemporary security issues in Africa have become especially germane.

There have been numerous efforts to improve security on the continent. On July 9, 2002, the African Union (AU) crafted a protocol calling for the creation of a Peace and Security Council. On December 26, 2003, the AU placed the protocol into force, and on March 16, 2004, the council became operational. The Peace and Security Council of the AU has encountered opportunities and dilemmas in improving security on the continent. Fifteen AU member states, elected for terms of up to three years, comprise the council, which has sought to address contemporary security issues in at least 15 nations in Africa, including the Democratic Republic of the Congo, Eritrea, Ethiopia, Mauritania, Rwanda, and Togo, among others. In several cases, the council has intervened with an AU peacekeeping force, including in the Comoros, Somalia, and Sudan.[19] Much more toil to solve security challenges in Africa waits to be accomplished, however.

This book analyzes contemporary security issues in Africa, centering on sub-Saharan Africa geographically, concentrating on the past three decades chronologically, and aiming at contemporary security issues topically. While I touch on political, cultural, and social factors throughout, my focus is contemporary security issues. Subjects include weak and fragile states, ethno-religious conflict and civil wars, natural resources and environmental security, violent extremism and terrorism, piracy and maritime security, food security and extreme poverty, and international responses, as well as linkages and future prospects. My intent is not for this book to

Senior military leaders from countries across the African continent applaud during an introductory session before the opening ceremony of the African Land Forces Summit 2017, in Lilongwe, Malawi. May 8, 2017. (Courtesy United States Africa Command)

be a comprehensive account of every security issue on the continent but rather an introduction for audiences interested in contemporary security issues in Africa, including students, scholars, policy makers, and general readers alike. Presenting both overviews of these vital concerns as well as specific case studies, this book is an excellent starter for anyone drawn toward contemporary security issues in Africa and their critical implications for Africa and international security. As a result, it covers many of the most important contemporary security issues in Africa while acknowledging that there are others that space limits prevent from detailing in this volume. My hope is that this work will provide a useful primer for readers unfamiliar with these matters and deliver helpful guidance toward additional sources, further readings, and existing debates about specific problems, all in the hopes to spur additional research regarding how conflict exists in Africa and why it matters to the rest of the world.

The core contribution of this book is its detailed analysis of the nexus between culture, politics, and security in Africa. The volume examines the key security issues affecting Africa and their implications at the national, regional, and international levels. Thus, this book explores the vital and dynamic role that countries in Africa play in influencing international security. It also investigates and articulates the causes resulting in the rising importance of Africa in global affairs. As a result, this work fills a significant void in modern security studies and contributes a unique addition to the literature of Africa's security by bridging the gap between historical context and contemporary analysis.

To research this volume, I utilized a plethora of primary and secondary sources, including international institution reports, regional organization accounts, government documents, NGO records, interviews, testimonials, memoirs, magazines, newspapers, scholarly books, and journal articles. To organize it, I employed a topical approach using a case-study methodology. For each chapter that follows, I introduce a particular contemporary security issue, provide a brief overview of its presence in Africa, and then highlight two case studies that each explores it within the context of a specific country, with the chapter on piracy and maritime security charting particular bodies of water instead. My hope is that each chapter will provide readers with a general introduction to an important contemporary security issue in Africa, a couple of relevant case studies that explore it in detail, and useful suggestions for additional readings and further research.

As a result, this book furnishes broad coverage of contemporary security issues in Africa while situating these matters within the setting of individual countries. This introduction sets the background for African security and frames the methodology informing subsequent chapters. Chapter 2, "Weak and Fragile States," explores central foundations undergirding all security issues in Africa—namely, poor governance and

endemic corruption, including case studies on the Central African Republic and Mali. Chapter 3, "Ethno-Religious Conflict and Civil Wars," examines the consequences of weak states in Africa as they have unraveled
into unrestrained violence and scrutinizes case studies on Uganda and
Sudan, with an investigation of the reverberations for South Sudan as civil
war in Sudan has beget upheaval in a newly independent South Sudan.
Chapter 4, "Natural Resources and Environmental Security," sifts the role
that assets have played in conflict on the continent and the negative consequences that such violence has had on the environment; it mines case
studies on Angola and the Democratic Republic of the Congo. Chapter 5,
"Violent Extremism and Terrorism," reconnoiters the rise of terrorism in
Africa, including the reign of al-Shabaab in Somalia and the emergence
of Boko Haram in Nigeria. Chapter 6, "Piracy and Maritime Security,"
navigates the critical importance of security off the coasts of Africa and
charts two key bodies of water, the Gulf of Aden and the Gulf of Guinea.
Chapter 7, "Food Security and Extreme Poverty," digests the substance of
food and livelihood to human security in Africa.[20] This chapter highlights
the recent progress that several African nations have accomplished in this
arena, as well as emphasizing other countries that have witnessed the
opposite dynamic, including case studies on Ethiopia and Malawi. Chapter 8, "International Responses," considers Africa's emergence as a major
actor in global affairs, spurring heightened attention and engagement
from the international community to Africa generally and contemporary
security challenges on the continent specifically, including case studies on
the United States and China. Chapter 9, "Linkages and Future Prospects,"
concludes the work with some overarching themes on African security, a
consideration of the interconnectedness of many contemporary security
challenges in Africa and the linkages between them, and some projections
on what future prospects might hold for security issues on the continent.

Of the 50 weakest states in the world, more than 30 have been in
Africa.[21] Ethno-religious conflict and civil wars have ravaged the continent, including brutal violence by the Lord's Resistance Army in Uganda
and a vicious civil war in Sudan, which resulted in the creation of South
Sudan but little cessation of conflict. While Africa has abundant natural
resources, oil in Angola and mineral resources in the Democratic Republic
of the Congo have proven that riches often have fueled conflict instead of
providing stability. Al-Shabaab and Boko Haram have demonstrated that
violent extremism and terrorism have been clear and present dangers on
the continent, while piracy in the Gulf of Aden and the Gulf of Guinea
has extended insecurity from land outward into the maritime domain.
Food security and extreme poverty have proven perennial challenges
for many African countries, including Ethiopia and Malawi. Partly in
response, such international powers as the United States and China have
amplified interaction with Africa in myriad ways. As a result, an informed

understanding of contemporary security issues in Africa is essential. Providing a comprehensive resource for students, scholars, policy makers, and general readers interested in contemporary security issues in Africa, this book details how complex security problems have impacted Africa and reinforces why addressing them is critical to Africa and international security. Overall, *Contemporary Security Issues in Africa* provides a useful introduction to many of the most important security challenges on the continent and details numerous case studies that explore these obstacles within definite milieus. By contributing to an understanding of these vital matters, it is my hope that they can be lessened in the years to come.

CHAPTER 2

Weak and Fragile States

OVERVIEW

Weak and fragile states in Africa have been critical security issues for a long time.[1] Extensive study has highlighted their prevalence on the continent. The Fund for Peace's Fragile States Index annually has evaluated countries around the world based on numerous variables and has placed them into 11 categories, ranging from "very sustainable" for the world's strongest countries to "very high alert" for the weakest states. The key indicators include such social ones as demographic pressures, refugees and internally displaced persons (IDPs), group grievances, and human flight; such economic ones as uneven development, poverty, and economic decline; and such political and military ones as state legitimacy, public services, human rights and rule of law, security apparatus, factionalized elites, and external intervention.[2] For 2017, South Sudan received the worst rating out of 178 countries around the world, edging out perennial failed state Somalia. Six nations received the weakest rating; four of these countries resided in Africa, including the Central African Republic, Somalia, South Sudan, and Sudan. In addition to these most prominent examples, there has been an overabundance of weak and fragile states in Africa: of the 50 weakest states in the world, 33 have been in Africa.[3]

Such a situation has not been a recent anomaly. Analyzing the past decade, the pervasiveness of weak and fragile states in Africa has become even more pronounced. Unlike the annual categories, which rank state fragility based on a specific year, the decade trends chart changes over time. The two worst categories are "critical worsening" and "significant worsening" and include 12 countries; 9 of them have been in Africa, including the two case studies analyzed in this chapter, the Central African Republic and Mali.[4] Such developments indicate two things: the vast majority of current weak and fragile states around the world have been in Africa, and the substantial bulk of countries worldwide deteriorating the most over the past 10 years have been on the continent. Geography has played a critical role. Jeffrey Herbst has shown that leaders in Africa have encountered great opportunity and immeasurable difficulty in state creation and consolidation because of one "fundamental problem": "how to broadcast power over sparsely settled lands."[5] This impediment has highlighted an important dichotomy in Africa between centralized and decentralized political institutions and the roles that they play within the state.[6]

Most constant among these weak and fragile states has been Somalia, which has lacked a functioning government for much of the past three decades. Noel Anderson documented, "Without a central authority for over twenty years, the country earned the unenviable distinction of serving as the longest running instance of complete state collapse in contemporary history."[7] The consequences of fragile state institutions have been significant and wide-ranging. Weak states have created power vacuums that have reverberated throughout their territory and have had secondary and tertiary effects. Oscar Gakuo Mwangi detected, "Under conditions of state collapse, social order is not persevered and societal cohesion is not enhanced; this leads to the emergence of moral decay and subsequently 'anarchy' becomes a way of life." Mwangi concluded, "In order to restore its legitimacy and its right to rule, the state must therefore transform society, restore and preserve social order and societal cohesion. When it is unable to do so, non-state actors often attempt to perform this role."[8] Mwangi's last point about nonstate actors is especially relevant: weak states have created voids within which armed groups often have emerged to foster violence, thereby further weakening governance in a vicious cycle detrimental to legitimacy.

One of the most critical elements contributing to weak and fragile states has been pervasive corruption. Founded in 1993, Transparency International tracks and combats fraud around the world. The group's ultimate goal is "a world in which government, business, civil society and the daily lives of people are free of corruption."[9] With chapters in more than 100 countries worldwide, Transparency International is the most recognized and respected nongovernmental organization (NGO) monitoring fraud and produces an annual Corruption Perceptions Index, rating countries around the world on a scale from 0, signifying high levels of venality, to 100, denoting little evidence of vice. Transparency International has found that corruption is widespread in most countries, with the worldwide average being 43. Most African nations have fared quite poorly, with only 8 countries in Africa beating the global average, including Botswana (60), Cape

Verde (59), Mauritius (54), Rwanda (54), Namibia (52), São Tomé and Prín-
cipe (46), Senegal (45), and South Africa (45). Of the 20 countries ranked
with the most corruption, 12 have been in Africa, including the Democratic
Republic of the Congo (21), Burundi (20), Central African Republic (20),
Chad (20), Republic of Congo (Brazzaville) (20), Angola (18), Eritrea (18),
Guinea-Bissau (16), Libya (14), Sudan (14), South Sudan (11), and Somalia (10).
They have joined at the bottom of the list such countries as Iraq (17),
Afghanistan (15), Yemen (14), Syria (13), and North Korea (12). Consistent
with its abysmal Fragile States Index ranking, Somalia scored the worst
among all countries worldwide for corruption with a score of only 10.[10]
Transparency International has related graft directly to the strength of a state,
stating that it "is a major obstacle to democracy and the rule of law[,] . . .
depletes national wealth[,] . . . corrodes the social fabric of society[,]" and
leads to "environmental degradation."[11] As a result, corruption has been a
significant impediment to state legitimacy in Africa. Because Somalia has
been covered extensively in other literature as a weak and fragile state and
will be analyzed later as a case study in the piracy and maritime security
chapter of this book, the two case studies on weak and fragile states that follow are the Central African Republic and Mali.[12]

CENTRAL AFRICAN REPUBLIC

The Central African Republic (CAR) is a landlocked country of more
than 5.6 million people, covering 622,984 square kilometers. The nation
has a primarily agricultural economy coupled with forestry and mining
industries. Cotton, coffee, tobacco, cassava, yams, millet, corn, bananas,
timber, gold, and diamonds all contribute. The CAR, like most countries
in Africa, is ethnically diverse, including Baya, Banda, Mandjia, Sara,
Mboum, M'Baka, and Yakoma ethnic groups, among others. The country
was formerly the French colony of Oubangui-Chari, named after the two
rivers that formed its northern and southern borders. The CAR declared
independence on August 13, 1960.

In 1993, Central Africans elected Ange-Félix Patassé as president.
A decade later in March 2003, a military coup d'état overthrew him, and
General François Bozizé, former army chief of staff, came to power. Military elements from neighboring Chad assisted Bozizé, antagonizing
relations between the two nations.[13] Bozizé continued as president after
winning elections in 2005 and again in 2011, although many observers
characterized the balloting as corrupt. In December 2012, a coalition of
rebel groups known as Seleka, meaning "alliance" in the national language of Sango, coalesced and moved toward the capital of Bangui. Many
Seleka fighters were from northeastern CAR, while others mobilized from
Chad and Sudan. On March 24, 2013, Seleka militants seized the capital

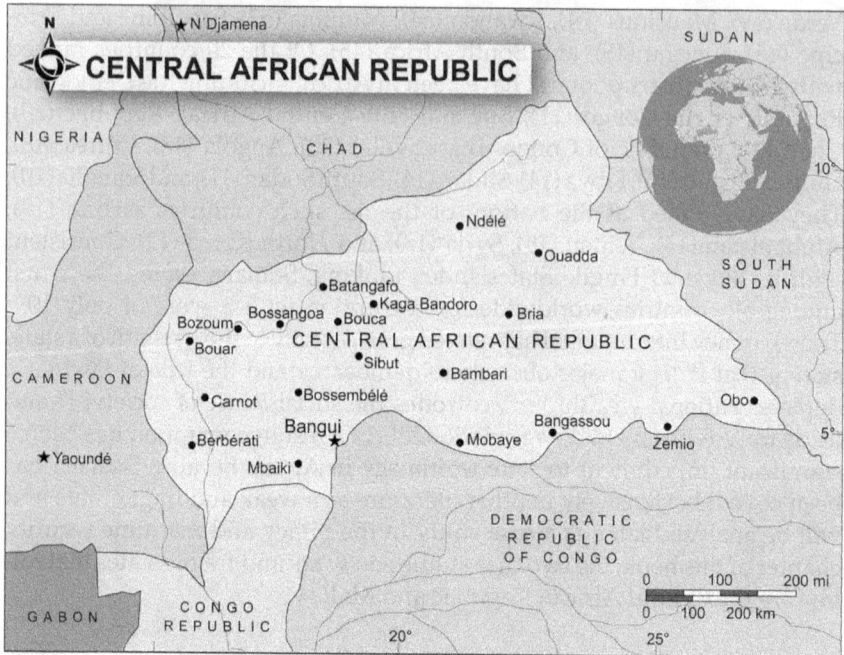

of Bangui and overthrew Bozizé's government, descending the country into violent chaos and fundamental anarchy. President Bozizé fled, and, on the following day, Seleka installed its leader, Michel Djotodia, as the new president of the CAR.

In April 2013, rebel groups formed the National Transitional Council (NTC), although bloodshed throughout the country continued unabated. Amnesty International reported, "Over the following 10 months, Seleka forces killed countless civilians, burned numerous villages, and looted thousands of homes."[14] In many significant ways, religious differences acted as an accelerant to this conflict, as leaders willingly and purposely inflamed religious hostilities. Religion and geography have played a visible role in hostilities in the CAR since 2012, as rebel groups such as Seleka have been predominately Muslim and have controlled much of the northeast part of the country. In contrast, Bozizé's government and the militias subsequently fighting the Seleka, known as Anti-Balaka, meaning "anti-machete" or "machete-proof" in Sango, have been largely Christian and have commanded much of the southwest part of the country. Overall, approximately 15 percent of the country is Muslim, with the remainder Christian or animist, although most faiths had coexisted peacefully prior to the current crisis.

In September 2013, purportedly in response to Seleka's numerous atrocities, Anti-Balaka militias began committing many brutalities of their own. From September to December 2013, Anti-Balaka fighters ravaged Muslim communities around the northwest town of Bossangoa. By the end of October 2013, John Ging, UN director of humanitarian operations, characterized the overall situation as "chaotic," with more than 50 percent of the nation's population in dire need of humanitarian assistance and escalating violence characterized by religious overtones. "The scale of suffering is among the worst in the world and getting worse," Ging feared.[15] By February 2014, most of the Muslim population had fled the country or were in the process of doing so. One Central African man escaping the carnage despaired, "I was born here, I don't understand the hate towards us. . . . I want to come home when there is peace in Central Africa."[16] During January and February 2014, Anti-Balaka massacres erupted in the capital of Bangui, while other onslaughts occurred simultaneously in Boyali, Boda, and Mbaiki. As a result, religious violence decimated entire communities. Human Rights Watch lamented, "Yaloké, a major gold trading center, had an estimated Muslim population of 30,000 and eight mosques prior to the conflict. When Human Rights Watch visited on February 6[, 2014], fewer than 500 Muslims and one mosque remained."[17] While acknowledging Seleka's numerous human rights abuses, Amnesty International characterized Anti-Balaka's "forced expulsion of Muslims from CAR" as "ethnic cleansing," primarily due to Anti-Balaka's stated objective of "ridding the country of its Muslim population."[18] On February 12, 2014, Peter Bouckaert, emergencies director at Human Rights Watch, dreaded, "At this rate, if the targeted violence continues, there will be no Muslims left in much of the Central African Republic."[19]

A spiteful sequence of reprisals quickly spiraled out of control.[20] On January 10, 2014, Michel Djotodia, former Seleka leader and interim president, resigned. Voters elected Catherine Samba-Panza as interim president on January 20, 2014, and she took office three days later. She and the NTC commenced planning for national elections to promote unity, which they originally slated for February 2015. Numerous fighters, however, layered ostensibly nationalist tinges to their overt and negative religious depictions of their opposition. Anti-Balaka militants framed Seleka as foreigners because many Seleka soldiers were from Chad and Sudan. Human Rights Watch revealed, "Muslims are often described as 'Chadians' rather than citizens by anti-balaka leaders, even though the vast majority of Muslims have citizenship."[21]

The conflagration that emerged was not entirely new to the CAR.[22] Violent conflict has been endemic to the country since its independence. The nation has experienced at least eight coups since 1960, including five successful ones. The turmoil has undermined the stability and legitimacy of political and state institutions across the country and created a combustible cloud within which any spark might ignite hatred and prompt deadly violence.[23] In a painstaking investigation of the historical prevalence of vengeance and popular punishment in the CAR, most often for suspected theft or witchcraft, Louisa Lombard and Sylvain Batianga-Kinzi discovered, "Two main conclusions emerge from this brief history. First, there has been a pronounced withering of the already-limited official state structures for adjudication. Second, the prerogatives of the Central African state have always been popularized and privatized in certain respects, and they have long included violence, including execution as spectacle, whether extrajudicial or official." Lombard and Batianga-Kinzi concluded, "The weakness of the Central African states is in some ways new but in other ways old, as is the move to take punishment and threat management into one's own hands."[24]

The extensive and tragic violence throughout the CAR has not subsided. As a result of the pandemonium, the nation experienced in 2017 a significant increase in IDPs, with 200,000 more added in that year alone.[25] The chaos throughout the country has resulted in a total approaching 700,000 IDPs.[26] Understandably, Central Africans have termed the current situation of unrelenting fighting and persistent instability as the "Crisis," an apt name that unwittingly belies the magnitude of suffering for most Central Africans.[27] Due to the indefatigable killing, roughly 450,000 Central Africans have fled the country to neighboring Cameroon, Chad, and the Democratic Republic of the Congo, straining the capacity of those nations and leading to horrific conditions in refugee camps that are ill equipped for such large influxes. Of course, many of the dynamics undermining state legitimacy in the CAR could also impact other nations in Africa. Rama Venkatasawmy cautioned, "The Central African Republic's current crisis should more realistically be viewed as the product of a particular combination of factors (similarly expressed by many other African nations): localized economic discrimination (specifically in the Miskine district); power struggle between political leaders; opportunistic exploitation of popular ethno-religious fears."[28]

The crisis has garnered international attention and triggered numerous responses from regional and international groups concerned that the CAR has become a failed state, including the African Union, Economic Community of Central African States (ECCAS), European Union, and UN peacekeeping forces.[29] All these groups have sent forces to the CAR to mitigate the fighting and to assist with humanitarian efforts. On June 20, 2008, leaders signed the Libreville Comprehensive Peace Agreement, creating the Mission de Consolidation de la Paix en Centrafrique (MICOPAX), which ECCAS led. On July 19, 2013, regional policy makers established the Mission Internationale de Soutien à la Centrafrique sous conduite Africaine (MISCA), also known as the International Support Mission to the Central

African Republic. In October 2013, the UN Security Council approved a 250-soldier force, ostensibly to protect UN workers.[30] On December 5, 2013, the UN Security Council elevated the crisis to international proportions, arguing that "the situation in the CAR constitutes a threat to international peace and security," invoking Chapter VII of the UN Charter, and authorizing the deployment of international peacekeeping forces to the CAR in accordance with Resolution 2127 (2013).[31] On April 10, 2014, UN Security Council Resolution 2149 created the UN Multidimensional Integrated Stabilization Mission in the CAR (MINUSCA), as the most recent attempt to dampen the flames of war within the nation.

Even with significant notice of the crisis and considerable attempts to pacify the situation by bolstering the stability and legitimacy of state institutions in the CAR, regional and international responses have been divided and disjointed. Martin Welz established that "the AU, the ECCAS, the UN, and, to a lesser extent, the EU competed for control over crisis solution, but also for relevance and visibility." Welz concluded that among these vying interests, "Chad and France in particular were driving the organizations' agendas."[32] On November 15, 2017, the UN Security Council renewed the mandate of MINUSCA and increased its authorized strength to 11,650 peacekeepers, including 480 observers and staff officers and 2,080 police personnel.[33] The council explicitly tasked MINUSCA

Rwandan soldiers stand in formation awaiting orders after being dropped off in the Central African Republic to aid African Union and French operations against militants during a three-week-long operation. January 19, 2014. (Courtesy United States Africa Command)

"to continue to support the CAR Authorities to develop and finalize a nationally owned strategy to tackle the illicit exploitation and trafficking networks of natural resources which continue to fund and supply armed groups in the CAR."[34]

Amid the violence and with the government in a tenuous position, Samba-Panza delayed elections until December 2015, even though she had originally scheduled them for February earlier that same year. In a historic move that highlighted how much of the bloodshed in the CAR revolved around religious lines, Pope Francis in November 2015 visited the besieged country to urge a cessation to the pugnacity and to advocate religious tolerance as the answer to the crisis. In this historic trip to a conflict zone, something uncommon for the Vatican to schedule, Pope Francis visited a Muslim mosque in PK5, a neighborhood beset by viciousness, where gunfights have been a common occurrence. Local residents characterized PK5 as one of the most dangerous neighborhoods in Bangui, the capital of the nation. During his trip, Pope Francis urged dutiful forbearance and admonished listeners to resist "the temptation of fear of others, of the unfamiliar, of what is not part of our ethnic group, our political views or our religious confession." Many local observers hoped that his visit and words might calm the religious vehemence. Urbain, a young resident of Bangui, preached, "He is God's diplomat. Bandits don't listen to politicians, but they will listen to him." Many onlookers echoed Urbain's wistful optimism and yearned "that the pride and good will generated by this visit carried forward into the intense election cycle to follow."[35]

After the pope's remarkable visit, the CAR held presidential and legislative elections from December 2015 to March 2016. The result was generally peaceful elections, although "operational delays and insecurity in some areas" marred them. On December 8, 2015, Bozizé sought to campaign but became ineligible. Instead, Faustin Archange Touadéra emerged as the winner, gaining nearly two-thirds of the votes cast. Even though the voting proved calm, violence throughout the country continued afterward.[36] Christine Lagarde, International Monetary Fund (IMF) managing director, spoke before the national assembly on January 25, 2017, and advised, "After shrinking almost 40 percent in 2013, the Central African Republic's economy has a long way to go." Lagarde explained, "Infrastructure has been shattered. Agriculture, forestry, and mining have not returned to past levels of output. Institutional capacity remains weak. And the security situation in some parts of the country is still tenuous." Lagarde, however, expressed "some optimism" based on Touadéra's National Recovery and Peacebuilding Plan and estimated that with "successful implementation" it could result in sustained economic growth for the nation shattered with bloodshed.[37]

The central feature to the anarchy and carnage in the CAR has been poor governance. In extensive research into violence there, Conciliation

Resources, an independent NGO dedicated to fostering sustainable peace, disclosed, "Interviewees emphasized that the current crisis is the result of persistent poor governance by a centralized state over many years before the Seleka rebellion in 2012, especially in the handling of the country's security and economy."[38] As a result, poor governance set the underlying conditions for the rebellion, which in turn proved a spark that ignited open warfare. The presence of armed groups acted as an accelerant to the conflict because they purposely fanned the flames of sectarian violence and militant nationalism to instill intense fear and loathing of opposition groups. The weakness of state institutions also allowed armed groups, including former Seleka factions and the Lord's Resistance Army (LRA), to operate unabated within the CAR, thereby adding strain to an already-volatile situation. Of course, the fragility of state institutions within the country also aggravated legitimate complaints regarding the lack of government provision of necessary programs and services, high and persistent unemployment, and wholesale inability to redress group injustices. Elizabeth Murray and Fiona Mangan determined, "More broadly, disproportionate poverty and underdevelopment in the north and east of the country are legitimate grievances for local communities and will remain a powerful rallying call for militant groups until duly addressed."[39] The situation in the CAR has remained precarious at best. As a result of the chaos and bloodshed, international actors renewed on January 27, 2017, the sanctions regime against the CAR, hopeful that doing so would stymie the flow of weapons into the country and thereby mitigate the ongoing crisis.[40] Much of the violence has continued unrelenting. On May 2, 2018, assailants armed with automatic weapons and grenades killed more than a dozen people and injured another 96, most of them attending church services, in the PK5 neighborhood near Bangui.[41]

MALI

Mali is a western African nation, spanning more than 1.2 million square kilometers. It claims a population of almost 18 million people, about half of whom are from the Mande ethnic group. Ethnic minorities include the Fulani, Voltaic, Songhai, and Tuareg, among others. Mali is a landlocked nation, with its capital at Bamako, a bustling city of some 2.5 million residents. Nearly 95 percent of Malians are Muslim, and Mali is one of Africa's, and indeed the world's, poorest countries. More than half of its land is desert, and its economy is largely agricultural and mining endeavors, which are highly dependent on gold and cotton exports.[42] François Heisbourg commented that Mali is "framed by artificial colonial-era boundaries and lacking all but agricultural and pastoral resources."[43]

Formerly the Sudanese Republic, Mali gained independence from France on September 22, 1960. Authoritarian rule followed until a coup

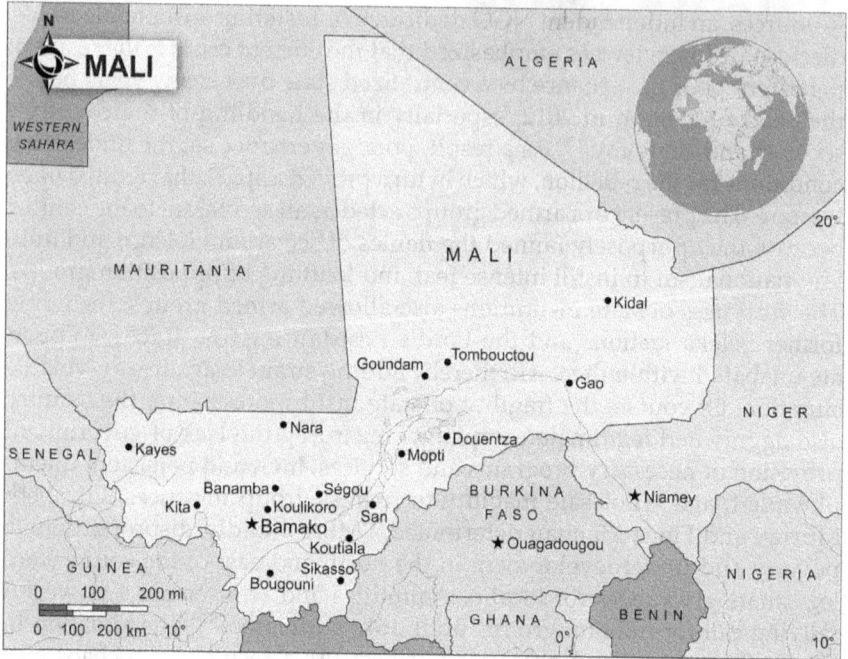

d'état in 1991, which overthrew the military dictator Moussa Traoré. These political limitations, however, did not prevent Mali from developing a nascent democracy. After the coup, Mali established itself as a young democracy and transformed into a relatively stable nation over the following decades. This occurrence had not only many positive but also some negative repercussions. Zachary Devlin-Foltz argued, "This created space for segments of civil society, including Islamists, to expand their role in social and political life. Some Islamists subsequently began challenging the government's handling of intergroup inequality and economic underdevelopment."[44] Voters elected Alpha Oumar Konaré as president in 1992 and did so again in 1997. They chose Amadou Toumani Touré as president in 2002 and 2007. This peaceful transition between civilian leaders strengthened Mali's reputation as a democratic success.

Mali, however, also has been an example of a successful democracy in Africa that quickly devolved into a weak and fragile state. Not long ago many international observers described Mali as the antithesis of an African weak and fragile state, shunning a trend that consumed many of its neighbors on the continent. Roger Kaplan concluded, "Mali was the paragon of political and economic progress."[45] Indeed. Even so, significant fissures shifted below the placid surface. Mali suffered from numerous dynamics that weakened its state institutions over time, making it ripe to become a weak and fragile state. One wide-ranging analysis documented many of these influences: "These include poor governance, the corrosive impact of drug trafficking and other illicit commerce, military fragmentation and collapse, limited implementation of previous peace accords with Tuareg rebel groups, and an uptick in regional arms and combatant flows from Libya since 2011."[46] Mali's coveted status as a stable democracy abruptly evaporated in 2012. Martin van Vliet discerned, "Long regarded as a poster child for democracy on the continent and a stable anchor in a troubled region, the authority of the Malian state corroded during the first months of 2012."[47]

Lurking beneath the relative calm in Mali were significant social cleavages. The country is home to a Tuareg minority in the north, representing roughly 10 percent of the nation's overall population.[48] Stark differences in ethnicity, religion, and geography combined to create significant internal divisions within Mali, especially between Malians residing in the northern deserts of the country, many of them Tuareg who pursue nomadic pastoralism, and those Malians living in the sub-Saharan south of the nation. Geography plays a significant and palpable role, dividing Mali physically and culturally. The Sahara is the world's largest desert, covering more than 9 million square kilometers. It separates North Africa from sub-Saharan Africa and therefore represents a major geographical boundary on the continent. Robert B. Lloyd observed, "Thus, the Sahara Desert is like a vast inland sea of sand, with the countries on its shores exerting little actual sovereignty over it due to vast distances and terrain."[49] The Sahara also has been a significant trade route throughout history, including considerable illicit trade involving everything from counterfeit cigarettes to trafficked drugs, arms, and humans.[50]

The Sahara desert demarcates significant cultural differences between northern Africa and sub-Saharan Africa. The Sahel, meaning "shore" in Arabic, spans across Africa from the Red Sea to the Atlantic Ocean and is a zone of transition between the Sahara desert in the north and savanna to its south. It also runs through central Mali with significant consequences. Morten Bøås and Liv Elin Torheim showed, "The Tuaregs' position in the northern region was turned upside down by French colonialism and made permanent by the postcolonial state system. . . . The Tuaregs therefore understand themselves as distinctly different from the other groups that constitute the Malian polity: differing from them in language, lifestyle and heritage."[51] While such a situation often has resulted in peaceful coexistence, at other times, especially in the recent past, cultural differences and historic grievances have produced frictions and outright conflict. Jean Ping added, "This long-time, millennial coexistence is at the center of many different types of tensions that have always been temporarily appeased but, unfortunately, never definitively eradicated."[52] This important distinction is not unique to Mali, however, but has existed throughout the region, where many countries have exhibited similar schisms related to the geography of the Sahara and the Sahel. François Heisbourg commented, "This historically deep divide between the peoples of the desert and those of the cultivated south exists in various forms in neighbouring Mauritania and Niger, as well as in Chad. It was also evident in pre-partition Sudan." Heisbourg determined, "In Mali, as in these countries, the handling, or mishandling, of this cultural chasm lies at the heart of post-independence strife."[53] Partly as a result, Mali's government experienced repeated clashes with the Tuareg, including during the 1960s, 1990s, and again in 2006.

The Sahel is also an area that exhibits a prevalence of weak and fragile states. Many observers have related this dynamic to the concept of ungoverned spaces. Robert B. Lloyd discovered, "Across the Sahel and Sahara regions of West Africa, large swaths of territory are essentially ungoverned. Criminal organizations, militant Islamist groups, and ethnic separatist movements created and now enjoy these ungoverned spaces of bases of operation." Lloyd also related this phenomenon to Mali: "The case of Mali is of particular interest due to the success of militant Islamist groups in capturing and holding territory, the impact of ungoverned space on the growth of such groups, and the means by which the international community and state checked the militants."[54]

In addition to geography, political upheavals and social uprisings weakened state institutions in Mali. The Arab Spring erupted in December 2010 when Mohamed Bouazizi, an unemployed student and street vendor in Tunisia, sought to sell fruits and vegetables to earn a living, but police confiscated them because he did not have a street vendor permit. In response, Bouazizi immolated himself on December 17, 2010, as a protest against poor living conditions under the regime of President Zine El Abidine Ben Ali. The underlying frustrations, especially the lack of employment prospects for youth, even ones with substantial education, combined with high living costs and seethed into outright struggle. Bouazizi subsequently died of his burns on January 4, 2011, yet his actions sparked a series of popular uprisings against authoritarian regimes throughout the entire region.[55] Protests and instability exploded across a series of North African countries, including Tunisia, Egypt, and Libya, as well as Yemen in the Middle East.[56] As a result, Libya in early 2011 devolved into savage clashes. In response, the UN Security Council on March 17, 2011, adopted Resolution 1973, which "demands the immediate establishment of a cease-fire and a complete end to violence and all attacks against, and abuses of, civilians."[57] The declaration also established a no-fly zone and compelled enforcement of an arms embargo against Libya. On March 19, 2011, the North Atlantic Treaty Organization (NATO) intervened in Libya with military force. NTC forces had captured by August 2011 Tripoli, Libya's capital, and deposed Muammar Gaddafi, the nation's longtime autocratic leader. On

October 20, 2011, they captured and killed Gaddafi.[58] The fall of Libya provided a shock to the region, and its reverberations impaired Mali.

An influx of Tuareg fighters returned from fighting in Libya to Mali, gathering abundant weapons, amplified aspirations, and augmented capabilities along the way. Their newfound arms cache included heavy weapons and numerous vehicles. Jean Ping resolved, "Mali therefore became the first collateral damage of the Libyan conflict."[59] Upon their return from Libya with augmented firepower and combat experience, Tuareg fighters formed in October 2011 the National Movement for the Liberation of Azawad (MNLA), a secular nationalist movement for Tuareg independence. By January 2012, a widespread Tuareg rebellion erupted in Mali, the fourth such uprising since its independence, much of it emanating from the Kidal region in northern Mali. As a result, the MNLA launched an insurgency, and rebel fighters seized large swaths of territory in northern Mali.

By 2012, Mali clung to the remnants of democracy but faced significant economic challenges. Martin van Vliet observed, "In 2012, Mali's per capita gross domestic product was only $1,100 and the country ranked 182nd (out of 186 countries) on the United Nations Human Development Index, while life expectancy at birth stood at just fifty-one years."[60] As a consequence of economic uncertainty from and political impotency against the insurgency, from March 21 to March 22, 2012, a coup d'état formed, led by Captain Amadou Sanogo and comprised of many junior officers in Mali's military. The coup began at the Sundiata Keita military camp in Kati, quickly spread to the capital of Bamako, and rapidly overthrew Amadou Toumani Touré, Mali's president, also known colloquially as President ATT. Much foment for the coup stemmed from rampant government corruption and the inability of Bamako to provide for the needs of its people. Critics also charged that the political leadership was rife with graft, siphoning off resources meant for the military's counterinsurgency campaign and redirecting them toward ulterior purposes. One detailed report claimed, "High-level corruption, reportedly tied, in part, to criminal networks, contributed to public distaste for the government and to reported initial support for the coup," which did not extinguish the insurgency but rather strengthened it by fracturing the government's response, thereby ceding momentum to the rebel fighters.[61] After the coup, insurgents quickly seized additional vast territory in northern Mali, weakening governance and heightening distress. Their offensive culminated with the MNLA overrunning most of northern Mali and on April 6, 2012, declaring Azawad, a territory encompassing most of Mali's northeast and comprising nearly two-thirds of Mali, an independent state.

Tuareg fighters were not alone in their aspirations to exert influence in Mali. Islamist groups have thrived in the ungoverned spaces of the Sahara and Sahel regions, including in northern Mali. One such group expanding its operations in the region was al-Qaeda in the Islamic Maghreb (AQIM), which originated from Algeria's civil war. After defeat there, the Salafist Group for Preaching and Combat (GSPC) relocated to the Sahel and in 2007 became AQIM. Afterward, the Islamist group gained momentum in northern Mali. Other Islamist groups in the north emerged, including Ansar al-Dine, roughly translated as "Defenders of the Faith," which garnered a great deal of strength in Kidal, and the Movement for Unity and Jihad in West Africa (MUJWA), also known as MUJAO after its French acronym, which gathered significant force in Gao. In a combination of convenience for two disparate groups, MNLA and Ansar al-Dine joined forces on May 26, 2012.

A schism between the two distinct groups sharpened, however, largely over the Islamist faction's imposition of strict sharia law and wanton destruction of historical shrines in such vaulted places as Timbuktu, which had been an Islamic cultural center since the 15th and 16th centuries. Its libraries housed hundreds of thousands of ancient manuscripts and sacred Muslim texts. Upon entering the city, Ansar al-Dine destroyed numerous historical artifacts that they deemed sinful, including Sufi tombs and religious manuscripts. Many local residents in Timbuktu went to heroic lengths to rescue the relics from ruin, often stashing them in metal trunks and moving them out of the city at night. Abdel Kader Haidara, a local preservationist, estimated that these labors saved from destruction nearly 300,000 pages of ancient manuscripts. "We took a big risk to save our heritage," Haidara acknowledged. "This is not only the city's heritage, it is the heritage of all humanity."[62]

As a result of differing approaches to sharia law, infighting among various insurgent groups erupted, complicating the rebellion and fracturing it into several embedded conflicts. MNLA, the secular separatist group, seized control of Azawad and declared its independence, but Ansar al-Dine, the jihadist group with links to AQIM, commandeered direction of the overall revolt. Roland Marchal revealed, "It is clear that the MNLA on the ground committed crimes and was basically dismantled by Ansar ed-Din. Today, as the MIA, its new strength is artificial and is derived from the need of fighters to join a more respectable movement at a time when they may lose everything. Such political nomadism is not new and happened in the previous 'Tuareg wars.'"[63] During June and July 2012, fighting between these groups intensified, with Ansar al-Dine routing MNLA in Timbuktu, and MUJWA overpowering MNLA in Gao. By July 2012, Islamist groups defeated MNLA and seized the initiative in the rebellion against Mali's government. As a result, Islamist groups imposed strict sharia law throughout the territories that they held, thereby further inflaming tensions. They also benefited from controlling increasing tracts of land used for trade. Terje Østebø divulged, "In northern Mali, the intertwining of Islamic militancy and illicit smuggling has produced a complicated mix of incentives. While details remain opaque, it is known that Mokhtar Belmokhtar, the emir of AQIM, has utilized smuggling revenues in the Sahel as a source of support for AQIM since the early 2000s."[64] Trafficking cigarettes, arms, drugs, and humans as well as kidnapping for ransom all have proven lucrative for AQIM, and by extension Ansar al-Dine, have helped fund their operations, and have provided resources for their military offensives.

In July 2012, the situation was dire. A flurry of activity at the UN Security Council sought to save Mali from state collapse. UN Security Council Resolution 2056 approved the Economic Community of West African States' (ECOWAS) involvement in restoring state control in Mali.[65] In October of that same year, UN Security Council Resolution 2071 authorized planning for the use of force under Chapter VII of the UN Charter.[66] On December 20, 2012, UN Security Council Resolution 2085 sanctioned an African-led International Support Mission in Mali (AFISMA).[67] The intent of this decision was for member nations from ECOWAS to stand up, train, and deploy a military force to stabilize Mali, known as the Mission Internationale de Soutien au Mali (MISMA).[68]

Time was not on MISMA's side, however. In January 2013, a menacing force of heavily armed Islamist fighters numbering between 2,000 and 3,000 attacked south toward the capital of Bamako, instigating a new phase in the revolt. They defeated Malian military forces in the town of Konna, advanced toward a key airport near Mopti, and threatened Sevaré, where the Malian army operated its headquarters. The crisis had reached a crescendo. On January 10, 2013, interim president Dioncounda Traoré requested international assistance. The next day, African and French intervention in Mali began, involving more than 5,000 MISMA soldiers and approximately 4,000 French soldiers. The French named the intervention Opération Serval, which sought to remove the Islamist militants and restore the Malian state.[69] In response, Alghabass Ag Intalla, a key Tuareg leader, created on January 23, 2013, the Movement for the Islamic Azawad (MIA), further delineating his faction from Ansar al-Dine. In approximately one month, African and French units overwhelmed Islamist forces in northern Mali. In late February, African and French forces killed Abdelhamid Abou Zeid, an AQIM senior leader, in fighting near the Ifoghas Mountains in northern Mali.[70] The terrorist group quickly named Yahia Abou El Hammam as successor to Abou Zeid.[71]

Due to their previous split from Islamist groups, the MNLA cooperated with anti-Islamist initiatives. The French intervention ended in March 2013, and on April 25, the UN Security Council approved Resolution 2100, calling for elections and a UN peacekeeping mission in Mali, named the United Nations Multidimensional Integrated Stabilization Mission in Mali (MINUSMA), which sought to overtake AFISMA on July 1,

2013.[72] In June 2013, Mali's government signed a peace agreement with Tuareg nationalists. As scheduled, the UN peacekeeping mission in Mali (MINUSMA) began on July 1, 2013, involving initially 6,000 police and soldiers, although the United Nations quickly doubled the size of the mission to 12,000 personnel.[73] Amid the chaos, voters elected President Ibrahim Boubacar Keïta on September 4, 2013. Many observers have argued that the elections marked a significant turning point in restoring strength and legitimacy to Mali's political and state institutions. Martin van Vliet contended that "the Malian case demonstrates that strengthening parliamentary performance is a socio-political process as much as it is an institutional matter." Van Vliet explained, "The profound crisis that the country has endured has given rise to increased political awareness across the country. More citizens than ever were mobilized in the recent presidential elections and people have continued to protest against poor governance performances of state officials."[74]

Mali's geography compounded the difficulties associated with weak and fragile states. Once again, the concept of ungoverned spaces applied to Mali. Several characteristics of ungoverned spaces were pertinent: difficult geography making physical access problematic; competing factions vying for power; a government's inability to control part or all of the country; and the free flow of people and goods, often illicit, through the space with the government unaware or unable to prevent it.[75] Robert B. Lloyd clarified, "An 'ungoverned space' is marked by the absence of central government control over a region and its people and challenges to the state's authority by one or more groups. . . . All contenders for control lack, to varying degrees, the capacity to enforce their rule."[76] As a result, ungoverned spaces have created power vacuums, have become sanctuaries for armed groups, and therefore have led to or have exacerbated conflict. They also have allowed militant groups to gain momentum and increase their capabilities. Costas M. Constantinou and Sam Okoth Opondo observed, "Yet, the more 'ungoverned' or violent the space the less diplomatic the encounter, as security and defence become the priority."[77] This dynamic was most evident in Mali's north, where the Sahara and Sahel created a desolate environment often utilized for smuggling and illicit trade, which has existed for centuries. Morten Bøås and Liv Elin Torheim explained, "Thus, to a certain extent, the current increase in informal trade and/or illicit trade also represents a revitalisation of the ancient routes of trade, commerce and pilgrimage, connecting West Africa to the Mediterranean, the Middle East and the Persian Gulf, which used to pass through this area."[78]

While Opération Serval was successful in military terms, Mali has persisted as a fragile state. Islamist groups operating in the ungoverned spaces of the Sahara and Sahel have maintained significant ability to threaten the country. On November 20, 2015, AQIM assailants terrorized the Radisson

Blu hotel in Bamako. Two attackers besieged the hotel and took 170 hostages. The raid and subsequent standoff with local law enforcement and military personnel lasted nine hours, killing 20 people and sending the nation into yet another state of emergency.[79]

The result has been a consistent worsening of Mali's state institutions over the past 10 years. The Fund for Peace ranked the country as one of the "four most critically worsened for the decade."[80] The consequences have been especially devastating for Malians. The insurgency and resulting conflict have caused more than 50,000 IDPs and refugees. Roland Marchal noticed, "The coup in Bamako illustrated a crisis of the political system that goes far beyond Tuareg or northern Mali issues." Marchal continued, "For elections to make for a more inclusive and legitimate government, it must first be clear that the main parties are committed to building a new form of social contract that does not rest on the Mali or Ségou empires, which *de facto* exclude parts of the population in the north."[81]

On May 15, 2015, Mali's government, pro-administration armed groups, and rebel militias signed a peace accord. Much of the fighting, however, has persisted undiminished.[82] France has continued Operation Barkhane, which has sought to continue counterinsurgency operations in the Sahel with its headquarters in neighboring Chad.[83] The African Union has studied the African Union Mission for Mali and the Sahel's lessons for both Mali and the broader region.[84] By 2017, MINUSMA had achieved some success in northern Mali, although the fragility of the state has endured profound and problematic.[85] Overall, the insurgency, coup, and resulting chaos greatly weakened Mali, which previously had been regarded as a stable democracy and strong government in Africa. Morten Bøås and Liv Elin Torheim resolved, "The combined force of the 2012 coup in Bamako and the rebellion in the north entailed an unmasking of Mali. What had been presented as a showcase of democracy, good governance, and peace and reconciliation proved to be a facade for institutional weakness and mismanagement."[86] The result has been chronic bloodshed. The Society for Threatened Peoples, an NGO dedicated to human rights, warned that the situation in Mali had deteriorated in 2018, citing multiple attacks against Tuareg camps in late April in the northern region of Menaka, bordering neighboring Niger, in which assailants killed more than 40 civilians, most of them elderly or children.[87]

CONCLUSION

Weak and fragile states have been prevalent in Africa for much of the past three decades. In addition to Somalia, the world's weakest state for most of that time, Africa has been home to 33 of the 50 weakest states in the world.[88] This trend has been consistent over the past decade. Corruption has been one of the most significant contributors to state weakness in

Africa, which again claimed the world's most corrupt government, Somalia, as well as 12 of the 20 countries with the most vice in the world.[89] The CAR has epitomized weak and fragile states in Africa. The government has been impotent in the face of Seleka and Anti-Balaka atrocities. While the fighting has exhibited some ethno-religious overtones, its primary feature is the lack of good governance, leading to group grievances prior to conflict and contributing to an inability to quell violence once it erupted. As a result, the CAR nears existence as a failed state. In a different way, Mali has demonstrated the dangers of weak and fragile states in Africa. Consistently touted in the past as a stable democracy, Mali descended into violent conflagration at the hands of Tuareg separatists and Islamist terrorist groups. Ultimately requiring international assistance and benefiting from internal divisions within the insurgency, Mali suffered a great deal, weakening its political and state institutions. While the African and French military intervention was largely successful, the reverberations of Mali's weakening have lingered. Of course, weak and fragile states have been only two contemporary security issues confronting Africa. Ethno-religious conflict and civil wars also have plagued the continent for much of the past three decades.

CHAPTER 3

Ethno-Religious Conflict and Civil Wars

OVERVIEW

Warfare has been a perennial force in Africa in the recent past. Rama Venkatasawmy declared, "More than half of all African countries have experienced at least a year of armed conflict during the past three decades."[1] The results of those clashes have been devastating, especially for Africans caught in the middle of them. Deaths from combat have been rampant, as well as injuries, disruption, and displacement. Robert Picciotto documented, "African casualties of conflict exceed those of all other regions combined. About one-fifth of the African population lives in areas severely disrupted by conflict," including more than 30 countries affected by an excess of 125 combined clashes since 1980.[2] Many of these struggles have revolved around, at least on the surface, ethnicity and religion.

Ethnicity is a vital force on the continent. Africa is the most ethnically diverse continent in the world, claiming 3,315 distinct ethnic groups.[3] Ethnic conflict, however, is quite difficult to define in theory and even more arduous to isolate in practice. Jan Angstrom characterized ethnic skirmishes as "organized large-scale violent conflict among ethnic groups of which at least one has not achieved statehood or is not in possession of the state apparatus."[4] Some observers have argued that ethnicity is a primary, if not the central, driver of fighting on the continent. Donald L. Horowitz identified ethnic conflict as a causal factor resulting in bloodshed in Burundi, Chad, the Democratic Republic of the Congo (DRC), Rwanda, and Uganda.[5] While discussing the crisis in Mali that erupted in 2012, Jean Ping maintained, "These events show that ethnicity represents the most important cause of African internal conflicts. The civil wars in Rwanda,

Congo, Burundi, Sudan, Sierra Leone and Liberia are amongst the many tragic examples."[6] Other instances of ethnic conflict in Africa abound, including Darfur, Côte d'Ivoire, Nigeria, and Kenya.[7]

In its most atrocious manifestation, ethnic conflict has led to genocide. In the aftermath of World War II, the UN General Assembly on December 9, 1948, adopted the Convention on the Prevention and Punishment of the Crime of Genocide, and it went into force on January 12, 1951.[8] This resolution defined genocide as deliberate acts "committed with intent to destroy, in whole or in part, a national, ethnical, racial or religious group."[9] The United Nations applied the convention to the Rwandan genocide, where in the short span of roughly 100 days Hutu militias killed nearly 1 million Rwandans, most of them Tutsis. The killing began on April 7, 1994, and did not cease until mid-July of that same year. As a result of this genocide, the UN Security Council created the International Criminal Tribunal for Rwanda (ICTR).[10] Adama Dieng, UN special adviser on the prevention of genocide and former registrar of the ICTR, reflected, "The Rwanda genocide was tragic evidence of how easily the flames of violence could be fanned."[11] Exactly one decade later on April 7, 2004, the United Nations created an action plan to prevent genocide, including the appointment of a special adviser on this vital matter. In his remarks to commemorate the somber occasion, Kofi Annan, UN secretary-general, made a solemn entreaty and asked a searing question: "We must never forget our collective failure to protect at least 800,000 defenceless men, women and children who perished in Rwanda 10 years ago. Such crimes cannot be reversed. Such failures cannot be repaired. The dead cannot be brought back to life. So what can we do?"[12] Recently, Adama Dieng, special adviser on the prevention of genocide, related official inequity to the possibility of genocide. "One of the most significant risk factors associated with genocide is a record of identity-based discrimination, in other words, discrimination that targets individuals or groups based on their religious, ethnic, racial or national identity," warned Dieng.[13]

Other observers, however, have cautioned that while many analysts have touted ethnicity as a cause of discord in Africa, factions often have wielded it for political or economic gain. Clement Mweyang Aapengnuo advised, "Ethnicity is typically not the driving force of African conflicts but a lever used by political leaders to mobilize supporters in pursuit of power, wealth, and resources."[14] Likewise, one study of ostensibly ethno-religious struggle in Jos, Plateau State, Nigeria, found that, contrary to popular portrayals, differences in ethnicity and religion were not the fundamental triggers of violence in that city. Instead, official government discrimination limiting access to power and resources for certain ethnic and religious groups was at the core of the hostilities.[15] As a result, communal bloodshed erupted in Jos in 2001, 2004, 2008, and 2010 between various ethnic and religious groups, pitting predominately Christian

Anaguta, Afizere, and Berom against largely Muslim Hausa and Fulani, killing thousands of civilians, and displacing as many as 250,000 residents from the energetic city of 1 million people.[16] Nigeria's established, but often arbitrary, practice of distinguishing between *indigenes*, or original, residents of an area and settlers, many of whom had lived in the area for generations, created flashpoints because indigeneship certificates excluded settlers from access to political power and economic opportunities and thereby stoked ethno-religious tensions.[17] Chris Kwaja disclosed, "Nigeria's statutory framework grants local officials the authority to extend or deny basic rights to citizens in their jurisdictions, thereby creating incentives for politicization of ethnicity and escalating intercommunal violence."[18] The bloodshed in Jos was even more significant because the city resides in the Middle Belt of Nigeria, a region where the predominately Muslim north blends with the largely Christian south. As a result, aggression in this region exacerbated existing hostilities in Nigeria's northeast.

As a result, ethnicity per se has not been at the root of conflict in Africa, but rather tensions over perceived ethnic discrimination have become a volatile and combustible atmosphere that local leaders either have mitigated, as was the case of Ghana, or have inflamed, as was the situation in Rwanda. Therefore, established efforts to protect the rights of minority groups have been crucial to assuage ethno-religious tensions and prevent them from erupting into violence. Ghana created the Commission for Human Rights and Administrative Justice (CHRAJ), which allowed redress for victims of ethnic discrimination and alleviated frictions as a result. In brutal contrast, political leaders in Rwanda stoked the embers of ethnic conflict into a raging fire, leading to the 1994 genocide.[19] Much evidence has suggested that ethnicity is not an intrinsic factor in conflict in Africa, most notably the ability of many groups to live in harmony. Clement Mweyang Aapengnuo advised, "While the ethnic group is the predominant means of social identity formation in Africa, most ethnic groups in Africa coexist peacefully with high degrees of mixing through interethnic marriage, economic partnerships, and shared values."[20] Such dynamics even existed in Rwanda, which most observers have characterized as the archetype of ethnic conflict in Africa.

Even when ethnic conflict has not erupted into combat, however, other causes have resulted in numerous civil wars on the continent. Civil wars have ravaged many countries in Africa during the past three decades. Sierra Leone was one prominent example.[21] Rachel Glennerster, Edward Miguel, and Alexander D. Rothenberg discovered that "despite the leading role of ethnic appeals in national politics, ethnic divisions have been much less damaging in Sierra Leone than in many of its African neighbors, and in particular were not a leading factor in the 1991–2002 civil war."[22] Nonetheless, civil war raged for over a decade, displacing more than 1 million people and killing another 50,000.[23] Regarding the prevalence of civil wars in Africa, the structure of political institutions in a particular country has mattered a great deal. Tore Wig showed that "excluded groups with centralized traditional institutions can rely on these institutions to more credibly bargain with the state, and that this reduces their risk of conflict," especially civil wars.[24]

One of the most common triggers for civil wars in Africa has been the coup d'état. The role of military coups in ethnic conflict and civil wars on the continent has been pronounced. Military leaders often have intervened and have seized political power with force. Jean Ping recorded, "Africa has become the continent most prone to military coups. The history of Africa shows that it has experienced, since its various dates of independence after decolonization, more than 70 overthrows of government. In addition, 31 African Heads of State have been assassinated."[25] Of course, this large sum of successful coups does not include the many more unsuccessful ones. When combined, Africa has experienced more than 200 total coups since independence, with Burkina Faso claiming 10 all its own.[26]

Put simply, a desire to accumulate power usually has driven conflict in Africa. Power has manifested itself in various situations as economic resources, political authority, corrupt dealings, or personal gain. Local elections where winners take all and official government discrimination have exacerbated tensions between different ethnic and religious groups. Struggles have erupted, however, not from those ethno-religious distinctions themselves but rather when political leaders purposely have used them for ulterior motives or a government has favored certain ethnic and religious groups over others, thereby accentuating and hardening preexisting differences within a diverse society. Most important, ethnic conflict and civil wars in Africa have existed within particular environments. Two countries that have embodied these types of contemporary security issues in Africa have been Uganda and Sudan.

UGANDA

The Republic of Uganda is a landlocked nation in eastern Africa comprising more than 240,000 square kilometers, of which water covers one-fifth, including Lakes Victoria, Albert, and Kyoga. With its capital located at Kampala, Uganda borders the DRC, Kenya, Rwanda, South Sudan, and Tanzania. Uganda's major terrain feature is a plateau surrounded by mountains, and the nation has abundant natural resources, including arable land, copper, cobalt, and gold. Regular rainfall ensures that fertile soil is one of Uganda's major assets, making agriculture the main sector of the economy and largest employer in the nation. Nearly three-quarters of the land is agricultural, with one-third arable and another one-quarter permanent pasture. Agricultural products include coffee, tea, cotton, tobacco, cassava, potatoes, corn, millet, and pulses, as well as abundant livestock.[27] Coffee is the nation's largest export, although oil deposits discovered in 2006, roughly 2.5 billion barrels of proved reserves, will likely play an increasing role in Uganda's economy. The nation trades widely throughout the region, including lucrative commerce with the DRC, Kenya, and Rwanda, which are all valuable markets for Uganda's exports. The country suffers, however, from several environmental problems, including deforestation, overgrazing, and especially poaching.[28] As with many African nations, Uganda has numerous ethnic groups, including the Acholi, Bakiga, Banyankole, Basoga, Buganda, Iteso, and Langi, among others, that make up its population in excess of 39 million people. The Buganda and Acholi ethnic groups in Uganda have provided an interesting dichotomy.[29] Tore Wig observed, "The Buganda have relied on their traditional centralized pre-colonial structures to bargain with the state, and have largely avoided full-scale war." Wig juxtaposed that dynamic with the Acholi, "a group with *decentralized* and fragmented political institutions. . . . The group has dominated the Ugandan army, and been on the sending and receiving end of numerous coups and rebellions, most recently seen in the revolt of the Acholi-dominated Lord's Resistance

UGANDA

Army (LRA). A bloody civil war has raged in Acholiland since the 1980s [emphasis in the original]."[30] The vast majority of Ugandans are Christian, with roughly 40 percent Roman Catholic, 32 percent Anglican, and 11 percent Pentecostal. Muslims comprise approximately 14 percent of the population. Uganda's population is also very young, with nearly 70 percent under the age of 25.[31]

Uganda gained independence from the United Kingdom on October 9, 1962. A series of brutal authoritarian regimes followed. Idi Amin ruled Uganda from 1971 to 1979, presiding over a horrific reign of terror and killing roughly 300,000 Ugandans in the process.[32] The dictatorial rule of Milton Obote followed from 1980 to 1985, resulting in another 100,000 deaths and wanton human rights abuses.[33] Yoweri Museveni seized power on January 26, 1986. There have been some limited political reforms in the intervening period. In 2005, a constitutional referendum allowed multiple political parties, although it also removed limits on presidential terms. On February 18, 2016, Museveni won reelection, although there were widespread allegations of corruption, fraud, and intimidation. Kizza Besigye, a challenger to Museveni in the election, vowed to contest the results.[34]

Violence has been a near-constant occurrence in Uganda during much of the past three decades. In addition to dictatorial control and flagrant maltreatment by ruling governments, ethno-religious conflict and civil wars have been a common facet of life in Uganda, producing numerous civilian deaths, immense numbers of internally displaced persons (IDPs), and significant refugees fleeing the country. The consequences have been tragic. The ethno-religious conflicts and civil wars in Uganda have resulted in tens of thousands of inhabitants killed and as many as 30,000 children kidnapped to serve as soldiers, thereby fueling grievances and prolonging violence. In addition, these conflicts at their worst displaced nearly 2 million Ugandans, and more than 30,000 have remained so. The reverse also has been true; warfare in such neighboring countries as Burundi, the DRC, Rwanda, Somalia, and South Sudan has produced a steady refugee stream into Uganda from those countries, totaling more than 500,000 refugees.[35]

The LRA is an Ugandan rebel group that has sought to use violence to establish theocratic rule over Uganda and has perpetrated the most recent occurrence in Uganda.[36] Even though ethno-religious conflict and civil wars have plagued Africa for decades, the LRA has incarnated this contemporary security issue while adding a dimension of religious extremism. The Acholi ethnic group has had a long history in northern Uganda and lives in a region of the country known as Acholiland with its capital at Gulu. Throughout the 1970s and 1980s, Uganda's government abused the Acholi, discriminating against them and committing atrocities on their people. In response, they launched a determined insurgency, purportedly to end bigotry against and improve living conditions for all Acholi. The LRA, however, seized upon the nascent uprising and turned the movement ever more violent, even against other Acholi. Regardless of its lofty rhetoric, the LRA has sought power through violence. At its peak, it mobilized several thousand fighters, although that number has dwindled to roughly 100 militants. The insurgent group has adhered to syncretism, which is the blending of various religious traditions and has been common throughout sub-Saharan Africa.[37] In the case of the LRA, syncretism has amalgamated Christian ideology, Acholi beliefs, and spiritual mediums, striving to establish theocratic rule over Uganda through violence based on a radical interpretation of the biblical Ten Commandments and Acholi traditions.

In 1986, Alice Auma, claiming to be a medium for the spirit Lakwena, sparked the Holy Spirit Movement, which intermingled religious syncretism with purported aspirations to improve circumstances for the Acholi people in northern Uganda. The following year, the Uganda People's Democratic Army rebelled against the central government and launched a fierce insurrection. Alice Lakwena led rebels, regaling them with promises of turning stones into grenades and rubbing oil that she blessed over their bodies, professing that it would shield them and thereby prevent enemies' bullets from hurting them.[38] Her campaign climaxed in 1987 at Magamaga in Jinja, only 80 kilometers from Uganda's capital of Kampala. After a crushing defeat there by government forces, the Uganda People's Defense Force (UPDF), Joseph Kony seized the mantle of leadership of the uprising, even though Lakwena had shaken the very foundations of Uganda's political system. Juliys Barigaba insisted, "The famous Magamaga battle was a mere 80 km east of Kampala, and had Lakwena managed to overrun the force at Magamaga, her spirit-nourished fighters would have captured Kampala overnight."[39]

After Lakwena's exit, Kony converted the Holy Spirit Movement into the LRA and assumed absolute rule; he also steered the group further toward religious extremism and tremendous violence.[40] Kony, claiming to be a spirit medium and messiah, first attacked Uganda's government, arguing that Yoweri Museveni, president of Uganda, and his government oppressed the Ugandan people, especially the Acholi. While still professing to seek a theocracy in Uganda based on his extreme interpretation of the biblical Ten Commandments and Acholi traditions, Kony plunged the LRA into fanaticism, violence, and callousness. He glorified cruelty and used it more and more against the Acholi people, contrary to his purported motives. Such an incongruity exposed the fact that Kony's ulterior motive was an unrelenting pursuit of power rather than his claimed purpose of improving living conditions for the Acholi. Kony's ascension to leadership also marked a clear shift in the revolt in Uganda. Theo Neethling asserted, "The movement's basic aim was always to restore national reconciliation, democracy, peace and economic prosperity in Uganda and to reverse the political marginalisation of the Acholi people in northern

Uganda." Such a purpose contrasted sharply with other portrayals of the violent group. "In the public domain, the LRA is known as a terrorist organisation that wishes to establish a theocratic state in Uganda based on the Ten Commandments," Neethling concluded.[41]

In response, Uganda's government launched a series of military offensives targeting the LRA, including Operation North in 1991. In 1996, Uganda's government compounded problems by displacing the Acholi from their homes into government-run camps, which worsened conditions and increased disease in crowded sites with little humanitarian aid. Tens of thousands died from illness alone. Richard Dowden perceived that in a failed attempt to protect the Acholi, "the Ugandan army forced more than 90 per cent of the Acholi population—about two million people—out of their scattered homesteads into 'protected' camps." The dire situation lasted for more than a decade. Dowden explained, "That began in 1996 and lasted until 2009. During those 13 years, the people in these camps lost everything. In the early years, conditions were appalling. Unprecedented mortality levels were recorded."[42] In a perennial and persistent struggle against the LRA, Uganda's government launched Operation Iron Fist in 2002 and Operation Lighting Thunder in 2008. With increased military campaigns targeting them, the LRA shifted its attacks from government personnel to the local populace, committing numerous human rights violations in the process.

In the decades that followed, the LRA waged a brutal campaign in northern Uganda. Partly in response to government pressure, the group also expanded its range of operations into neighboring countries. The LRA first shifted toward the area that would become South Sudan, then to the Democratic Republic of Congo, and most recently into the Central African Republic. Everywhere its militants went, they left devastation in their wake. Their ruthless campaign led to approximately 2 million IDPs and another 350,000 refugees. In the process, the LRA destabilized Uganda and the surrounding region. Among many heinous acts, the radical group employed significant numbers of child soldiers, kidnapping the vast majority of them and then forcing them to participate in their odious attacks.[43] The LRA used abduction as its primary recruiting strategy, waging violence to seize children and thereby sustaining the group's capacity to conduct cruelty. As a result, the LRA fueled its campaign of terror with kidnapped children forced to fight. In a vicious cycle, the kidnappers targeted refugee camps for the conscription of child soldiers.[44] The LRA strategy was as simple as it was inhumane: kidnap children, indoctrinate them, and then force them to kill others, including their own family members. Estimating that the LRA abducted approximately 30,000 child soldiers, James Bevan compared this recruiting through kidnapping scheme to plunder: "In the absence of economic and social endowments with which to reward membership, the LRA abducts potential fighters from the civilian population in a way that is analogous to resource exploitation."[45] The results of this inhumaneness were terrific. The LRA embarked on a campaign of horror in Uganda and surrounding areas. In the aftermath of its carnage, the group left 2 million people displaced in Uganda and tens of thousands dead from brutality and disease.

In addition to efforts by Uganda's government, there have been numerous international efforts to stop the LRA. On July 8, 2005, the International Criminal Court (ICC) issued arrest warrants for Kony and four senior accomplices, including Vincent Otti, Okot Odhiambo, Raska Lukwiya, and Dominic Ongwen. The ICC charged these commanders with numerous crimes against humanity, including murder, rape, mutilation, and kidnapping, among many others. Legal efforts did little, however, to halt the group. Several senior commanders died prior to apprehension, including Lukwiya in 2006, Otti in 2007, and Odhiambo in 2013, although authorities could not confirm Odhiambo's death until two years later. Kony and Ongwen eluded apprehension. Kony expanded his group's viciousness into bordering countries. In 2005, the same year that the ICC charged him and his lieutenants with crimes against humanity, the LRA extended its reach from Uganda and began operating in neighboring DRC. In 2006, the United Nations Organization Mission in the Democratic Republic of the Congo (MONUC) sought to apprehend LRA leaders but failed multiple times.[46] In 2008, the group moved its base of operations once again, this time to the Central African Republic. Even though on the run and with its number of fighters dwindling, the LRA remained callous and vehement. In December 2009, several dozen LRA fighters attacked Makombo, located in the Haut Uele district of the DRC. In four days of monstrous viciousness, LRA fighters killed almost 350 civilians and kidnapped 250 more. Combined with several other assaults, local residents collectively characterized these reprehensible raids in northern DRC as the "Christmas massacres," which resulted in over 600 total deaths at the hands of a weakened but still deadly LRA.

The group's atrocious acts and seeming impunity garnered regional and international attention, including exertions to stop it by the African Union, European Union, United States, and United Nations. In 2010, U.S. president Barack H. Obama signed the LRA Disarmament and Northern Uganda Recovery Act, aimed at capturing the group's leaders and ceasing its atrocities.[47] Social media sparked additional awareness and shined a spotlight on the terrible acts of Kony and the LRA. In 2012, Invisible Children, Inc., produced the video "Kony 2012," which spotlighted many abuses of the organization and its notorious leader; the video went viral, as more than 100 million people viewed it. It consequently fostered public awareness and revulsion at the group's sadism. The captivating documentary exposed Kony's callousness and sparked a public campaign to "Stop Kony," which aimed to apprehend him and end his cruelties.

In 2012, regional leaders activated the African Union Regional Task Force to combat the LRA. Two thousand soldiers from the UPDF joined 500 troops from the Sudan People's Liberation Army (SPLA) to mobilize the task force. Throughout 2013, this unit sought to capture Kony and his senior accomplices. Exertions continued as international partners trained African militaries to contest the LRA and apprehend its leadership. The effort was tedious but achieved some successes.[48] In 2014, the African Union appointed a new special envoy to coordinate its responses to the LRA.[49] In 2015, Dominic Ongwen surrendered to soldiers from the task force. As a result, the ICC began his trial on December 6, 2016, on charges of war crimes and crimes against humanity surrounding his atrocious human rights abuses as commander of the notorious Sinia Brigade of the LRA.[50] This was the first trial of an LRA commander and continued through January 2017. Throughout the hearings, the ICC received testimony from 4,000 victims of the LRA. Ongwen, a former child soldier himself, faced more than 70 counts of crimes against humanity. Personifying the ruthlessness of the group, the LRA had abducted Ongwen at the age of 10 and had trained him to become a soldier, and, in the process, he had grown to become one of Kony's most vicious accomplices.

In 2016, international partners continued to work with the African Union Regional Task Force to hunt for Kony and his remaining fighters,

A Uganda People's Defense Force soldier fires a rocket-propelled grenade during live-fire training at Camp Singo, Uganda. August 20, 2014. (Courtesy United States Africa Command)

although Uganda's interest in continuing the costly operation waned. Paddy Ankunda, UPDF spokesperson, vowed, "The LRA has been degraded. They no longer have the means to make war." Ankunda also argued that international support had failed to fund the full costs of the effort.[51] On April 19, 2017, Uganda halted the search for Kony, which had spent more than $750 million from its launch in 2011. The UPDF spokesperson claimed that even though Kony remained at large, Uganda's goal had been achieved due to the LRA's inability to function.[52] Kony has evaded apprehension at the time of this writing, most likely hiding in the border region of Kafia Kingi between the Central African Republic, South Sudan, and Sudan. These military offensives, however, have significantly damaged the LRA's capability. The possibility of limited atrocities has persisted, but with only 100 soldiers, the group lacks the capability to wage the broad and sustained violence that they previously had wielded throughout the region for much of the past 30 years. While Richard Karemire, Ugandan army spokesperson, maintained that Kony, and by extension the LRA, "no longer poses any significant threat to Uganda's security and Northern Uganda in particular," the African Union on June 6, 2017, released a report that cautioned against viewing the threat in other countries as extinguished. "The LRA has maintained an active presence in CAR, DRC and parts of South Sudan where it continues to raid, ambush, loot, torture, abduct and detain civilians, as well as traffic ivory poached from the Garamba National Park in the DRC, and minerals looted from CAR to sustain itself and its leader, Joseph Kony," cautioned Moussa Faki Mahamat, head of the African Union commission. Mahamat warned that the "LRA has not yet been eliminated and still maintains the potential to rejuvenate itself."[53] In early April 2018, UN Multidimensional Integrated Stabilization Mission in the Central African Republic (MINUSCA) peacekeepers rescued 15 hostages that the LRA had kidnapped near the city of Obo, Central African Republic.[54] Even with the organization largely defeated, however, tribulations in Uganda have lingered. Freedom House reported that Yoweri Museveni, Uganda's president, "sought to remove the presidential age limit of 75, which would permit him to run again in 2021. Museveni had just won reelection the previous year in a process that featured police violence, internet shutdowns, and treason charges against his main challenger."[55] After achieving his goal, Museveni has initiated the process to change Uganda's presidential term limit from five to seven years, thereby further entrenching him in power after more than three decades of rule already.[56]

SUDAN

The Republic of Sudan is an eastern African nation and part of the Nile valley, comprising nearly 1.9 million square kilometers and bordering the

Central African Republic, Chad, Egypt, Eritrea, Ethiopia, Libya, and South
Sudan. With its capital at Khartoum, Sudan's key geographic features
include flat plains and northern deserts, which suffer from frequent dust
storms and periodic drought. Other environmental troubles include wildlife poaching, soil erosion, and desertification. Sudan also has 853 kilometers of coastline on the Red Sea. Although riddled with rampant poverty,
oil has dominated Sudan's economy for much of the past three decades.
Sudan produces roughly 105,000 barrels of crude oil per day and boasts
proved reserves of 5 billion barrels. It also possesses nearly 85 billion cubic
meters of proved reserves of natural gas. Approximately 75 percent of its
former oil production now resides in South Sudan, whose independence
roiled Sudan's economy and resulted in rampant inflation, peaking near
50 percent in 2012 and remaining around 35 percent thereafter. Sudan
exports gold, but oil remains Sudan's largest export, most of it transiting
to Egypt, Macau, Saudi Arabia, and the United Arab Emirates.

Even though oil overshadows its exports, the vast majority of Sudanese
work in the agricultural sector, most as subsistence farmers. Agricultural
products include cotton, peanuts, sorghum, millet, wheat, sugarcane, cassava, and sweet potatoes, among others. Sudan is also the world's largest
producer of gum arabic, accounting for three-quarters of global supply.
Sudan has a population of more than 37 million people, of whom approximately 60 percent are younger than 25 years old. The largest ethnic group

is Sudanese Arab, representing roughly 70 percent of the population, joined by minorities of Fur, Beja, Nuba, and Fallata. Most Sudanese are Sunni Muslim. Civil war has had a major impact on Sudan: the nation has had more than 2 million total IDPs, largely due to ethno-religious conflict and civil war.[57]

The Republic of South Sudan, which gained independence from Sudan on July 9, 2011, is a landlocked country, spanning roughly 645,000 square kilometers and bordering the Central African Republic, the DRC, Ethiopia, Kenya, Sudan, and Uganda. With its capital located at Juba, South Sudan's terrain consists of highlands in the south, which transition to vast plains in the center and north of the country. The White Nile River runs through the middle of South Sudan, creating the Sudd, a wetland of more than 100,000 square kilometers, one of the world's largest swamps. The lengthy civil war resulting in its creation devastated South Sudan's infrastructure, especially its road network. Even so, South Sudan has abundant natural resources. Agricultural products include sorghum, maize, rice, millet, wheat, mangoes, papayas, and bananas, as well as nearly 20 million head of cattle. Most South Sudanese pursue subsistence farming and live in poverty. South Sudan benefits from fertile soil and abundant water; it also possesses the majority of oil between the two countries, producing more than 150,000 barrels per day at peak production and holding nearly 3.8 billion barrels of proved reserves, as well as more than 63 billion cubic meters of natural gas proved reserves. South Sudan relies on oil revenue for its entire budget. Because South Sudan is landlocked, however, its valuable oil exports must transit by pipelines north to Port Sudan on the Red Sea. This situation has been a source of tension between the two nations, as Sudan's demands for increased transshipment fees led South Sudan to cease all production of oil in January 2012. This impasse battered both economies, with inflation in South Sudan peaking near 80 percent but subsiding by 2013, whereas inflation in Sudan was less severe, peaking at 50 percent but lasted much longer.[58] South Sudan's population stands at approximately 13 million, with nearly two-thirds of South Sudanese younger than 25 years old. As with most African nations, South Sudan is home to numerous ethnic groups, with the two largest, Dinka and Nuer, accounting for roughly half of the population. Most South Sudanese are Christian, with some practicing animist beliefs. Like its neighbor to the north, South Sudan is home to numerous refugees, including more than 260,000 from Sudan. In addition, South Sudan has had nearly 1.8 million IDPs, some from the war with Sudan and many more from the internal struggle that began in December 2013 and has shattered South Sudan.[59]

In order to understand the two countries, one must first comprehend the historical context of Sudan. Muhammad Ahmad, known colloquially as the Mahdi or Expected One, ruled Sudan until 1898, when British and Egyptian forces seized control of the region.[60] In 1955, civil war ignited,

SOUTH SUDAN–SUDAN

largely along the geographical and cultural divide between north and south. Kenneth Omeje and Nicodemus Minde discovered, "From the perspective of the southern elite, northern domination of political and administrative offices in government meant that the south became a colony of a colony at a time when Sudan was yet to attain independence."[61] The resulting civil war would become known as Anyanya, which, if translated, means roughly "snake venom." On January 1, 1956, Sudan gained independence from British and Egyptian rule, although fighting persisted. As a result, civil war raged from 1956 to 1972 and again from 1983 to 2005. In 1989, a military coup resulted in Omar al-Bashir assuming the presidency, and civil war again broke out between the predominately Muslim north and the largely Christian south. One tragic consequence of the fighting was the migration of the Lost Boys and Lost Girls, a refugee stream of as many as 20,000 orphaned children, most of them destitute and malnourished, who fled the civil war in Sudan to neighboring Ethiopia and Kenya. The plight of these children spurred efforts by aid organizations to care for them in refugee camps, reunite them with their families, or resettle them in peaceful locations.[62]

These two civil wars ravaged the population and resulted in more than 2 million civilian deaths. Not all conflict, however, was between Muslims and Christians. In 1991, Riek Machar, an ethnic Nuer and leader of a faction of the Sudan People's Liberation Movement (SPLM), massacred 5,000 ethnic Dinka in Bor, Jonglei State, Sudan, which was the hometown of John Garang, himself a Dinka. "It's an act not even the government we are fighting has done before," lamented Kwol Manyand, an SPLA commander loyal to Garang.[63] This atrocity was both foreboding and foreshadowing, as the eventual civil war in South Sudan would follow similar tribal lines of ethnic conflict. The significant and persistent fighting garnered international attention, largely due to widespread human rights abuses in Darfur, located in western Sudan.[64] Fighting in Darfur erupted in 2003, rapidly degenerating into genocide. Deaths numbered approximately 300,000 while displacing another 2 million Sudanese. Among the many atrocities, the forcible recruitment of child soldiers was appalling and fueled additional cruelties. In January 2005, leaders from the two sides proposed a peace treaty, the North/South Comprehensive Peace Agreement (CPA). As a result of the agreement, rebel groups in the south gained six years of autonomy, at the conclusion of which there would be a referendum on southern independence. On January 9, 2005, the Khartoum government and the SPLA signed the CPA, thereby halting the civil war and opening a path toward self-determination for South Sudan. The CPA included provisions for the inclusion of SPLM leaders in Sudan's government, equal sharing of oil revenues, limitation of sharia law to northern Sudan, and a popular referendum on independence for southern Sudan to be held six years after the signing of the agreement, among other stipulations.

On July 30, 2005, John Garang, an SPLA colonel and leader, Sudan's vice president, and presumptive future president of South Sudan, died in a helicopter crash, and Salva Kiir replaced him. As a result of the subsequent political chaos and amid allegations of assassination, a tenuous peace dissolved and steady fighting resumed. The African Union attempted to maintain order: the African Union Mission in Sudan (AMIS) had approximately 2,000 troops but lacked financial resources. In 2006, the United Nations–African Union Mission in Darfur (UNAMID) sought to stop the genocide in Darfur with approximately 14,000 troops and a budget of $1.5 billion.[65] Thomas G. Weiss and Martin Welz commented, "The African Union-United Nations Mission in Darfur (UNAMID) was established amid genocide in Sudan's Darfur region and owes its existence to several factors: The Sudanese government's refusal to allow non-African troops into the country; the AU's inability to stop the ongoing genocide; and the urgent need, as articulated by the Security Council, to solve the crisis with the consent of the Sudanese government."[66]

In January 2011, South Sudan became destined to become the world's newest country as a result of a popular referendum in which more than

98 percent of voters in the south chose independence.[67] Conflict in Sudan did not end, however, with the creation of South Sudan. Jubilation quickly dissipated into ethnic tensions within the new country. The Sudan People's Liberation Movement-North continued to fight in South Kordofan and Blue Nile states, displacing more than 1 million Sudanese. In addition to its own conflict, Sudan has received more than 350,000 refugees from the Central African Republic, Chad, Eritrea, Ethiopia, and South Sudan.

On July 9, 2011, South Sudan celebrated independence. Juba is its capital and largest city, claiming some 400,000 residents. The young country has extensive oil but is landlocked, making it reliant on shipping oil in pipelines through Omdurman near Khartoum and ending at Port Sudan on the Red Sea. South Sudan's economy is almost exclusively reliant on oil, by some estimates as much as 98 percent, making dependence on pipeline transit absolute and the resulting volatility extreme.[68] Much of its oil rested in the disputed territory along the border between South Sudan and Sudan, which has led to additional and persistent antagonisms.[69] Kenneth Omeje and Nicodemus Minde publicized, "Between April and May 2012, Sudan and South Sudan came to the brink of a major war as armed hostilities and war rhetoric over the ownership of the Heglig oil fields (in the disputed Abyei region) and mutual recriminations regarding sponsoring rebel insurgencies to destabilise each other's territory reached a tipping point."[70]

Once held up as the embodiment of hope and optimism for democracy, South Sudan has become a troubling example of the difficulties of ethno-religious conflict and civil wars in Africa. James Harkin presaged, "It is a parable about the peril of dreaming up fragile new mini-states as a response to problems within troubled old countries. South Sudan is not so much a failed state as one that never truly came into being; it was born dead."[71] As a result, ethnic tensions resurfaced with a vengeance. In April 2013, Salva Kiir, South Sudan's president, restricted Riek Machar's power as vice president, and, in July 2013, Kiir fired Machar along with most of his cabinet. On December 15, 2013, pressures exploded, personified by Kiir, an ethnic Dinka, accusing Machar, an ethnic Nuer, of treason by plotting a coup d'état against him. This development was significant, and ominous, because these groups represent two of the largest ethnic groups in South Sudan: the Dinka comprise approximately 36 percent of the population and the Nuer make up another 16 percent.[72] As a result of countless accusations and recriminations, supporters of each faction launched a new civil war within South Sudan largely along ethnic lines, resulting in approximately 2 million persons displaced from the nascent nation and 50,000 civilian deaths.[73]

The Intergovernmental Authority on Development (IGAD) has attempted to broker the peace process, reaching several agreements only to have fighting resume again. In 2013, violence reemerged in Darfur, causing more than 5,000 deaths and displacing another 500,000 people. In a vicious cycle, civil war in Sudan resulted in the creation of South Sudan, which itself devolved into its own civil war. Sudan and South Sudan also have disputed the Abyei region along their respective borders, keeping tensions between the two countries combustible at best.[74] After significant pressure from the African Union and United Nations, Kiir, leader of the SPLM-in-Government, and Machar, leader of the SPLM-in-Opposition, agreed in August 2015 to end the struggle and share power in South Sudan. "Signing is not the difficult part, but implementation is the biggest challenge which we must collectively work with President Kiir and Machar to bring the lasting peace to our beloved Nation," commented Gatwech Koak Nyuon, South Sudan peace ambassador, in an ominous foreboding of the difficulties of achieving peace in the young country.[75] In April 2016, Machar returned to Juba and joined Kiir to form the Transitional Government of National Unity (TGONU).[76] Indicative of the elusive prospect of peace in South Sudan, compromise failed in July 2016 as Machar left Juba for a second time and violence reignited.[77]

The lack of progress for South Sudan since independence has led some observers to call for a "clean break" in which both Kiir and Machar would leave power and an international transitional administration established by the African Union and the United Nations would govern the country until it has sufficient stability and capacity for self-rule.[78] South Sudan, however, has continued to experience near-constant warfare.[79] Even though leaders signed a cessation of hostilities agreement on December 21, 2017, fighting has continued largely undiminished.[80]

The devastation has been significant.[81] The civil war has resulted in 4.5 million IDPs and refugees from South Sudan alone. The Africa Center for Strategic Studies recorded that this was "the same number of southern Sudanese displaced during the entire three-decade Sudan civil war." As a result of this newest clash, 7 million people, nearly two-thirds of South Sudan's entire population, have required humanitarian assistance. The situation has only gotten worse. The Africa Center for Strategic Studies alerted, "The humanitarian situation in 2018 is expected to be worse than 2017 as conflict persists, farming is disrupted, humanitarian access is restricted, the economy is further destabilized, and household coping capacity dwindles."[82] Such dire predictions have borne out, as violence indeed has surged. In late April 2018, the UN peacekeeping mission in South Sudan cautioned that conditions in the fledgling country had deteriorated. David Shearer, special representative of the UN secretary-general for South Sudan and head of the UN Mission in South Sudan (UNMISS), warned, "Our teams on the ground are reporting incidents of killing, sexual violence, homes being burnt to the ground, cattle raiding, and the looting of hospitals and schools."[83] Hope still has flickered for the young nation, but the winds of carnage have made it faint indeed.

CONCLUSION

Ethno-religious conflict and civil wars have been significant contemporary security issues in Africa. In excess of 125 total wars during the past three decades have impacted more than 30 countries on the continent.[84] Many observers have argued that ethnicity has been a pivotal driver in these fights. Extreme ethnic conflict occasionally has led to genocide, as was the case in Rwanda and Darfur. Other observers, however, have pointed out that leaders often have leveraged ethnicity for political or economic gain. Ultimately, these clashes have revolved around power. Official government discrimination against certain groups has prevented their access to political clout and economic opportunities; as a result, it also has created volatile discontent. When leaders have fanned the flames of ethno-religious differences, discord has erupted. Civil wars in Africa also have been rampant over the past three decades. Often triggered by military coups, civil wars have been about power and have devastated countries. Uganda has exemplified ethno-religious conflict in Africa. The emergence of the LRA and its subsequent campaign of terror wracked the nation and undermined its neighbors. The LRA also revealed that when left to their own devices, militant groups have gained momentum and expanded operations; when targeted relentlessly, they have been vanquished. In contrast, Sudan has shown the impact of civil wars in Africa. With a lengthy history of violence, Sudan embarked on a civil war that lasted for nearly three decades and exhibited ethno-religious fault lines. The conflict resulted in the world's newest state, South Sudan, and the accompanying jubilance and optimism that came with such creation. Ultimate reality, however, differed greatly from initial aspiration. Begot from civil war, South Sudan descended in short order into its own civil war, one that has continued to confound the fledgling nation. The costs of ethnic conflict and civil war have been tremendous. Kate Almquist Knopf accounted, "UN peacekeeping in the two Sudans since 2004 has cost approximately $20 billion, the costliest peace interventions in the last decade."[85] While ethno-religious conflict and civil wars have been important contemporary security issues in Africa, they have not been alone. Natural resources and environmental security also have been quite important.

CHAPTER 4

Natural Resources and Environmental Security

OVERVIEW

Natural resources and environmental security have been significant contemporary security issues in Africa. Many observers have characterized a resource curse in which the presence of abundant assets in a particular nation, especially a developing one, can exacerbate conflict rather than provide stability. Although a country rich in resources is not destined for war, in many cases resource wealth hampers diversification, emboldens corruption, entrenches despotism, and subsidizes violence; therefore, copious natural resources can become an accelerant to discord, providing volatility and tension rather than steadiness and peace.[1] Dominik Kopiński, Andrzej Polus, and Wojciech Tycholiz wrote, "On a political level, the resource curse hypothesis suggests that resource-rich developing states are more prone to bad governance, corruption, and rent-seeking behaviour that can lead to a weaker democracy." They explained, "It is based on the observation that the very resources that should be used for the benefit of the population often end up in the hands of a very small and exclusive elite, and in the long term bring adversity rather than prosperity to the majority of people."[2] Along similar lines, many scholars have described a phenomenon known as the Dutch disease, wherein reliance on a specific commodity can set an economy off-balance. *African Business* commented, "Resources have historically proved to be a curse for many nations, either due to the corruption they may foster or due to the Dutch disease, whereby the rest of the economy is distorted as a result of commodity income driving up the currency."[3]

Ample innate means may not cause warfare, but they can act as kindling to fuel violence and to sustain fighting. Income from natural resources, often referred to as rents, has allowed political bribes, arms purchases, and recruitment pay, which all provide tinder that can spark bloodshed. Mick Moore reasoned, "Schematically, the existence of these rents establishes incentives for two different types of actors to militarize political conflict. Those who enjoy government power are tempted to use some of the rents to ensure that they stay in power through non-democratic means: through buying over leading political opponents, recruiting well-paid armed forces and intelligence services, and spending generously on military equipment." Moore continued, "At the same time, knowledge that those in power are unlikely to cede it peacefully motivates 'out' groups to resort to military strategies to try to obtain their share of temptingly-large rents. In sum, the evidence tells us that existence of resource rents, especially those from oil and minerals, tends to generate both non-democratic forms of rule and internal armed conflict."[4]

Nowhere in the world has the resource curse been more evident than Africa. Many countries on the continent possess rich inherent possessions, yet, instead of strength, resulting struggles often engulf them. Jessica Moody declared, "The impact of the so-called resource curse on African countries has been widely documented. A country rich in natural resources on the continent has typically fallen victim to poor economic management and attendant increases in poverty and unemployment."[5] Examples have included Angola, Chad, the Democratic Republic of the Congo (DRC), Ghana, and the Republic of the Congo (Brazzaville). In a detailed examination of the impact of natural resources and environmental security on Angola, Philippe Le Billon maintained, "Rents generated by narrow and mostly foreign-dominated resource industries allow ruling groups to dispense with economic diversification and popular legitimacy, often resulting in rent-seeking, poor economic growth, and little social mobility outside politics and state patronage."[6]

In addition to the complex relationship between natural resources and struggle in Africa, the expropriation of natural resources has had severe consequences on the continent. Environmental security issues such as desertification and deforestation have been banes across Africa. International actors have attempted to address some of these problems through environmental initiatives, including the UN Convention to Combat Desertification (UNCCD) established in June 1994. The convention is global, with 196 countries party to it, most recently South Sudan on May 18, 2014.[7] The UNCCD defined desertification as "land degradation in arid, semi-arid and dry sub-humid areas resulting from various factors, including climatic variations and human activities."[8] The convention also recorded "the high concentration of developing countries, notably the least developed countries, among those experiencing drought and/or

desertification, and the particularly tragic consequences of these phenom-
ena in Africa."[9] As a result, the convention adopted a 10-year strategy in
2007, running from 2008 to 2018. The convention also related desertification to food security.[10]

Security issues in Africa have impacted natural resources and environmental security on the continent and vice versa. O. P. Godwin observed,
"These are exacerbated by recurrent floods and droughts as well as
by other natural disasters, which set back the economies of a number of countries—and thus sustainable development."[11] Of course, climate change also has been a major issue for Africa.[12] The African Union
dreaded, "Whilst Africa at present contributes less than 5% of global car-
bon emissions, it bears the brunt of the impact of climate change."[13] As a
result, the African Union has prioritized addressing climate change as a
major conundrum for the continent over the next five decades. In addition to desertification and climate change, deforestation in Africa has been
a perennial problem.[14] Deforestation has hurt many countries in Africa,
including the DRC, Nigeria, Sudan, Tanzania, Zambia, and Zimbabwe,
among others.

Many of the tribulations with natural resources and environmental security in Africa have involved multinational corporations. The UN
Universal Declaration of Human Rights (UNUDHR) formed the foundation of contemporary international human rights law. The Norms on the
Responsibilities of Transnational Corporations and Other Business Enterprises with Regard to Human Rights applied human rights law to multinational corporations, which the United Nations approved in 2003 largely
in response to natural resource and environmental security difficulties.
In addition, the Extractive Industries Transparency Initiative (EITI) has
proven crucial to combating corruption associated with natural resources,
lessening conflict emanating from competition over them, and improving accountability in the extractive industries, a move that has been
essential to Africa addressing these contemporary security issues. Omeje
and Minde pronounced, "EITI is a voluntary multi-stakeholder regulatory regime that is based on soft governance mechanisms. EITI aims to
improve public revenue management through voluntary disclosure, by
operating companies and states, of payments resulting from the sale of
natural resources (solid minerals and hydrocarbons)."[15] As a result, EITI
seeks transparency, traceability, and accountability with regard to natural
resources, which helps to mitigate clashes over them. Based on the perceived success of this initiative, another enhanced version, EITI++, has
sought to assist weak states with natural resource management through
World Bank partners.

Natural resources have been the source of great potential and significant struggle for Africa; as a result, they have exhibited a dual nature,
presenting both promise and risk. The exigency for natural resources in

Africa has risen during the past three decades, especially for oil and minerals. M. J. Morgan projected, "Iron ore demand, for instance, is expected to increase by 50% between 2010 and 2016."[16] Much of this pressure has had negative consequences, and some of it has resulted in bloodshed.[17] Even when there has not been overt fighting, natural resources often have failed to achieve the potential that they hold for many countries in Africa. In 2007, Ghana discovered oil off its coast in the Atlantic Ocean and began production in 2010, initially generating more than 100,000 barrels per day. Preliminary estimates counted the possible revenue at $3.5 billion, capable of completely transforming Ghana's economy.[18] Some observers held early hope that Ghana would mark a departure from the natural resource curse. Dominik Kopiński, Andrzej Polus, and Wojciech Tycholiz identified "the inherent, structural features of Ghana's political and economic systems that, in our view, render the country less vulnerable to the NRC [Natural Resource Curse]: the strength of its civil society; the institutionalization of its political process; and the relative predictability of its economic performance."[19] Their optimism was well founded. Ghana had a relatively diversified economy and a strong democracy, although oil was a newfound, and significant, addition. Previously, fishing and agriculture had controlled Ghana's economy, with more than half of its population reliant upon those sectors, and the nation has had historical connections to gold and cocoa exports. Even with such "cautious optimism," however, the authors admitted that "in the Ghanian case, there is every chance that the resource curse will prove to be a treatable 'disease.'"[20] Nearly a decade of oil production has done little to improve Ghana's economy or the living conditions of its citizens. *African Business* reported, "The UN's Human Development Index indicates that Ghana has made no substantial progress in improving the standard of living of its citizens since it was buoyed by its first production of oil."[21] Other cases in Africa have emerged, ripe with hopefulness about the renovating potential of natural resources. In January 2016, Senegal discovered possibly as much as 450 billion cubic meters of gas off its coast, which "marked the biggest ever offshore gas discovery in West Africa."[22] Although the first gas likely will not be extracted until at least 2021, managing it successfully will be an opportunity and trial for Senegal. Two case studies that have typified the critical importance of natural resources and environmental security in Africa have been Angola and the DRC.

ANGOLA

The Republic of Angola is a coastal nation in southern Africa, boasting approximately 1,600 kilometers of coastline along the South Atlantic Ocean. Deriving its name from the Ndongo Kingdom and with its capital at Luanda, Angola borders the DRC, Namibia, Republic of the Congo

(Brazzaville), and Zambia and comprises roughly 1,250,000 square kilometers, including its discontinuous Cabinda Province.[23] Angola's dominant terrain feature is its narrow coastal plain that transitions rapidly to a large interior plateau, which is prone to occasional flooding. The oil industry governs Angola's economy, with the diamond trade playing a secondary, but much less prominent, part. Most of the nation's population pursues subsistence farming and raises livestock, although pasture overuse, soil erosion, desertification, and deforestation are all perennial trials for this nation.[24] Abundant rainfall ensures fertile land, and Angola's major agricultural products include bananas, sugarcane, coffee, corn, cotton, cassava, and tobacco; its environment is especially conducive to coffee. Much of this agricultural potential, however, goes unrealized. The Food and Agriculture Organization (FAO) conceded, "With around 10 percent of Angola's arable land currently under cultivation, the country's agricultural productivity and crop yields are extremely low. Given that more than half of Angola's poor are located in rural areas and depend almost exclusively on agriculture for their livelihood, it was fundamental to boost the agriculture sector's institutional capacity."[25] As a result, the FAO funded more than 500 farmer field schools in Bié, Huambo, and Malanje, which trained more than 13,000 smallholder farmers.

On November 11, 1975, Angola gained independence from Portugal. The Alvor Accords envisioned coalition government between the Popular

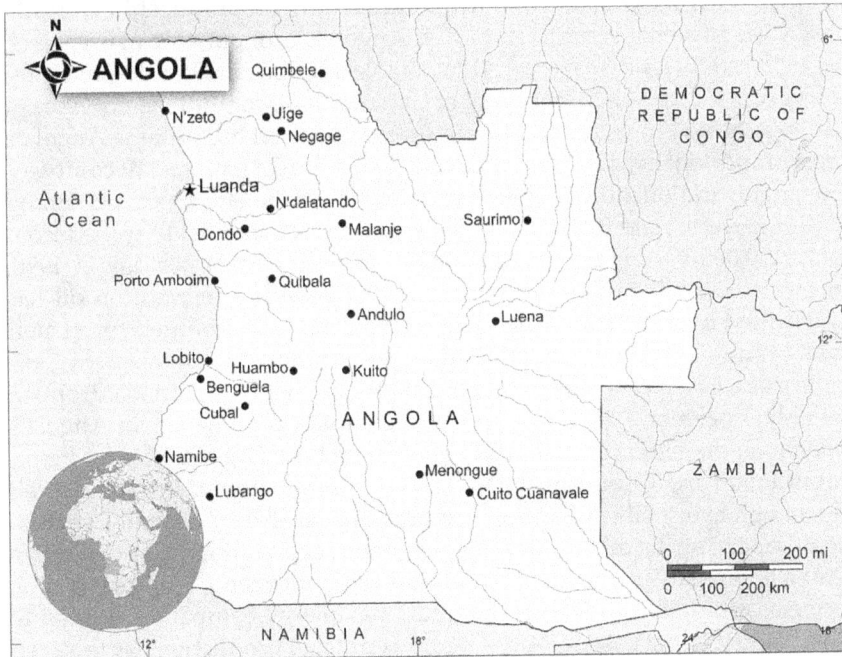

Movement for the Liberation of Angola (MPLA), National Union for the
Total Independence of Angola (UNITA), and National Liberation Front
of Angola (FNLA). The agreement ended, however, as the various factions resorted to force and fighting resumed. As a result, the MPLA seized
power in Luanda, and the international powers enmeshed in the global
Cold War attempted to influence the resulting civil war through support
to various sides. Even though outside forces placed Angola within the ide-
ological paradigm of the Cold War, natural resources were always at the
center of the bloodshed in Angola. Philippe Le Billon insisted, "The industrial economy of the twentieth century and the spread of luxury consumption provided a demand for Angola's oil and diamonds that partly fueled
four decades of war. Angola's wealth appears to be a curse for its people."[26] Angola's wealth in natural resources has not benefited the majority
of Angolans; despite its many natural resources, the country ranks low on
human development. In the UN "Human Development Report," Angola
ranked 150th out of 188 countries.[27] Over the 15-year period from 1990 to
2015, Angola showed some slight improvement but gained only four spots
from 2010 to 2015 and remained in the "low human development" category.[28] Nearly three decades of civil war decimated Angola and required
a massive reconstruction effort after the conflict's end in 2002. The result
has been a dearth of intact infrastructure throughout much of the country.
Oil production spurred Angola's economic growth after its civil war, and
the nation is the second-largest oil producer in sub-Saharan Africa, behind
Nigeria.[29] Angola is also the fourth-largest diamond producer in world.[30]

Oil has played a significant part in Angola's economy for many years.
In 1955, explorers discovered oil in Angola's Kwanza valley. In the 1960s,
surveyors located oil off the coast of Cabinda, a discontinuous province of
Angola located to its north. Since independence, oil has become Angola's
most important export. The MPLA created in 1976 a national oil company,
Sonangol, and offshore oil fields proliferated in the late 1990s, beginning
with the Kuito field in 1999. Angola's oil production quickly spiked from
only 150,000 barrels per day in 1980 to 475,000 barrels per day in 1990,
rising to 735,000 barrels per day in 2000.[31] Angola's reliance on oil has
intensified over the past three decades. In 2000, oil accounted for 91 percent of Angola's exports, with diamonds accounting for 9 percent. In 2005,
oil's share of exports rose to 96 percent, while that of diamonds dropped
to only 4 percent.[32] As a result of oil's climbing prominence in Angola's
economy, the nation in December 2006 joined the Organization of Petroleum Exporting Countries (OPEC). To some industry experts, it seemed
as though every oil exploration has proven successful: "Globally, companies hope to strike oil in four out of every ten exploration wells drilled. In
Angola, that strike rate has been almost ten out of ten."[33] Oil production
boomed from 2002 to 2008 as international energy companies flocked to
the country. In the past decade, Angola's crude oil production has lessened

somewhat but has remained substantial. In 2010, Angola produced 2 million barrels per day, and, by 2015, that number dipped to 1.8 million barrels per day.[34] Oil has continued to dwarf Angola's economy. Angola is the second-largest producer of oil in sub-Saharan Africa behind Nigeria, producing approximately 1.7 million barrels per day of petroleum.[35] Virtually all the country's exports remain oil related, with proved reserves of crude oil at roughly 8.3 billion barrels, much of which the Cabinda province holds.

Even with such profuse means, Angola lags well behind in economic and human development. Once again, this dynamic has related to natural resources—in Angola's case, oil. Because oil comprises such a significant portion of Angola's exports, more than 90 percent, the government has relied on it exclusively, has paid little attention to diversifying Angola's economy, and has shown even less interest in improving the living conditions of its people. The UN Human Development Index ranked Angola 150th out of 188 countries.[36] As a result, Angolans have suffered while Angola's government and international corporations have reaped large dividends. Many ethnic groups comprise Angola's population of roughly 29 million people, with the Ovimbundu, Kimbundu, and Bakongo being the largest in number. Approximately two-thirds of Angola's population is below the age of 25. Much of the population holds indigenous religious beliefs, while more than 41 percent are Roman Catholic and another one-third is Protestant.

Angola gained independence from Portugal on November 11, 1975, but quickly erupted into internal combat. A vicious civil war raged from 1975 to 2002 between the Popular Movement for the Liberation of Angola (MPLA) led by José Eduardo dos Santos and UNITA commanded by Jonas Savimbi. Situated within the context of the global Cold War, fighting in Angola attracted external largesse in the form of support from the Soviet Union and the United States for the various factions.[37] Military intervention by foreign fighters from Cuba, South Africa, and Zaire (modern-day DRC) ensued. In 1987, Angola joined the International Monetary Fund (IMF) and World Bank, marking a turn away from socialism and toward integration into the global economy. The MPLA and UNITA waged a brutal civil war, with violence hitting a peak from 1992 to 1994. The endemic warfare also attracted private security companies, most notably the South African firm Executive Outcomes.[38]

Fighting in Angola impacted neighboring countries, including the DRC, Namibia, and Republic of the Congo (Brazzaville) and destabilized much of the region. Renato Aguilar and Andrea Goldstein explained, "Thus, at the beginning of the 2000s, Angola's economy suffered from enormous distortions—excessive reliance on the oil and diamond sectors, with few linkages to the domestic sector, a small services sector, a large army with non-transparent expenditures, and a large and overstaffed public sector."

The economic and human costs were staggering. Aguilar and Goldstein continued, "In the second half of the 1990s, the destruction of infrastructure, especially in the hinterland, was enormous, as were the human costs—half a million dead and four million internally displaced people. The deterioration of the infrastructure and the presence of mines have had a particularly high cost on agriculture."[39] Angola has rebuilt much of its infrastructure, but the fighting resulted in more than 1.5 million deaths and 4 million internally displaced persons (IDPs). In February 2002, MPLA soldiers killed Jonas Savimbi, thereby removing the indefatigable leader of the insurgency against Angola's government.[40] Savimbi's death weakened UNITA, and the group reached a cease-fire and peace agreement with Angola's government on April 4, 2002.[41] As a result, UNITA transitioned from a rebel group to a political party, albeit a contentious opposition one.

Corruption has been a major challenge in Angola. In October 2008, a scandal colloquially named "Angolagate" went to trial where allegations accused powerful French citizens of ignoring the UN arms embargo and illegally supplying from 1993 to 1998 amid the civil war heavy weapons worth nearly $1 billion, including tanks, helicopters, and warships to José Eduardo dos Santos through a Slovakian arms company in exchange for oil concessions in Angola.[42] The incident demonstrated the tangible way that natural resources aggravated and lengthened conflict in Angola by providing funding for arms purchases, both to actors within the state and from those outside the country. More recently, Angola held elections on August 31, 2012, which reinstalled President José Eduardo dos Santos; his latest inauguration was roughly one month later.[43]

Much of the civil war hinged on natural resources, especially oil and diamonds. Jedrzej George Frynas and Geoffrey Wood observed, "While the origins of the Angolan war were of political nature, the contours of the war are closely related to fluctuations in oil revenues, and access by the competing sides to other natural resources, most notably diamonds, but also tropical hardwood, and—until Angola's great herds of elephants were virtually wiped out in the 1980s—wildlife products." Frynas and Wood continued, "The presence of oil resources, as well as other natural resources, can help to explain the duration and character of the conflict and, to some extent, even the timing of government offensives in the 1990s."[44]

There have been signs of optimism in Angola after such a violent and chaotic recent past. Angola's government established in 2009 Kimpa Vita University, providing education to more than 10,000 students. Other significant development projects have flourished, many of them to repair or replace the infrastructure devastation wrought by the civil war. Such gestures have buoyed public confidence. Afonso Luviluku, vice governor of Uíge, professed, "Since the opening up of new roads, industrial activity

Angola's Fuzileiros Operações Especiais Marines prepare to clear buildings after disembarking a boat during room-clearing training in Lobito, Angola. October 7, 2015. (Courtesy United States Africa Command)

in the province is taking shape. Coffee plantations that were stagnant for 40 years are finally starting production (we used to have the biggest coffee production of the country and were the second in Africa) and we are now in the process of reviewing the exploration of our mineral resources."[45] Angola's mineral resources are vast and include copper, silver, cobalt, diamonds, gold, lead, manganese, vanadium, and zinc, many of which went underdeveloped due to the raging civil war.

In 2017, President José Eduardo dos Santos announced that he would step down, thereby ending his rule of nearly 40 years. Elections followed on August 23, 2017. The MPLA won more than 60 percent of votes cast compared to less than 30 percent for UNITA.[46] Voters elected João Lourenço, Angola's former defense minister, as the nation's third president.[47] The consequences of misallocation, corruption, and conflict related to natural resources and environmental security for Angola have remained: two-thirds of Angola's population live on less than $2 per day.[48]

A recent development related to natural resources and environmental security has been China's enhanced involvement in Angola.[49] Some observers have articulated concerns about the role that China has taken in Angola, not only in terms of economic development but also connected to postconflict reconstruction. Estimates have placed the number of Chinese workers in Angola at more than 100,000 migrants. The China International Fund has led many construction projects in Angola, including more than 215,000 housing units, 2,500 kilometers of railway lines, 1,500 kilometers of roads, 70 factories, and an international airport in Luanda.[50] Marcus Power reported, "The growing importance of Chinese credit lines and increasing presence of Chinese corporate agencies across Angolan territory raise important questions about development, poverty reduction and inequality; governance and labour relations; and Angola's institutional capacity and the social structure of its cities."[51] Other commentators have taken a more ominous tone. Referring to the nearly 40-year presidency of José Eduardo dos Santos, Rafael Marques de Morais portrayed China's enlarged role in Angola as "The New Imperialism" and warned, "The concentration of power in the presidency has turned Sino-Angolan relations into a new stream for looting."[52] Time will tell whether the administration of João Lourenço will differ from his precursor in this regard. Freedom House, an independent nongovernmental organization (NGO) committed to political freedom and civil liberties around the world, cautioned, "Newly elected president João Lourenço moved to weaken the control of his predecessor's family in 2017, but it remains to be seen whether he will make a serious effort to stem endemic corruption or ease restrictions on politics, the media, and civil society." As a result, Freedom House listed Angola as one of its "Countries to Watch in 2018."[53] Regarding natural resources, Angola has faced not only momentous obstacles but also many opportunities. Nigeria has overtaken Angola as Africa's leading oil producer, a feat that surprised many analysts.[54] In addition, Angola's economy has suffered for several years due to a sharp downturn in oil production, which has resulted in collapsing oil values, falling currency devaluation, ballooning budget deficits, and rising price inflation, peaking at more than 20 percent. Such a situation has reinforced the absolute necessity for Angola to diversify its broader economy, combat its state fraud, and reinvigorate its energy industry.[55]

DEMOCRATIC REPUBLIC OF THE CONGO

The Democratic Republic of the Congo (DRC) is a central African nation comprising roughly 2.3 million square kilometers, making it the largest country in sub-Saharan Africa. With its capital located at Kinshasa, the DRC is largely landlocked, although it possesses a small coastline on the South Atlantic Ocean. The population of more than 83 million Congolese includes more than 200 ethnic groups, although the Bantu and Hamitic ethnic groups comprise nearly half of the population. Roughly 70 percent of Congolese are Christian, with the vast majority of them being Roman Catholic. The country has plentiful natural assets, including coffee, sugar, palm oil, rubber, tea, cotton, cocoa, cassava, bananas, plantains, peanuts, corn, and timber and is also a major producer of cannabis. Its mining sector is extensive and lucrative, including copper, cobalt, gold, diamonds, coltan, zinc, tin, and tungsten; mining also produces the most exports for the DRC. The nation's mineral wealth largely resides in the north and northeast, making it vulnerable to cross-border incursions from armed groups in such neighboring countries as Burundi, Central African Republic, Rwanda, South Sudan, and Uganda. In the DRC, control of natural resources, particularly minerals, has driven and exacerbated much fighting. Trade in illicit resources from the country, especially diamonds and coltan, has sparked, spread, and sustained conflict in the DRC, funding weapons purchases, paying soldiers, and fostering bribes. This militarization repeatedly has tightened a particular group's control of the natural resources, thereby creating a malicious sequence.

The DRC has a lengthy and tragic history of violence emanating from natural resources. King Leopold II of Belgium brutalized the Congo under colonial rule.[56] Much of his devastating reign involved seizing natural resources, first ivory and then rubber. Formerly the Republic of the Congo, the country gained independence from Belgium on June 30, 1960. Struggles over control of the nation's abundant natural resources persisted after independence. In November 1965, Colonel Joseph Mobutu led a coup and seized the presidency of the country. He changed his name to Mobutu Sese Seko, switched in 1971 the moniker of the country to Zaire,

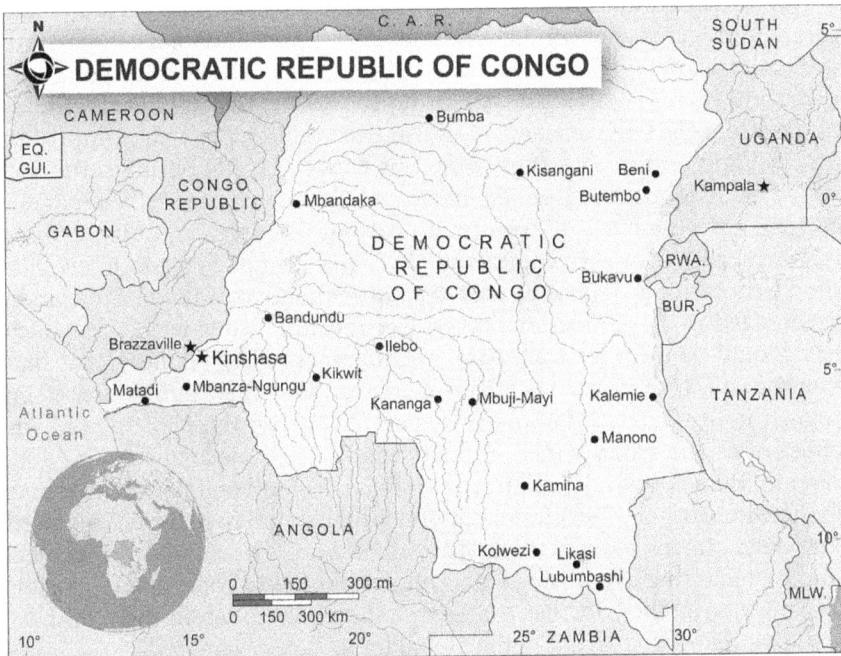

and ruled from 1965 to 1997.[57] Delivering insatiable violence, looting natural resources, and encouraging rampant corruption were all hallmarks
of Sese Seko's 25-year reign. Toward the end of his regime, in 1990, Zaire
became a nominal democracy.

Geography played a significant role in the relationship between natural resources and environmental security in Zaire because many of the
nation's natural resources existed in the eastern and northeastern region
of the country, near the borders of Uganda and Rwanda. Eastern Zaire,
including the areas bordering Burundi, Rwanda, and Uganda, exhibited
the severest tensions regarding conflict minerals, especially the provinces
of North and South Kivu, known collectively as the Kivus. In 1994, conflict
in neighboring Rwanda and Burundi sparked massive migration from
those two countries into eastern Zaire.[58] Some estimates numbered refugees at more than 120,000, while IDPs exceeded 2.5 million people. Such
mass migration overwhelmed Zaire's inherent capacity and destabilized
much of the eastern and northeastern portion of the country. Devastating conflict ensued, with involvement and complicity from neighboring
Rwanda and Uganda. As a result, Laurent Kabila came to power in 1997
and renamed the country the Democratic Republic of the Congo (DRC).
In January 2001, an assassin killed Laurent Kabila; Joseph Kabila, his son,
assumed the presidency on January 17, 2001, inaugurating what many
observers hoped would be a transition from the country's violent past
toward a more buoyant future.[59]

The illicit diamond trade became the first major hurdle for the DRC.
A rampant increase of conflict diamonds, or blood diamonds, emanating
from such African countries as the DRC, Liberia, and Sierra Leone garnered international attention.[60] During the 1990s, illegal exports of diamonds from the DRC reached as high as $400 million per year, comprising
nearly 50 percent of all exports from this nation.[61] Neighboring countries,
including Rwanda and Uganda, participated in much of the illicit market,
crossing into the DRC to expropriate natural resources and then exporting them from their own capitals at Kigali and Kampala, respectively. The
problem of blood diamonds and the subsequent worldwide opposition
to them led to the Kimberley Process Certification Scheme (KPCS), which
has sought to improve transparency and traceability of the global diamond trade. Certification schemes, however, have had limitations. Pelin
Ekmen noticed, "As a voluntary system, however, the KPCS is only as
effective as the participants' own internal control mechanisms."[62] More
recently than diamonds, coltan has emerged as a pivotal natural resource
in the DRC. Coltan, short for columbite-tantalite, is a metallic ore required
for power-storing parts, semiconductors, and capacitors in consumer elec-
tronics, including everything from cellular phones to computer chips; it is
also very rare. The DRC has the largest supply of coltan in the world, by
some estimates 80 percent of the global total.[63]

In the DRC, conflict and natural resources regularly have intertwined. Two civil wars ravaged much of the country: the First and Second Congo Wars. The seeds of the first war grew in 1994 when a horrendous genocide occurred in Rwanda, pitting ethnic Hutus against Tutsis and resulting in the deaths of approximately 800,000 civilians in little more than three months. When a new government came into power in Rwanda after the genocide, more than 1 million Rwandans, mostly Hutus and many of those involved in the mass murders, fled across the border into eastern Zaire, thereby destabilizing that country. For two years, a rebellion led by Laurent Kabila simmered against the central government in Kinshasa. Two years later in 1996, Rwanda and Uganda intervened in the rebellion and invaded Zaire. Bolstered by external support, insurgent forces seized the capital of Kinshasa the following year, removed Mobutu Sese Seko, and installed Kabila as president. Whereas the First Congo War pitted Rwanda and Uganda against Zaire, the Second Congo War in 1998 expanded pre-existing tensions into a regional conflagration between two alliances. In the second war, Burundi, Rwanda, and Uganda united against Kabila, while Angola, Namibia, and Zimbabwe united for Kabila. In the process, Uganda began expropriating gold from the nation, now named the DRC, while Rwanda did the same with diamonds, accentuating the connections between natural resources and violence and revealing those two nations' economic motives in spite of their purported political impulses. The two wars were devastating, killing in excess of 3.5 million people. Exhausted from perennial violence, leaders signed the Lusaka Ceasefire Agreement in July 1999, ensuring a shaky peace between the DRC and five neighboring countries: Angola, Namibia, Rwanda, Uganda, and Zimbabwe.

Natural resources were at the center of both deadly conflicts. Christopher W. Mullins and Dawn L. Rothe maintained, "As nations mired in their own civil disorder, both Rwanda and Uganda had a lot to gain economically and politically through controlling territory within the DRC." The bonds between natural resources and conflict were as fatal as they were profound. Mullins and Rothe continued, "As the UN Security Council has established, both nations funneled much of the profits from the illegal mineral expropriations into their militaries. Early profits were used to continue to fund the occupations or diverted to other struggles. Additionally, once the resources were transferred out of the nation to the open market, these resources were viewed by the international community as exports from either Uganda or Rwanda, as the case may be. This provided another set of rewards for the action: the annual balance of payment evaluation each nation would undergo by the IMF and WB [World Bank]."[64] As a result of the constant violence in the DRC since its independence, international organizations have interceded multiple times. The first attempt to mitigate fighting was the UN Operation in the Congo (ONUC), which was a UN peacekeeping mission in that country launched in July 1960 and authorized by UN Security Council Resolution 143 of July 14, 1960.[65] ONUC ran from July 1960 to June 1964 and was one of the first UN peacekeeping missions ever. The operation deployed almost 20,000 peacekeeping troops, but violence endured. The peacekeeping mission failed, and 250 peacekeepers died, including UN secretary-general Dag Hammarskjöld.[66]

More than three decades later, the UN Organization Mission in the Democratic Republic of the Congo (MONUC) began in 1999 after the signing of the Lusaka Ceasefire Agreement; the new operation claimed its authority from UN Security Council Resolution 1279.[67] MONUC lasted from November 30, 1999, to June 30, 2010, and deployed more than 16,000 peacekeepers. Over time, its mission grew. The United Nations created the newer peacekeeping mission to the DRC "initially to plan for the observation of the ceasefire and disengagement of forces and maintain liaison with all parties to the Ceasefire Agreement. Later in a series of resolutions, the Council expanded the mandate of MONUC to the supervision of the implementation of the Ceasefire Agreement and assigned multiple related additional tasks."[68] After another decade, the UN Organization Stabilization Mission in the Democratic Republic of the Congo (MONUSCO) took over from MONUC on July 1, 2010, under the authority of UN Security Council Resolution 1925.[69] Its goal was "to use all necessary means to carry out its mandate relating, among other things, to the protection of civilians, humanitarian personnel and human rights defenders under imminent threat of physical violence and to support the Government of the DRC in its stabilization and peace consolidation efforts."[70] With an annual budget of more than $1 billion, MONUSCO deployed in excess of 21,000 total personnel, including 15,424 peacekeeping troops, mostly from Pakistan, India, and Bangladesh.[71]

Increased international demand for hard commodities, including minerals, has tightened the relationship between natural resources and conflict in the DRC. Analyzing that country specifically, Bruce Guenther contended that "the recent shift in the global terms of trade in favour of hard commodities due to the growing demand of China and India will present significant challenges for governance and peace-building as state and non-state actors attempt to gain control over lucrative natural resource rents. . . . This will be particularly challenging in fragile states such as the Democratic Republic of Congo."[72] As a result, international commentators have perceived a strengthened nexus between natural resources and conflict in the DRC.

There have been some positive developments. Since the 2003 transitional government and peace accords, the nation has experienced economic growth.[73] The potential of carnage, however, has continued to smolder. On July 31, 2006, UN Security Council Resolution 1698 formally recognized the relationship in the DRC between natural resources, illicit resource trade, and conflict.[74] Nicolas Cook defined conflict minerals as "ores that, when mined, sold or traded, are widely reported to play key roles in fueling armed conflict and human rights abuses in several far eastern provinces of the Democratic Republic of the Congo."[75] In general, conflict minerals have included tantalum, tin, tungsten, and gold and have been used to fund militias, extend violence, and commit abuses.[76]

In response to the contemporary security issues of natural resources and environmental security in the DRC, the international community progressively has focused on certification and regulatory schemes, including the Kimberley Process (KP) rough diamond trade regime, fair trade movement, and environmentally sustainable resource use. The Organisation for Economic Co-Operation and Development (OECD) has created due diligence standards, which is "the primary due diligence standard that a wide array of interests groups has proposed."[77] Of course, many of these disputes have not only related to violence but also have impacted environmental security. In the DRC, wildlife poaching, water pollution, deforestation, and extensive mining have all caused significant environmental problems, especially the extracting of coltan. As a result, recent efforts have focused on tracking that industry. In 2010, the Federal Institute for Geosciences and Natural Resources in Hannover, Germany, created a novel way to "fingerprint" coltan to combat its illicit trade. Pelin Ekmen observed, "Thus, the geochemical fingerprinting for coltan is one way to enhance transparency of the mineral's trade and attract companies to draw the raw mineral from the suppliers at the mines directly and not through a number of devious middle men."[78] Conflict minerals in the DRC have attracted substantial transnational awareness. Nicolas Cook remarked, "The most extensive U.S. law aimed at halting the trade in conflict minerals, specifically the 3TGs, is Section 1502 of Title XV of the *Dodd-Frank Wall Street Reform and Consumer Protection Act* (P. L. 111–203)."[79] While laudable in intent, these regulatory schemes also have had unintended consequences. *African Business* revealed, "Dodd-Frank has allegedly led to a collapse in incomes in eastern DRC as companies wait for clarity on the proposals."[80] Of course, this dynamic only applied to lawful actors; others with fewer reservations simply proceeded unrestricted with illicit trade in conflict minerals.

As the extensive resource curse literature has discussed, those in control of a country's ample intrinsic possessions usually have clung to power, using violence if necessary and thereby engendering fierce reactions in response. This has been the case in the DRC. The nation's constitution mandated a two-term limit for president. President Kabila's term limit ended on December 19, 2016, but he refused to step down, sparking protests in the capital of Kinshasa and across the country. In response, Kabila instituted a harsh crackdown on any and all opposition. On January 21, 2018, police opened fire on protestors, killing 5 people and wounding another 17 onlookers. One of the victims was a 16-year-old girl exiting a church. This tense situation has prompted violence throughout the DRC, as armed groups have used it as an excuse to reignite simmering embers.[81]

The results of natural resources and environmental security have been devastating for the DRC. Bruce Guenther recorded, "The human costs of this resource curse are extremely high, with the most recent conflict (1998–present) resulting in approximately 4 million Congolese deaths from malnutrition and disease and with 350,000 dying as a direct result of violence. Moreover, 3.4 million people are internally displaced."[82] The DRC has continued to experience bloodshed. Human Rights Watch revealed, "Since August 2016, violence involving Congolese security forces, government-backed militias, and local armed groups left up to 5,000 people dead in the country's southern Kasai region," resulting in the destruction of 600 schools and the displacement of more than 1 million people. Other areas of the country have suffered similar outbreaks of brutality. During the same period in the southeastern province of Tanganyika, another 250,000 people became displaced. As a result, violence in the DRC has degenerated. Human Rights Watch continued, "The humanitarian situation in Congo has severely worsened, with Africa's largest displacement crisis in 2017, famine expected to affect 7.7 million Congolese, and a national cholera epidemic that has spread across the country."[83]

African leaders have made significant efforts to address natural resources and environmental security, including moving away from centralized resource management to community-based natural resources management (CBNRM). Leo Charles Zulu advocated, "Following widespread failure of centralized resource management, CBNRM is widely seen as *the* solution to deliver both ecological (sustainable resource use) and social goals of poverty reduction and more relevant, equitable, efficient and inexpensive environmental governance."[84] African Union efforts include the Action Plan for Accelerated Industrial Development of Africa, African Mining Vision, and creation of the African Minerals Development Centre.[85] Some reporters have depicted the DRC in 2018 as "the panoramic chaos of a vast and troubled nation spinning out of control." Ida Sawyer, Human Rights Watch director for central Africa, stated that some senior officials in the nation described a "strategy of chaos" by Joseph Kabila, president of the country, to cling to power at all costs. Natural resources have been at the heart of the pandemonium. The contrast is both tangible and tragic: Kabila has significant stakes in more than 80 companies throughout the nation and is worth tens of millions of dollars, while more than 4.5 million people in the country are IDPs and 2 million children are starving.[86] Therein lies the rub.

CONCLUSION

Natural resources and environmental security have been significant contemporary security issues in Africa. Commentators have long utilized the natural resource curse and the Dutch disease to describe the relationship between abundance in natural resources, uneven economic development, and outright conflict. Of course, natural resources have not always caused conflict, but they frequently have exacerbated and sustained it. Many nations in Africa have struggled with these difficulties, including Angola, Chad, the DRC, Ghana, and Republic of the Congo (Brazzaville), among others. Extensive appropriation of natural resources and confrontation over their control has degraded the environment, complicating economic progress and human development. The presence of multinational corporations has exacerbated both issues, often encouraging African governments to rely exclusively on a specific foreign export such as oil in lieu of diversifying their economies and improving the livelihoods of their populations. Likewise, multinational corporations have been complicit in the trade of conflict resources and have contributed to environmental degradation through unchecked oil and mining operations. The international community has sought to address such problems through human rights laws and certification regimes such as the KP, EITI, and EITI++, among others. Angola exemplified the dangers of copious physical possessions prolonging conflict when it descended into a vicious 30-year civil war, much of it sustained by control of the country's vast oil resources. The resulting violence decimated the country, leaving it one of the world's least developed nations. The fighting from 1975 to 2002 left more than 1 million Angolans dead and another 4 million displaced from their homes. While there has been a guarded optimism that Angola has been on a path toward economic growth and stability, concerns over China's actions in that country have emerged. In a different way, the DRC has revealed how abundant natural resources can fuel conflict. First diamonds and later minerals, especially coltan, have sparked fighting, including the First and Second Congo Wars. The international community has launched several efforts to keep peace in the DRC, including most recently MONUC and MONUSCO, but it has remained a volatile country where leaders have sought to hold on to power at all costs, largely because of the lucrative assets at stake. Natural resources, however, have not been the only spur to bloodshed on the continent. Violent extremism and terrorism also have been significant contemporary security issues in Africa.

CHAPTER 5

Violent Extremism and Terrorism

OVERVIEW

Since 2000, the Institute for Economics and Peace has produced a comprehensive annual index on global terrorism, charting results, trends, characteristics, groups, and economics of terrorism around the world. This guide provides key insights and valuable analysis on terrorism at the global, regional, and country levels and draws from the Global Terrorism Database, a comprehensive data set containing specific information on more than 170,000 terrorist incidents. In order to provide an overview of violent extremism and terrorism in Africa, several dynamics bear mentioning. As of late, deaths from terrorism have declined globally, from 29,412 in 2015 to 25,673 in 2016. The prevalence of this contemporary security issue around the world, however, has increased. Recently, terrorism has scarred more countries globally as represented by at least one death, expanding from 65 countries in 2015 to 77 countries in 2016. The combined effect of these developments has been an overall deterioration of the Global Terrorism Index score by four percentage points, thus indicating a total rise in the brunt of terrorism around the world.[1]

The effect of violent extremism and terrorism in Africa has been pronounced and significant. Of the 50 countries around the world most hurt by terrorism, 22 have been in Africa. The regional shock of violent extremism on Africa has become even more explicit as the overall force of terrorism has escalated. Of the top 20 countries around the world most ravaged by terrorism, 10 have been in Africa, including Nigeria (3rd) and Somalia (7th). In 2016, sub-Saharan Africa experienced 1,450 terrorist attacks and suffered 4,715 deaths as a result. These rankings have not been just theoretical or academic: terrorism in Africa has had devastating consequences for people and communities. Three of the most fatal terrorist attacks in the world during 2016 occurred in Africa. On January 30, 2016, Boko Haram assailants killed 88 people in a vicious onslaught in Dalori, Nigeria. Another 283 people, most of them assailants, died in an assault on August 19, 2016, by the Sudan People's Liberation Movement-in-Opposition (SPLM-IO) in Pajut, South Sudan. On November 23, 2016, another 85 people died in an attack by Front Populaire pour la Renaissance de la Centrafrique (FPRC) combatants in Bria, Central African Republic. The shock of violent extremism and terrorism in Africa is not a new phenomenon; it has been a persistent scourge on the continent during the past three decades. From 2002 to 2016, sub-Saharan Africa experienced nearly 10,000 attacks, claiming the lives of 35,559 people. Unfortunately, these contemporary security issues have persisted. In 2016, Nigeria and Somalia combined to account for 10 percent of all deaths from terrorism worldwide.[2] As a result, violent extremism and terrorism have been critical contemporary security issues in Africa.

Many of these violent extremist and terrorist groups have been militant Islamist organizations. There have been numerous terrorist clusters in Africa, including factions linked to al-Qaeda such as al-Qaeda in the Islamic Maghreb (AQIM) and its affiliates, al-Shabaab, Boko Haram, and Islamic State in Iraq and the Levant (ISIL), among others.[3] In sub-Saharan Africa, the two most prominent violent extremist and terrorist outfits have been al-Shabaab and Boko Haram. These two units have committed roughly 65 percent of all fatalities and approximately 70 percent of all attacks in sub-Saharan Africa.[4] In addition to a variety of terrorist groups, their destructive capabilities have been vast and deadly. Deaths in Africa from militant groups have exploded from approximately 2,500 in 2010 to nearly 20,000 in 2015 before leveling off around 10,500 per year from 2016 onward. Even though the number of fatalities in Africa from terrorism has dropped somewhat, it has remained considerable. In addition, the activity of these groups has increased as of late, with the number of violent strikes rising from 2,317 in 2016 to 2,769 in 2017.[5]

There has been a critical bond between weak and fragile states and violent extremism and terrorism in Africa. A state's inability to secure its territory and to provide basic necessities for its people has had a dual effect. First, it has allowed violent extremists the physical geography to operate freely and with little restraint. Second, it has created grievances about government corruption and blatant disregard for people, thereby allowing radicals the opportunity to fill the void with local security, albeit usually with brutality, and basic social services, which increase the public's support, or at least acquiescence, of them and therefore elevate violent extremist organizations' local legitimacy. Both of these dynamics have permitted terrorism to flourish in weak and fragile states. Zachary

Devlin-Foltz stated, "In stable contexts, extremists tend to occupy a marginal fringe of the political space. As the level of fragility increases, however, they tend to move to center stage," something that he characterizes as the "fragility-extremism nexus."[6] Examples have included Ansar al-Dine, Movement for Unity and Jihad in West Africa (MUJWA), and AQIM in Mali, al-Shabaab in Somalia, and Boko Haram in Nigeria. Violent extremism and terrorism in Africa have had significant repercussions. In Mali, these contemporary security issues nearly split the country into two halves, one northern and another southern. In Somalia, al-Shabaab has decimated the already-fragile government, further complicating economic and political stability. Regarding Nigeria, Terje Østebø observed, "The rise of Islamic militancy in parts of the Sahel and Horn of Africa poses growing threats to regional stability. The appeal of these militants stems from their ability to tap into and persuade marginalized communities, particularly youth, that their grievances can be rectified by the establishment of a more pure Islamist culture."[7] Overall, the sway of violent extremism and terrorism on Africa has strengthened notably since 2002. Since then, only 14 countries in sub-Saharan Africa have experienced fewer ramifications from violent extremism and terrorism, while 21 nations have seen significantly more consequences. In its regional analysis for sub-Saharan Africa, the Institute for Economics and Peace declared, "Since 2002, terrorist activity has increased markedly in terms of both the number of attacks and fatalities."[8]

SOMALIA

Somalia would make an excellent case study for any chapter of this book, as all contemporary security issues in Africa presented have applied to this country. The fact that Somalia has been a failed state has created conditions that have sparked ethno-religious conflict and civil war, violent extremism and terrorism, piracy and maritime security, and food security and extreme poverty, among others. Noel Anderson discerned, "Since 1991 Somalia has been the exemplar failed state, plagued by seemingly endless civil war, chronic food and water shortages, piracy, and militant Islamic extremism."[9] Somalia is a relatively large nation, covering 637,657 square kilometers and bordering Djibouti, Ethiopia, and Kenya. It is also a littoral country, maintaining more than 3,000 kilometers of coastline along the Gulf of Aden and the Indian Ocean. Somalia counts a population of approximately 11 million people, the vast majority of whom are younger than 25 years old. Nearly 98 percent of Somalia's population is Muslim. Within the country exists the self-declared Republic of Somaliland in the northwest and the semiautonomous state of Puntland in the northeast.[10]

Politically, Mohamed Siad Barre ruled Somalia from 1969 to 1991, but a clan system has dominated power relations in Somalia. From 1977 to 1978,

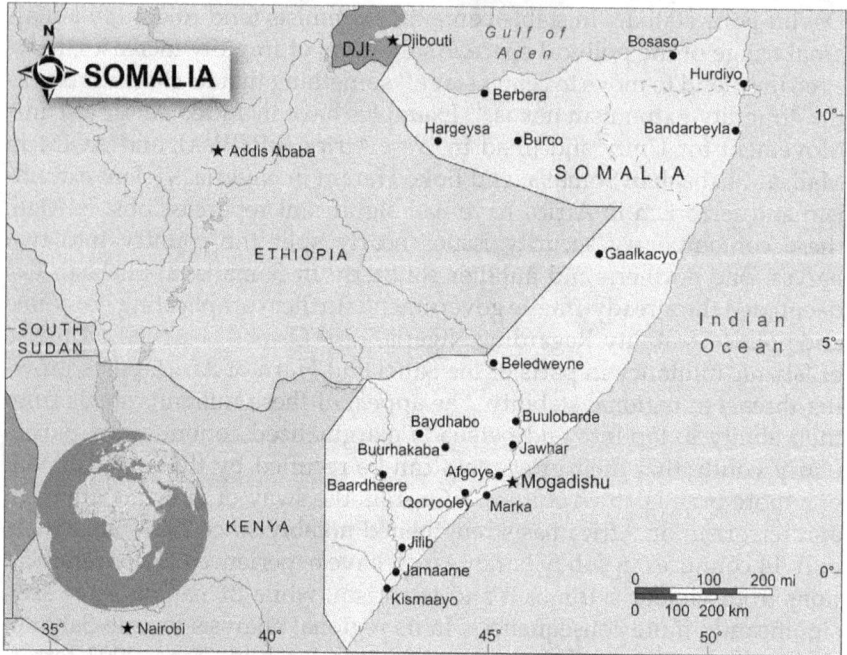

a border war erupted between Somalia and Ethiopia over disputed territory in the Ogaden region. Since Barre's dictatorial rule ended in 1991, Somalia has persisted as a failed state.[11] At that time, clan violence erupted throughout southern Somalia.[12] The United Nations engaged in a large humanitarian effort in Somalia from 1993 to 1995.[13] In 2000, the Somalia National Peace Conference (SNPC) launched the Transitional National Government (TNG), which failed. In 2004, a new interim government, the Transitional Federal Government (TFG), emerged. The TFG and Abdullahi Yusuf Ahmed, its leader, sought to govern Somalia and instill stability throughout the struggling country. The Union of Islamic Courts (UIC), however, seized control of Mogadishu in May 2006 and established sharia law throughout much of the nation. In response, the TFG attempted to provide governance but was unable to stop the UIC's aggressive advances. As a result of the chaos, neighboring Ethiopia intervened militarily in Somalia in 2006.[14]

While the TFG and Ethiopia eventually stopped the UIC, Somalia has remained chaotic at best. An increase in Islamic militancy in general and the emergence of al-Shabaab specifically were the dire results. Al-Shabaab grew in size and strength as a direct consequence of Ethiopia's intervention.[15] Within this tumult, violent extremism and terrorism have flourished in Somalia, making it the seventh-most impacted nation in the world and the second-most in Africa. From 2000 to 2016, Somalia suffered

4,466 deaths from attacks, rising steadily after 2006. Al-Shabaab committed the vast majority of these incidents.[16] Out of this bedlam grew an ever
more aggressive form of Islamic militancy. Prior to al-Shabaab, al-Itihaad
al-Islamiya (AIAI), or Islamic Unity, and the UIC had led Islamist extremism in Somalia. AIAI emerged in the 1980s and grew until the mid-1990s.
In the mid-2000s, the United Islamic Courts, also known as the Union of
Islamic Courts, arose. The UIC established sharia courts throughout much
of the country. In 2006, the UIC seized Mogadishu, but a swift intervention
in December 2006 by Ethiopian forces dealt it a major blow and secured
the capital. The forceful move, however, also had negative ramifications.
Terje Østebø cautioned, "The broad-brush branding of UIC as an Islamic
militant threat, leading to the Ethiopian intervention in 2006, was crucial
for paving the way for the emergence of al Shabaab and for further radicalizing developments in Somalia."[17]

From the ashes of this defeat, al-Shabaab arose to become the most for-
midable terrorist organization in Somalia. Much of this had to do with the
presence of a foreign army intervening in Somalia, which itself resulted
from the inability of the Somali government to provide security. In this
sense, weak and fragile states often have provided the underlying conditions enabling the emergence and spread of violent extremism and terrorism. Abdisaid Musse Ali-Koor warned, "These tensions have not emerged
suddenly or spontaneously. Rather, they reflect an accumulation of pressure over decades. The genesis of this is largely the externally-driven dif-
fusion of Salafist ideology from the Gulf States. . . . Salafism, which had
been a fringe off-shoot of Islam in East Africa in the 1990s, has become
mainstream today."[18] Out of this setting emerged Harakat al-Shabaab
al-Mujahideen (Mujahideen Youth Movement), also known as al-Shabaab.
Oscar Gakuo Mwangi noticed, "The TFG is, however, functionally ineffective in that it cannot perform the core functions of providing basic political
and economic goods and services. *Al-Shabaab*, an Islamist non-state actor,
is now providing these goods and services in the absence of a functional
central authority."[19]

While purportedly claiming to be a youth movement, al-Shabaab has
used violence to achieve its political and religious goals, committing suicide bombings, assassinations, and assaults; as a result, it has been a brutal
terrorist group. Al-Shabaab has perpetrated the vast majority of assaults
in Somalia and has done so for more than the past decade. The Institute
for Economics and Peace reported in its Global Terrorism Index, "Terrorism in Somalia continues to be synonymous with al-Shabaab," which
has executed more than 70 percent of all strikes in Somalia since 2000.[20]
Al-Shabaab has roughly 5,000 core militants, although it claims as many
as 100,000 sympathizers around the world. The violent extremist organization has leveraged foreign intervention and has argued that it alone
was protecting both Islam and Somalia in response. Al-Shabaab has

espoused Salafi-jihadist ideology and has desired to establish an Islamic
state in Somalia and to rule by sharia law. Ahmed Abdi "Mukhtar Abu
al-Zubayr" Godane was the first leader of al-Shabaab, which he founded
in 2004. The group came to the forefront in 2006, largely in response to
Ethiopia's incursions into Somalia from 2006 to 2009. Ethiopia aided the
TFG and quickly defeated the UIC, although al-Shabaab strengthened
greatly during this time. Ethiopia withdrew from Somalia in January 2009,
but recruits flocked to al-Shabaab afterward, swelling the organization's
ranks as a result of their perceived influence in Ethiopia's withdrawal.
Public support also rose, allowing al-Shabaab the ability to move more
freely throughout Somalia. As a result, the violent extremist organization
seized large swaths of territory throughout southern Somalia, triggering first angst and then a military response from the African Union (AU).
Al-Shabaab is heavily armed and highly funded. Analysts have estimated
that the group wields a plethora of weapons, including such heavy weapons as artillery, antitank and antiair weapons, and armored personnel car-
riers, among others, and estimates of their revenue have ranged from $70
to $100 million annually.[21]

There have been numerous international responses to al-Shabaab. In
2007, UN Security Council Resolution 1744 authorized AU intervention

A Kenyan Defense Force major updates a map of Somalia with the latest
AMISOM and al-Shabaab troop movements at the International Peace Support
Training Center in Nairobi, Kenya. August 25, 2015. (Courtesy United States
Africa Command)

to combat the violent extremist organization. The African Union Mission in Somalia (AMISOM) had more than 10,000 troops but minimal financial resources.[22] AMISOM replaced Ethiopia's military presence, which many Somalis had come to view as an occupation by a foreign power. The United Nations and the AU hoped that such a move would provide more legitimacy to the TFG and stabilize the fragile country. AMISOM was quite costly, however, and suffered numerous casualties. Thomas G. Weiss and Martin Welz dreaded, "The AU Mission in Somalia alone has incurred over 3,000 deaths since its inception in 2007—a total rivalling the full number of fatalities (some 3,100) among UN peacekeeping operations since 1948."[23]

Al-Shabaab responded to international efforts by targeting countries that assisted AMISOM and thereby turned its ire toward neighboring countries. Abdisaid Musse Ali-Koor remarked, "Over time, these tensions have turned violent. Attacks by militant Islamists against civilians in East Africa (outside of Somalia) rose from just a few in 2010 to roughly 20 per year since then. The vast majority of these have been in Kenya."[24] On July 11, 2010, al-Shabaab bombed a restaurant and rugby club in Kampala, Uganda, where many patrons had gathered to watch the World Cup finals. The dual bomb blasts killed 74 civilians, ostensibly in retaliation for Uganda's provision of soldiers for AMISOM. The event marked al-Shabaab's first deadly attack outside of Somalia and signified an extension of its violent extremism beyond Somalia.[25] In response, countries neighboring Somalia deployed additional forces to border regions and into Somalia to combat al-Shabaab. In August 2011, the Kenya Defense Forces (KDF) launched an operation in Somalia aimed at the group, and that October Ethiopia redeployed soldiers to western Somalia. These operations weakened al-Shabaab but did not eliminate the group. Noel Anderson reported, "With the assistance of Kenyan and Ethiopian forces, which launched coordinated offensives in the fall of 2011, the mission has enjoyed some progress toward [its] objective, recapturing several cities and dislodging insurgents from Mogadishu to consolidate control of the capital."[26]

On February 9, 2012, al-Shabaab announced an alliance with al-Qaeda, presumably to internationalize itself and to counteract perceptions that transnational efforts had weakened the Somalia-based group. In July 2012, the KDF became an official participant in AMISOM. As a result, al-Shabaab more and more targeted Kenya and launched its most heinous attacks against that country. Paul D. Williams recorded, "In more general terms, one recent analysis concluded that Al-Shabaab was probably responsible for approximately 15 attacks a month between October 2012 (after Kenyan and allied militia forces took control of Kismayo) and February 2014. On average, these attacks killed over 40 people each month."[27] Religion played a major role in al-Shabaab's wrath toward Kenya. In stark contrast to Somalia's population, which is 98 percent Muslim, Kenya's population represents a vast majority of Christians, upward of 83 percent with only 11 percent Muslims.

From August to September 2012, the Federal Government of Somalia (FGS) materialized and replaced the TFG, providing a modicum of stability and increased vigilance against al-Shabaab. In May 2013, UN Security Council Resolution 2102 created the UN Assistance Mission in Somalia (UNSOM), which sought to support the FGS and AMISOM.[28] Al-Shabaab remained capable of mass violence, unleashing a growing number of attacks on those that it deemed supported the FGS. On September 21, 2013, al-Shabaab carried out a vicious terrorist attack on Westgate Mall in Nairobi, Kenya. Newspaper reports immediately characterized the carnage as "the worst terrorist attack Kenya has suffered since the US embassy bombings in east Africa that brought al-Qaida to international attention in the 1990s."[29] The violent siege resulted in a four-day standoff, at the conclusion of which local law enforcement officials had killed all four terrorists. During the assault, however, assailants murdered 67 civilians and wounded more than 200 others. Al-Shabaab claimed responsibility for the raid, purportedly in retaliation for Kenya's deployment of troops to Somalia, which began in 2011. Paul D. Williams explained, "First although it was not the first Al-Shabaab terrorist 'spectacular', the siege received unprecedented international media attention that shone a spotlight on the state of Al-Shabaab and efforts to defeat it. Second, the attack gave renewed impetus to those calling for a new, more offensive phase in the war against Al-Shabaab."[30]

In August 2014, the Somali military and AU forces, supported by international partners, launched Operation Indian Ocean, which focused on combating al-Shabaab.[31] A U.S. air strike on September 1, 2014, killed Ahmed Abdi Godane, al-Shabaab's founder and leader, in the Sablale district of Somalia, along with six of his senior commanders.[32] Ahmad Umar replaced Godane as the leader of al-Shabaab, and Umar increased links between al-Shabaab and al-Qaeda.[33] In the early morning hours of April 2, 2015, al-Shabaab launched a merciless terrorist raid on Garissa University College in Garissa, Kenya, using suicide bombs and assault rifles. In what analysts branded as one of the deadliest terrorist attacks in Kenya's history, al-Shabaab militants killed 147 students, and the group once again publicly declared culpability. The carnage was significant because it mirrored the earlier strike on the Westgate Mall but claimed nearly twice as many victims.[34] In response, KDF launched in September 2015 Operation Linda Boni, which deployed to Kenya's Boni Forest to eradicate al-Shabaab militants in that area.

The counterterrorism exertions of the FGS, Somali National Army, AMISOM, neighboring countries, and international allies have greatly weakened al-Shabaab. During 2015, AMISOM reclaimed large areas of land from the terrorist group, much of which the violent extremist organization had held for several years. This included liberation of the town of Algen, which al-Shabaab had occupied since 2005. Many of these successes against al-Shabaab were due to Operation Juba Corridor, a major offensive by AMISOM, which focused on regaining territory in the Gedo, Bakool, and Bay regions within Somalia. Hassan Sheikh Mohamud, Somalia's president, praised "the latest offensives by our army and AMISOM forces to liberate key towns in the country" and declared that as a result of this offensive, al-Shabaab was on the verge of "military collapse."[35] Internal disputes within al-Shabaab, centered on whether to continue its affiliation with al-Qaeda or instead to join the more extreme ISIL, have created fissures within the Somali group.

Violent extremism and terrorism in Somalia have existed within the milieu of a failed state. The void of authority in Somalia created conditions that allowed al-Shabaab first to surface and then to flourish, with deadly and devastating consequences. Oscar Gakuo Mwangi explained, "State collapse in Somalia has created opportunities for *Al-Shabaab* to adopt strategies aimed at seeking community support and legitimising itself," including "the deployment of Somali nationalism and xenophobia, the use of propaganda, social transformation, and the provision of social services."[36]

During 2016, Ethiopia's forces once again left Somalia, and al-Shabaab exhibited renewed lethality, escalating its forays and seizing more territory.[37] During that year, al-Shabaab committed 359 attacks, killing 740 people and injuring another 943. As a result, 2016 became the second deadliest year for al-Shabaab since 2000, evaporating any hope that regional and international exertions had defeated the group.[38] To make matters worse, al-Shabaab has increased its violent spasms and fatalities resulting from them. In 2017, the group committed 1,593 violent attacks, which resulted in 4,557 fatalities. The Africa Center for Strategic Studies documented, "Al Shabaab continues to be linked to the highest escalation of violence. It was involved in more than three times the number of violent events related to militant Islamist groups in Africa than the next most active group, Boko Haram. . . [and] accounted for almost 44 percent of all reported fatalities involving militant Islamist groups in Africa that year."[39]

On February 8, 2017, voters elected Mohamed Abdullahi "Farmajo" Mohamed as president of Somalia.[40] The victory for Farmajo, who defeated incumbent Hassan Sheikh Mohamud, was quite significant. Calling for anticorruption and transparency, Farmajo provided hope that Somalia would be on the path toward improved stability. The task before him would be large: "A looming famine threatens the lives of millions. Al-Shabaab is still unleashing havoc in Mogadishu and many parts of southern and central Somalia. The Somali Army is weak and underfunded; the government has been relying on Amisom forces for security for almost a decade."[41] Farmajo's ascendancy was also meaningful because it was the only peaceful transition of power in Somalia's history; it also marked the first moment since 2006 that Somalia was not under a transitional government. The AU has studied AMISOM and learned many lessons from its operation.[42] Even so, after more than a decade of exertions against al-Shabaab, the terrorist group has remained quite lethal, averaging more than five strikes per day. In 2018, al-Shabaab claimed two dubious distinctions: it was the deadliest violent extremist organization on the continent and the most implacable insurgency in Africa. The militant Islamist group executed 1,749 attacks from April 2017 to March 2018, representing 58 percent of the total incidents on the continent during that time frame.[43]

NIGERIA

The Federal Republic of Nigeria is located in western Africa with an extensive coastline of 853 kilometers along the Gulf of Guinea and its capital at Abuja. Nigeria claims two main rivers, the Niger and Benue, spanning nearly 9,000 kilometers. Neighboring countries include Benin, Cameroon, Chad, and Niger. Nigeria has a varied climate and terrain, ranging from tropical hills and plateaus in its center to arid plains in the north, and has vast resources, including natural gas, petroleum, tin, iron

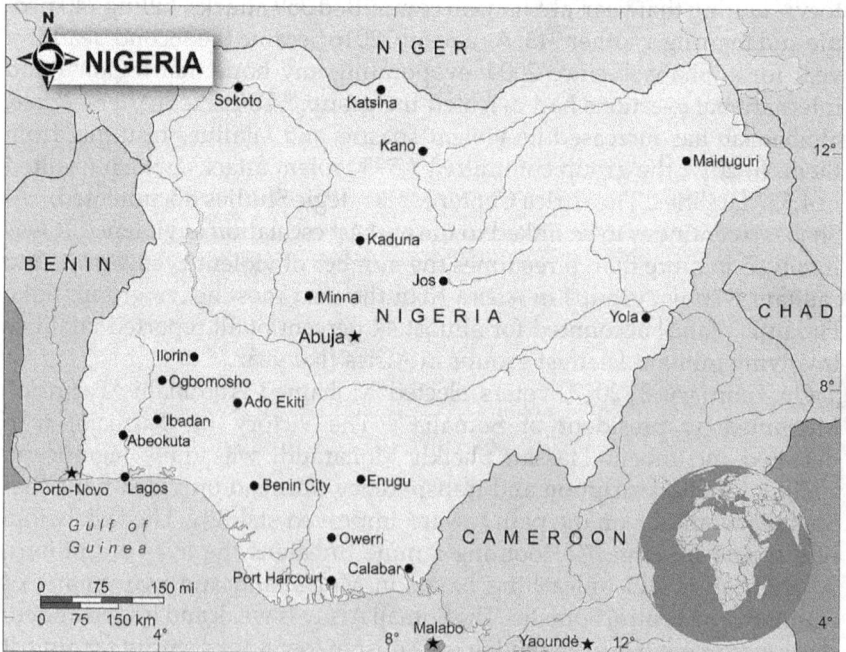

ore, coal, limestone, lead, zinc, cocoa, peanuts, cotton, palm oil, corn, rice, yams, rubber, and fish, among others.

A former British colony, Nigeria gained independence on October 1, 1960. Most observers break Nigeria's recent political history into four republics. The First Republic existed from 1960 to 1966. From 1967 to 1970, Nigeria erupted into a civil war, as the southeast portion of the country attempted to secede as independent Biafra. The consequences were staggering. The vicious and prolonged conflict resulted in more than 2 million deaths.[44] The Second Republic ran from 1979 to 1983, and then military rule reigned supreme from 1983 to 1999, during which time the Third Republic from 1992 to 1993 attempted to take off in June 1993 but failed. In 1999, a new constitution ushered in a civilian government and the Fourth Republic, which has governed ever since. Goodluck Jonathan, Nigeria's vice president, assumed the presidency on May 5, 2010, after the death of Umaru Yar'Adua, Nigeria's president. Born on November 29, 1957, Jonathan is a Christian from Bayelsa State and spent the early part of his adult life as a teacher. Voters subsequently elected Jonathan president on April 16, 2011. His election, however, reinforced divisions within the country. John Paden cautioned, "Nigeria's presidential election of 2011 split the country along both ethno-religious and regional lines."[45] In January 2014, Nigeria joined the UN Security Council as a nonpermanent member, illustrating the nation's ascendancy in international leadership in a way similar to its appearance as an important economic power represented by the grouping of Mexico, Indonesia, Nigeria, and Turkey (MINT) as emblematic of the gathering strength of emerging markets.[46]

Nigeria is Africa's most populous country, claiming a population of more than 190 million with important geographical and religious distribution. Divided by geography, Nigeria has a predominately Muslim population in the north, a mixed religious composition in the southwest, and a largely Christian population in the southeast. Nigeria is also home to the largest population in the world that equally divides between Muslims and Christians.[47] Nigeria's residents are culturally diverse and very young. Central Nigeria is unique in the country and is home to the Middle Belt, a region where the predominately Muslim north blends with the largely Christian south. Nigeria claims as many as 400 ethno-linguistic groups, the three largest of which are Hausa-Fulani (29 percent), Yoruba (21 percent), and Igbo (18 percent).

Nigeria's diversity, however, also has presented obstacles. For much of Nigeria's recent past, various ethnic groups have jostled for control of the central government, often resulting in discrimination, tensions, and even outright violence.[48] Over 60 percent of the population is under the age of 25, and Nigeria is Africa's largest economy, with a gross domestic product nearing $400 billion. Its largest export partners are the United States and India, while its principal import associates are China and the

United States. Oil has formed the foundation of Nigeria's economy since the 1970s, with nearly 1.9 million barrels of crude oil produced per day. A vibrant economy has not translated into widespread benefits for most Nigerians, however, as more than 60 percent of Nigerians live in poverty.[49]

Context is important for understanding the contemporary security issues of violent extremism and terrorism in Nigeria. The Sokoto Caliphate was a significant historical development. Usman dan Fodio waged jihad in the region during the early 19th century and established the Sokoto Caliphate in 1804. This occurrence created a chronological precedent for Islamic law in Nigeria. In addition, Nigeria is a former British colony. Discontent with colonial rule spawned the Maitatsine movement, which preceded the contemporary threat of Boko Haram. The Maitatsine movement coalesced in the early 1970s, and Mohammed Marwa led it. During the 1980s, this faction sparked extensive riots, killing more than 4,000 people. The Yan Shi'a, another Islamist group, followed suit in the 1990s. Violent extremism and terrorism have escalated in Nigeria since the 1990s and have wrought a devastating toll. From 2000 to 2016, terrorist attacks have killed 18,914 people in the country. Many violent extremist groups have operated in Nigeria; 37 different groups have committed incidents since 2000, and 13 perpetrated assaults in 2016 alone.[50] Most prominent among groups executing these atrocities in Nigeria is Boko Haram.

Boko Haram is a violent extremist organization whose formal name is Jama'atu Ahlis-Sunnah Lidda'awati Wal Jihad or Sunni Community for the Propagation of the Prophet's Teaching and Jihad. The group is known colloquially as Boko Haram, derived from the Hausa word for book and the Arabic word for forbidden. When combined, the name roughly translates as "western education is forbidden." Beginning as a regional organization, Boko Haram eventually established ties with al-Qaeda and ISIL, aligning first with al-Qaeda and then in 2014 shifting toward ISIL, although there has been considerable disagreement within Boko Haram over these strategic choices, which in turn has led to its splintering into three distinct factions.[51] Eeben Barlow revealed that Boko Haram "recently rebranded itself as the Islamic State's West Africa Province (ISWAP)," which has illustrated its intent to align with international terrorist groups.[52]

Boko Haram is an Islamist terrorist group led by Mohammed Yusuf, who was born on January 29, 1970. In 2000, Yusuf decreed sharia law in several states in northern Nigeria. Local militias, known as Hisbah, formed to enforce sharia law and claimed some level of state sanction, as the Kano State government helped to establish them.[53] In 2002, Yusuf founded Boko Haram, which has desired to impose sharia law throughout Nigeria and has operated most prominently in northeastern Nigeria on the borders of Cameroon, Chad, and Niger. The group gained strength in Nigeria with strikes throughout the northeast, and this trend has intensified. Some estimates count total casualties inflicted by Boko Haram at approximately

20,000, and the violence instigated by the group has produced hundreds of thousands of displaced persons.[54]

The group has been complicated, however, evolving over time. Marc-Antoine Pérouse de Montclos explained, "Boko Haram has been variously described as a radical religious sect, a violent insurgency, a terrorist organization, a network of criminal gangs, a political tool and a cult."[55] Nigeria's law enforcement personnel in 2009 killed Muhammad Yusuf, and Abubakar Shekau seized the mantle of leadership for Boko Haram, further radicalizing the group. At the time of Yusuf's death in July 2009, police in Maiduguri, Borno State, sought out Boko Haram fighters and killed hundreds of them, albeit with numerous accusations of extrajudicial killings and excessive brutality.[56] More generally, rampant corruption and extreme violence by the Nigeria Police Force (NPF) have complicated Nigeria's efforts against Boko Haram. Oluwakemi Okenyodo warned, "Low levels of trust in the Nigerian police limit public cooperation critical to combatting internal security threats from irregular forces such as insurgents, criminal gangs, and extremists," revealing that nearly three-quarters of Nigerians surveyed perceived the police as corrupt.[57] In 2012, Mohammed Abubakar, Nigeria's inspector general of police, admitted, "Police duties have become commercialized. . . . Our police stations, State [Criminal Investigations Divisions] and operations offices have become business centres and collection points for rendering returns from all kinds of squads and teams set up for the benefit of superior officers."[58]

In addition to endemic vice, uncalibrated violence by Nigeria's security forces has inflamed tensions, providing fodder for Boko Haram's presentation of its purported aims and distancing local populations who have found themselves caught in the middle. The Joint Task Force (JTF), a composite grouping of Nigeria's military, police, and security personnel charged with combating Boko Haram, has engaged in heavy-handed responses, including indiscriminate harshness against militants and civilians alike. The result has been an escalation of violence on both sides. Human Rights Watch reported, "Civil society activists in Nigeria say that ordinary citizens fear both Boko Haram and the JTF, whose abusive tactics at times have strengthened the Islamist group's narrative that it is battling government brutality. Indeed, the police's extrajudicial execution of Boko Haram's leader, Mohammed Yusuf, and dozens of other suspected members in July 2009 became a rallying cry for the group's subsequent violent campaign."[59]

Beginning in 2009, Boko Haram launched a ferocious insurgency against Nigeria's government and unleashed a pitiless campaign of terror throughout the country. As a result, "Nigeria's ranking on the Global Terrorism Index rose from 16th out of 158 countries in 2008 to 6th (tied with Somalia) by the end of 2011. There were 168 officially recorded terrorist attacks in 2011 alone."[60] Boko Haram has been fairly wholesale in its raids, which not only have resulted in thousands of deaths but also have shattered the sense of community for many Nigerians, especially those in the northeast. "The group has launched hundreds of coordinated attacks across the northern region since July 2009 that have resulted in the deaths of over 6,000 people and the displacement of tens of thousands more."[61]

In response, Goodluck Jonathan, Nigeria's president, strengthened in March 2011 Nigeria's National Human Rights Commission, presumably to mitigate ethno-religious tensions.[62] Such a move, while laudable, did little to stem the violence. Boko Haram reaped global notoriety in August 2011 when it deployed suicide bombers to attack the UN Nigerian headquarters in Abuja, thereby striking a physical and symbolic blow to Nigeria's aspirations to heightened leadership and increased engagement within the international community. On December 25, 2011, Boko Haram bombed numerous Christian churches, killing 37 people, and injuring 57 more in one attack on the St. Theresa Catholic Church in Madalla outside Abuja.[63] While remaining the major perpetrator of violent extremism and terrorism in Nigeria, Boko Haram also has inspired splinter groups. In January 2012, Jama'atu Ansarul Muslimina Fi Biladis Sudan (Vanguards for the Protection of Muslims in Black Africa), an Islamist group known colloquially as Ansaru, emulated Boko Haram's callousness. Boko Haram's pugnacity, however, has continued to gain worldwide awareness. On February 19, 2013, the violent extremist organization kidnapped seven French tourists visiting northern Cameroon, demonstrating Boko Haram's mobility across the porous border between the two countries.[64]

In May 2013, President Goodluck Jonathan declared a state of emergency in the northeast region states of Adamawa, Borno, and Yobe because of the scale of violent extremism and terrorism waged by Boko Haram.[65] Nigeria's exertions, however, proved woefully insufficient to combat the group. Local communities impacted by Boko Haram in Maiduguri, Borno State, formed the Civilian Joint Task Force (CJTF) in July 2013, largely due to the ineffective response from Abuja. This move represented a grassroots reaction to Boko Haram, and the CJTF, known colloquially as Yan Gora, sought to provide homegrown security in the absence of a federal solution from Abuja, often armed only with such rudimentary weapons as knives and axes.[66] The CJTF proved successful locally, pressuring Boko Haram to retire to the Gwoza Hills and the Sambisa Forest Reserve.[67] In September 2013, this violent extremist organization conducted one of its most deadly assaults to date in Benisheikh, Nigeria, killing more than 160 people, many of whom were women and children. By the end of 2013, Boko Haram reaped global condemnation among heightened concerns about the group's escalating viciousness. On November 13, 2013, the United States declared Boko Haram a terrorist organization, stressing its concerns regarding Boko Haram's potential links to AQIM while emphasizing the importance of Nigeria "protecting civilians and ensuring that human rights are respected" in its operations against Boko Haram.[68] In March 2014, Navi Pillay, UN high commissioner for human rights, feared that Nigeria was "currently facing its most daunting set of challenges for decades," in large part due to Boko Haram.[69]

Boko Haram's most high-profile attacks came in 2014. On April 14–15, 2014, Boko Haram kidnapped 276 schoolgirls attending Government Secondary School from the town of Chibok in Borno State, Nigeria, gaining transnational notoriety and prompting a worldwide "bring back our girls" campaign.[70] In extensive interviews with many of the girls, almost all of whom were Christians, Human Rights Watch determined, "The victims appear to have been targeted either because of their presumed religious affiliation or for attending western-style schools."[71] On April 14, 2014, Boko Haram also bombed a crowded motor park near Abuja, killing more than 90 people as they boarded mass transit buses for their morning commute.[72] On May 21, 2014, Boko Haram bombed cars in Jos, killing more than 100 people. Reports in the aftermath of the Jos bombing stressed that Boko Haram had become more deadly: "Bomb attacks are growing more frequent and sophisticated."[73] On July 23, 2014, Boko Haram blasted Murtala Mohammed Square in Kaduna, presumably to kill Sheikh Dahiru Bauchi, a critic of Boko Haram and moderate Muslim cleric leading prayers for thousands of Muslims gathered there. Another explosion at the nearby Kawo market followed. The two blasts killed more than 80 people combined.[74] In August 2014, Boko Haram declared an Islamic caliphate emanating out of Gwoza, Borno State, and operated out of the Gwoza Hills and Sambisa Forest Reserve largely due to geography. Gwoza is a hilly region, which delineates the border between Nigeria and Cameroon, while nearby Sambisa Forest, more than 500 square kilometers of pristine nature reserve, provided a sparsely populated space where Boko Haram established militant camps. The *Economist* discerned, "The grab for territory signals a change from Boko Haram's hit-and-run tactics. This may be in keeping with pronouncements by its firebrand leader, Abubakar Shekau, that chunks of Borno State are 'Muslim Territory.' "[75]

In August 2014, Mohammed Sambo Dasuki, Nigeria's national security advisor, warned that Boko Haram "is threatening our very democratic foundations. They strive not only to dismantle democratic structures but to prevent the provision of state services, such as health, education, commerce, and security." Dasuki explained, "Their activities have forced thousands to flee their homes, jobs, and communities, pushing them into poverty. It is therefore important to understand the effects of insurgency on governance and the additional challenges that leaders face in striving to deliver on their promises to citizens."[76]

On November 28, 2014, Boko Haram bombed the Central Mosque in Kano, thereby further extending their wanton violence to Muslim places of worship. At around 2 p.m. Boko Haram attackers raided the mosque during Jumat prayer, detonated several powerful bombs, and then fired upon survivors fleeing the chaos. The deadly attack killed 35 worshipers and injured another 150 participants. Ahmed Mohammed Soron Dinki, an eyewitness to the cruel incursion, recalled, "I was rushing to the mosque for prayers when I heard a big sound and heavy smoke followed. It was terrible. I saw more than fifty dead bodies on the ground and the majority of the dead bodies are kids and their parents." Boko Haram's violence against Muslims whom they deemed apostates not only instilled fear among many witnesses but also sparked backlash against the group from some influential Muslim leaders. Lamido Sanusi, the emir of Kano, resolved, "These people, when they attack towns, they kill boys and enslave girls. People must stand resolute." Sanusi called for his followers to take requisite actions "to defend themselves" in the perceived absence of government protection.[77]

In October 2014, Nigeria's government attempted to broker a cease-fire with Boko Haram, but the group continued to maraud and gain territory, seizing by the end of October Mubi, the second-largest city in Adamawa State. Sources estimated that Boko Haram controlled as much as one-fifth of all Nigeria's territory by the end of 2014.[78] In November of that same year, however, the National Assembly did not extend the state of emergency in the northeast, partly in response to abuses of civilians by Nigeria's military; to some degree this move was a tacit acknowledgment that the government's campaign against Boko Haram had not worked. By the end of 2014, Nigeria's response had proven itself a failure.[79] Boko Haram had captured large areas in northern Nigeria, especially Borno State, and had achieved the notorious distinction of being the deadliest terrorist group in the world for that year. The Institute for Economics and Peace labeled Boko Haram as "the most deadly terrorist group in the world" in its Global Terrorism Index: in 2014, the violent extremist organization more than tripled its carnage, causing 6,644 deaths through its ferocious terrorism. As a result of Boko Haram's dramatic increase in bloodshed, Nigeria became the country most battered by terrorism in the world, an unwanted distinction for any nation. In 2014, Nigeria lost 7,512 civilian lives to terrorism, an increase of more than 300 percent.[80] Marius Pricopi divulged, "For some, it may come as a surprise that, in 2014, Boko Haram was the deadliest terrorist organization in the world. . . . The same year, the terrorist activity of Boko Haram generated no less than 6,644 deaths, the total number of related Boko Haram kills since the start of the insurgency in 2009 reaching the stunning number of 20,000."[81]

To place this violent extremism and terrorism in Nigeria in global context, the impact of terrorism generally and Boko Haram on Nigeria specifically intensified dramatically from the group's founding in 2002 to 2014, claiming tens of thousands of victims and propelling Nigeria to the notorious accolade of being one of the countries in the world most harmed by terrorism. Marius Pricopi remarked, "Nigeria thereby came to hold the second highest number of terrorism-related deaths in the world, being exceeded only by Iraq—a country torn by war, insurgencies and sectarian violence."[82] Some international specialists warned that by the end of 2014, "the warning lights regarding the extremist group Boko Haram were flashing red."[83]

Boko Haram continued its onslaught and lethality in 2015. From January 3 to January 7, 2015, Boko Haram overran Baga, Nigeria, killing approximately 2,000 people and causing another 20,000 residents to flee. Reports characterized the incident as "the worst in its six-year insurgency." The strategic location of Baga near the borders of Cameroon, Chad, and Niger, as well as the broad scope and widespread devastation of the incursion, indicated that Boko Haram had the capacity to threaten not only Nigeria but its neighbors as well. The Baga attack prompted heightened efforts at regional cooperation to combat the group. Abubakar Shekau, Boko Haram's leader, claimed responsibility for the raid and warned of strikes to come: "We killed the people of Baga," Shekau boasted. "We indeed killed them, as our Lord instructed us in His Book." Symbolic of the group's professed goal of implementing a caliphate in Nigeria, Shekau burnt Nigeria's flag and replaced it with the black banner of Boko Haram, proclaiming, "Nigeria is dead."[84] The results of Boko Haram's violent extremism and terrorism in Nigeria have been staggering. Estimates have placed the number of internally displaced persons (IDPs) in Nigeria at more than 2 million, primarily due to violence between Boko Haram and Nigeria's government but also resulting from broader clashes between Christians and Muslims.[85] In addition, more than 400,000 refugees have fled the upheaval from Nigeria to such neighboring countries as Cameroon, Chad, and Niger.[86]

Under pressure from Nigeria's military, security, and police forces, Boko Haram has evidenced fissures. In August 2016, Boko Haram splintered into three distinct factions: an unaligned group bent on local violence, a faction allied with al-Qaeda, and another division affiliated with ISIL.[87] The one constant with the group, however, has been change. Boko Haram has proven flexible and resilient, often adapting and morphing based on specific circumstances. Marc-Antoine Pérouse de Montclos characterized the group as "one of the most complex, unique and poorly understood security crises Nigeria has ever faced."[88] Abdulkadir Abubakar, former chief intelligence officer and senior commander for Boko Haram whom the Nigerian military apprehended in June 2017, disclosed the existence of schisms within the group, two of which were disposed to end the insurgency against the expressed orders of Abubakar Shekau, largely due to Shekau's wanton violence against civilians. "The two factions are willing to cooperate with Nigerian Government to defeat Shekau," Abubakar confessed.[89] In a show of strength, Boko Haram extended its reach beyond

Cameroon soldiers assigned to the Battalion d'Intervention Rapide arrive at a humanitarian assistance site in Kourgui, Cameroon. The mission provided medical assistance and education to more than 1,250 people displaced due to Boko Haram violence. May 13, 2015. (Courtesy United States Africa Command)

Nigeria to the broader Lake Chad Basin, comprised of Cameroon, Chad, Niger, and Nigeria. Boko Haram's terrorism purposely has singled out countries as well, including Cameroon, purportedly because Cameroon has aided Nigeria's exertions against violent extremism.[90]

Violent extremism and terrorism have continued to plague Nigeria. Although receding from their peak levels, these contemporary security issues have lingered as critical obstacles for the country. In 2016, Nigeria ranked third worldwide on the Global Terrorism Index and first in Africa, suffering 466 attacks, which killed 1,832 people and injured another 919.[91] Although annual fatalities from Boko Haram's hostilities peaked at 11,519 in 2015, the group has continued to be lethal, inflicting 3,484 fatalities in 2016 and another 3,329 deaths in 2017. While casualties resulting from Boko Haram incidents have leveled off, they have endured as substantial. In addition, Boko Haram redoubled its number of violent spasms from 417 in 2016 to 500 in 2017, illustrating that it has renewed vigor.[92] In 2016, internal divisions led to the formation of another violent extremist organization, ISIS-West Africa, splintering off Boko Haram. As its name implies, the group officially has associated itself with ISIS, another moniker for ISIL. This scenario has made possible the group leveraging ISIS's capability, recruiting, and funding. Contrasted with the relative success against Boko Haram, this development has been an ominous sign, as ISIS-West Africa has demonstrated even more destructive capability than Boko Haram and has avoided much of the sectarian violence against Muslims that has characterized Boko Haram's attacks and weakened some of Boko Haram's perceived legitimacy in its insurgency against Nigeria's government.[93] During a visit to Borno State on January 12, 2018, Amina Mohammed, deputy secretary-general of the United Nations, cautioned, "One of our main messages is that while Nigeria has really made huge efforts in containing its space and pushing back the insurgency, it is not over yet."[94]

Major factors in combating Boko Haram specifically and violent extremism and terrorism in Nigeria generally have been improving public trust and strengthening the government's stability, including combating corruption and eliminating civilian abuses by military, security, and police forces. There is still much to accomplish in these regards, as Transparency International ranked Nigeria 136th out of 176 countries, making it one of the most corrupt governments worldwide.[95] Boko Haram's impact on education in Nigeria has been particularly devastating, which is not surprising given its nefarious mantra. The violent extremist organization has killed an estimated 2,295 teachers, has displaced another 19,000 educators, and has destroyed approximately 1,500 schools, mostly in the northeast region of the country. Adamu Adamu, Nigeria's minister of education, explained that the carnage not only was tragic in present terms but also has limited schooling prospects for the foreseeable future.[96] In 2018, Nigeria's military launched Operation Last Hold, which has replaced the previous Operation Lafiya Dole (Peace by Force). While Operation Lafiya Dole succeeded at driving Boko Haram from the Sambisa Forest, Operation Last Hold has focused on the Lake Chad Basin. Major General David Ahmadu, chief of training and operations of Nigeria's army, anticipated, "The operational end-state of Operation Last Hold is the total defeat of the Boko Haram terrorist sect." Such a laudable goal, however, has proven much harder to achieve than to avow. Over the course of its malicious insurrection, Boko Haram has killed as many as 20,000 civilians and displaced another 2 million people throughout Nigeria.[97]

CONCLUSION

Violent extremism and terrorism have been significant contemporary security issues in Africa. While global deaths from terrorism have dipped slightly in the past several years, the number of countries experiencing them and the frequency of attacks worldwide have both risen. This phenomenon has continued to impact Africa. Almost half of the 50 countries around the world most marred by terrorism have been in Africa, including Nigeria and Somalia, both of which have been in the top 10.[98] Africa has faced numerous violent extremist organizations, and the consequences from them have been devastating. In 2017, there were nearly 3,000 terrorist attacks in Africa, claiming more than 10,000 lives.[99] Weak and fragile states have exacerbated violent extremism and terrorism. Somalia has epitomized both contemporary security issues, existing as a failed state and suffering greatly from violent extremism and terrorism. A failed state for much of the past three decades, Somalia more recently has become engulfed by violent extremist organizations, especially al-Shabaab, which has committed nearly three-quarters of all terrorist incidents in this state since 2000.[100] With 5,000 fighters and as many as 100,000 supporters around the world, al-Shabaab has wreaked havoc on Somalia since 2006, extending its ire to such neighboring countries as Kenya and Uganda. Regional and international efforts to combat al-Shabaab have dampened the group's capabilities, although it has retained harmful intentions and deadly capabilities. In 2017, the group committed 1,593 attacks and killed 4,557 people, illustrating its lethal persistence. In a different way, Nigeria also has typified the contemporary security issues of violent extremism and terrorism in Africa. Whereas Somalia has revealed the dangers of failed states breeding terrorism, Nigeria has demonstrated that this dynamic has worked in the reverse direction: Boko Haram has weakened Nigeria. Founded in 2002, Boko Haram has waged a brutish uprising against Nigeria ever since, inflicting mayhem on the country and undermining its political system by contributing decisively to Goodluck Jonathan's electoral loss, the first such defeat of a sitting president in Nigeria's history. Triggering an official state of emergency in Nigeria in 2013, Boko Haram has cut a trail of death and destruction across large portions of land, extending its vehemence religiously from Christians to Muslims and geographically from Nigeria to Chad. By 2014, Boko Haram controlled 20 percent of Nigeria.[101] In the process, the group killed approximately 20,000 civilians and displaced as many as 2 million people.[102] While the group splintered into three factions in 2016, it has demonstrated a resilience that retains fatal purpose and destructive potential. In 2017, the group committed 500 terrorist attacks, which resulted in 3,329 deaths.[103] As much as violent extremism and terrorism have inflicted destruction on Africa generally and havoc on Somalia and Nigeria specifically, other contemporary security issues in Africa, piracy and maritime security, have manifested their importance in the same regions but in altogether different ways.

CHAPTER 6

Piracy and Maritime Security

OVERVIEW

Contemporary security issues in Africa have existed not only on land but also at sea. Water covers nearly three-quarters of the world's surface, and 6 out of 10 people globally live in coastal regions. As a result, sea lines of communication (SLOCs) are critical to trade. The majority of global commerce travels by ocean because of the cost-effectiveness of maritime transportation. Therefore, ships convey nearly 90 percent of goods and 65 percent of all energy around the world. As a result, the maritime environment is crucial to the international economy; it also houses abundant natural resources, especially hydrocarbons essential to energy security and fish vital to food security. Because the maritime environment is significant economically and environmentally, security at sea is paramount to international security.[1]

Maritime security has been especially important for Africa.[2] In its "Agenda 2063," a comprehensive framework for the continent during the next 50 years, the African Union envisioned, "Africa's Blue/ocean economy, which is three times the size of its landmass, shall be a major contributor to continental transformation and growth, through knowledge on marine and aquatic biotechnology, the growth of an Africa-wide shipping industry, the development of sea, river and lake transport and fishing; and exploitation and beneficiation of deep sea mineral and other resources."[3] Unfortunately, piracy and maritime security have been significant contemporary security issues in Africa. Piracy at sea disproportionately has impacted Africa.[4] Francois Vreÿ declared, "Piracy has become the epitome of maritime insecurity and Africa has risen to the number one spot in the world for piracy attacks."[5] Geography has played a major part in this development: 38 African countries have coastlines, and nearly all Africa's imports and exports travel through sea ports. As a result, two areas in the world most threatened by piracy at sea surround Africa, the Gulf of Aden and the Gulf of Guinea.

Even though piracy and maritime security have been critical contemporary security issues in Africa, ambiguity has shrouded them.[6] Two important and critical definitions have illustrated this conundrum. The 1982 United Nations Convention on the Law of the Sea (UNCLOS) defined piracy as an attack on a vessel outside of territorial waters or beyond 12 nautical miles from shore.[7] The International Maritime Organization (IMO) described armed robbery as an assault on a ship within territorial waters or less than 12 nautical miles from a nation's land.[8] Classification opacities and the complicating factor of international waters have made enforcement and prosecution difficult for any one nation. While legal definitions have made subtle distinctions between piracy and armed robbery at sea, these contemporary security issues have varied little in materialization, especially around Africa.[9] Even so, these categorical obscurities have been problematic for understanding the broad scope of the enigma, especially in Africa where many incidents have taken place in territorial waters.[10] Lisa Otto advised, "In the case of Nigeria this is especially so given that piracy, under international law, must take place on the high seas or outside a state's jurisdiction to be defined as such. Nigerian piracy, however, has been characterized by its territorial nature, with both on- and off-shore manifestations in Nigerian waters and the waters of neighbouring countries."[11] Indeed. For the purposes of this book, I focus on any attacks on naval vessels, including piracy in international waters and armed robbery at sea in territorial waters, to inform a broader comprehension of piracy and maritime security in Africa.

The causes of piracy at sea have been as diverse as they have been complex. Primary among them has been the weakness of state institutions on land nearby.[12] In many cases, instability, poverty, and corruption on land have prompted piracy at sea. In addition to fragile state institutions, economic factors have played an important part. In Africa, illegal fishing has been one of the most prominent ones; it has degraded the marine environment and has destroyed economic opportunities for local communities. Overexploitation has plagued roughly three-quarters of fisheries around the world, and the cost of this scourge to Africa has ranged in the tens of billions of dollars. As a result, some local youth have turned to piracy in lieu of viable economic alternatives. In addition to piracy, other related maritime security issues have multiplied. Drug trafficking has been a major one, with critical maritime transit routes transiting from South America and Asia through Africa into Europe. Weapons proliferation has been a troubling concern and an accelerant to conflict on land. On October 26, 2010, Nigeria's government seized at the port of Lagos a major arms shipment from Iran to fighters in the Niger Delta; this illegal arms cache included 107mm rockets smuggled in sealed shipping containers. Reports indicated that insurgent groups previously had not used this type of heavy weapons and their introduction into Nigeria "would mark a dangerous escalation in the level of violence."[13]

Piracy at sea has been multifaceted, including economic and political undertones, ostensibly addressing both types of grievances. In the Gulf of Aden, piracy at sea purportedly has sought to counteract the impact of illegal fishing and toxic waste dumping in the waters off Somalia. Those engaged in piracy have articulated that they merely sought to compensate for lost economic opportunity on land and at sea.[14] While admitting that his companions desired "just money," Sugule Ali, a Somali pirate, presented a complex mix of motives for pursuing piracy in the Gulf of Aden. "We don't consider ourselves sea bandits," Sugule reasoned. "We consider sea bandits those who illegally fish in our seas and dump waste in our seas and carry weapons in our seas. We are simply patrolling our seas. Think of us like a coast guard."[15] In conjunction with this complex fusion of intentions, piracy in the Gulf of Aden surged. Until roughly 2012, this region became the focal point of piracy at sea, not only in Africa but around the world as well.

After 2012, most attention on piracy and maritime security shifted to another region near Africa, the Gulf of Guinea. Political and economic motives amalgamated there as well, represented most visibly by the Movement for the Emancipation of the Niger Delta (MEND), which surfaced in late 2005. This militant group has attempted to address injustices throughout the Niger Delta, including the lack of infrastructure, elevated environmental concerns, and high youth unemployment, among others. Nigeria's federal government at Abuja failed to distribute oil wealth throughout the Niger Delta, and MEND fought to spread it more evenly. Significant environmental pollution, much of it related to oil, has degraded the Niger Delta, which the United Nations characterized as one of the world's most endangered environmental areas and launched on November 30, 2009, an extensive $9.5 million environmental impact assessment.[16] In that area oil operations and illegal bunkering, the practice of off-loading oil after the attack and seizure of a tanker, have spilled more than 1.5 million tons of oil into the delta, making it one of the ecosystems most damaged by oil in the world.[17] Partly as a result of this degradation but also for economic purposes, piracy off Nigeria swelled. Therefore, MEND pronounced economic, political, and environmental reasons for its attacks. Justin V. Hastings and Sarah G. Phillips explained, "Niger River Delta militants—and among them pirates engaged in kidnappings for ransom—have a narrative that constrains their behaviour: they are protectors of their land, using violence and especially kidnappings of foreign oil workers and attacks on oil facilities to stop environmental degradation committed by foreign oil firms, and to demand a greater share of the oil and natural gas income."[18] Beginning in 2012, the Gulf of Guinea became the focal point of piracy at sea, not only in Africa but also in the world. Once again, this situation has presented a conundrum for the UNCLOS definition of piracy, because MEND has not maneuvered in international waters and has not operated solely for financial profit. Lisa Otto clarified, "Another concern with the UNCLOS is the requirement that, for acts to be those of piracy, they must be committed for private ends. This then excludes cases of piracy committed for political reasons, as has been argued to occur in Nigeria (and to some extent in Somalia) in the past, and begs the question of how it is to be determined when the motivation shifts from being for political gain to being for private gain."[19] Sifting through the rhetoric of a particular armed group's articulated aims and discerning their true motivations have added imperviousness to definitional morass.

While the causes of piracy have been muddy, its consequences have been crystal clear. The results of piracy overwhelmingly have been negative for Africa, the world economy, and the vital relationship between the two. Estimates of stolen oil have ranged in the hundreds of billions of dollars. There also have been numerous and significant indirect costs. Piracy has hampered economic development by raising the expenses of routine trade, rerouting some vessels to other ports, and deterring other ships from any port visits whatsoever. Piracy also has endangered the marine environment, especially through toxic waste dumping and bunkering, which prompts leaks due to hurried transfers of oil by untrained hijackers.

While they are major contemporary security issues in Africa, piracy and maritime security have significant regional variations; as with all security issues, they exist within specific circumstances. That dynamic has been particularly true with this chapter's two case studies: the Gulf of Aden and the Gulf of Guinea. These have been two areas in the world most imperiled by piracy and most lacking in maritime security. While these two regions have some general similarities, they also have exhibited essential contextual differences. Most important, the location of piracy has differed markedly between the two regions. In the Gulf of Aden, piracy usually has taken place in international waters, increasingly farther out from the coast of Somalia and entering into the Indian Ocean, whereas in the Gulf of Guinea, piracy typically has occurred in territorial waters and exclusive economic zones, mostly off the coast of Nigeria, although there have been attacks off the coasts of Angola, Benin, Côte d'Ivoire, the Democratic Republic of the Congo, Ghana, Guinea, Republic of the Congo (Brazzaville), and Togo.

Countering piracy and ensuring maritime security have proven arduous tasks. Due to its vastness, the maritime environment has been a

major hurdle. Interdicting ships at sea is much more difficult than controlling vehicles on land, not least because the presence of roads limits
traffic to certain routes, unlike at sea where vessels have complete freedom of movement.[20] In addition to the previously discussed conundrum
between international waters, exclusive economic zones, and territorial
waters, there have been practical problems. Immense spaces make detec-
tion difficult, while there is a fundamental mismatch between large, slow,
and sparsely manned shipping vessels and fast, maneuverable, and easily armed pirate skiffs. In addition, naval capacity is expensive and out of
reach for many developing nations.[21] In Africa, the dearth of local naval
capacity has made countering piracy trying. Most nations in Africa that
have faced these threats, with such notable exceptions as South Africa and
Nigeria, have maintained only a handful of small coast guard vessels. As
a result, they have been reliant on regional cooperation and international
assistance for bolstering naval capacity to strengthen maritime security
and thereby to combat piracy.

Because piracy and maritime security transcend national security and
impact regional and international security, there have been numerous
efforts to combat piracy in Africa. In 1975, regional leaders created the
Maritime Organisation of West and Central Africa (MOWCA) to cooperate on maritime issues. On December 10, 1982, the United Nations crafted
the Convention on the Law of the Sea. Part V, Article 55 of this resolution demarcated exclusive economic zones between nations, extending
200 nautical miles from territorial waters.[22] In addition to international
attention to maritime security, regional efforts in Africa have addressed
these contemporary security issues. On June 11, 1994, the Organization of
African Unity adopted the African Maritime Transport Charter.[23] The Economic Community for West African States (ECOWAS) specially concentrated on piracy in the region, and local leaders in 1999 created the Gulf
of Guinea Commission to address maritime security in the region, whose
membership includes Angola, Cameroon, the Democratic Republic of the
Congo, Republic of the Congo (Brazzaville), Equatorial Guinea, Gabon,
Nigeria, and São Tomé and Príncipe. Meeting in Durban, South Africa,
during October 2009, African Union principals reinforced the African
Maritime Transport Charter, indicating an acknowledgment of the surg-
ing hardships from piracy and maritime security and a revamped commitment to combat them. The following year, the African Union on July 26,
2010, renewed the charter.[24] On November 29, 2012, the Gulf of Guinea
Commission signed the Luanda Declaration on Peace and Security in the
region, which "calls for the consideration of a permanent mechanism to
enforce and monitor peace and security in the region."[25] Representatives
of more than 50 countries met in Lomé, Togo, on October 15, 2016, to partner on maritime security in Africa. The result was the African Charter
on Maritime Security, Safety, and Development in Africa, also known as

the Lomé Charter, which aimed at crafting an African maritime security agenda.

Overall, piracy around the world has declined, although it also has concentrated in certain areas where it still plagues many nations. The IMO recorded that in 2015, there were 303 reported incidents, while in 2016, that number had dropped to 221. The organization explained, "This confirms the current downward year-on-year trend, with a reduction of about 27% at the global level."[26] Even though piracy has receded globally, it has lingered as a critical contemporary security issue in Africa during the past three decades, exploding first in the Gulf of Aden and then shifting more recently toward the Gulf of Guinea. At the same time that piracy declined worldwide by 27 percent from 2015 to 2016, it swelled in the Gulf of Guinea by 77 percent.[27]

GULF OF ADEN

Chaos on land often has spilt outward into the maritime environment.[28] The Gulf of Aden off the coast of Somalia has embodied this important dynamic with many negative repercussions. As discussed in the previous chapter, the Siad Barre government in Somalia collapsed in 1991 after more than two decades of rule. Extensive and persistent conflict ensued, which transformed Somalia into a failed state and allowed piracy in the Gulf of Aden to flourish. Even so, maritime security in the Gulf of Aden has existed within a specific political, social, and cultural context. Justin V. Hastings and Sarah G. Phillips showed, "In the Horn of Africa, pirates take structural and ideational cues from the licit economy and are constrained by the informal regulations that govern clan groups, rent-based economic activities, and collective security arrangements in Somalia."[29]

The Gulf of Aden holds strategic importance because it is a choke point, a geographical feature where a body of water narrows and forces vessels to journey through a constricted stretch, for transit through the Red Sea and the Suez Canal. A great deal of seaborne trade, including vast amounts of oil, passes on a daily basis through the Gulf of Aden, where piracy typically has pursued kidnapping and hijacking for ransom but has decreased in the volume of attacks and their consequences. Many observers have attributed this decline to heightened international responses in this region and enhanced operational capabilities onboard merchant ships plying those waters. At its peak in 2012, the reach of Somali pirates was vast, extending as far as Mauritius and Mozambique. This was quite different from the Gulf of Guinea where the majority of confrontations have occurred in territorial waters.

Since 2010, piracy in the Gulf of Aden has ebbed. One extensive report documented, "The number of attacks in this area, which had roughly doubled annually from 2007 to 2009, rising from 51 reported attacks to 217, appeared to level off in 2010, when 219 attacks were reported." The report continued, "Attacks in the Gulf of Aden declined by more than half in 2010, attributed in large part to international naval patrols. Attacks east and south of Somalia, however, increased substantially, up from 19 reported attacks in 2008 and 80 in 2009 to over 140 in 2010."[30] Many specialists have credited this reduction to augmented international maritime undertakings in this region and strengthened security measures aboard merchant ships. As a result, numerous policy makers have heralded these endeavors as a successful case study of combating piracy and bolstering maritime security through relentless regional and international cooperation.

The rise in piracy in the Gulf of Aden prompted the creation of the International Recommended Transit Corridor (IRTC) to consolidate shipping traffic, ease escorting duties, and deter unchecked piracy.[31] Despite the overall success of transnational endeavors in the Gulf of Aden, outbreaks have continued to occur. Most prominent of these was the assault on the *Maersk Alabama*, which gained global notice. Somali pirates successfully attacked the vessel in 2009, unsuccessfully harassed it again in 2010, and assaulted it a third time in March 2011.[32] During this period, Somali pirates intensified their efforts and confronted more ambitious targets. In 2010, emboldened bandits engaged two U.S. warships, the USS *Nicholas* and the USS *Ashland*. On March 31, 2010, a pirate skiff contested the *Nicholas*, a U.S. Navy Fletcher-class destroyer; the warship sank the smaller vessel and captured a larger bandit command ship, known colloquially as a mother ship. On April 10, 2010, Somali pirates battled the *Ashland*, a Whidbey Island-class dock landing ship, triggering a firefight in which the navy vessel sank the pirate skiff.[33] On February 18, 2011, brigands hijacked the sailboat *Quest*, which was cruising off the coast of Oman; Somali pirates held the four passengers as captives before eventually killing them.[34] Piracy in the Gulf of Aden peaked in 2011 with a flurry of strikes. In 2011, London's *Sunday Times* reported that "in 2010 alone a total of 4,185 seafarers were attacked with guns and rocket-propelled grenades. During the same period $111 m[illion] was paid out to pirates in ransoms. In the last 12 months, hijackings off the coast of Somalia accounted for 61% of all attacks on ships worldwide. . . . In the past four years, 3,500 seafarers have been kidnapped and held hostage by pirate gangs."[35]

One unique aspect of piracy in the Gulf of Aden has been the extensive international involvement to improve maritime security in this region. The United Nations addressed this contemporary security issue in Africa with UN Security Council Resolution 1816 in June 2008.[36] As a result, the United Nations called for international cooperation against piracy off the coast of Somalia and also sought to reinforce the role of Somalia's Transitional Federal Government. The European Union (EU) mobilized when EU Naval Forces conducted Mission Atalanta, while the North Atlantic Treaty Organization (NATO) conducted Operation Ocean Shield.[37] These two counterpiracy operations were independent, although organic cooperation has developed between them. Carmen Gebhard and Simon J. Smith divulged, "Two faces of EU–NATO cooperation become apparent: the political level is dominated by a permanent deadlock, while on the ground and at sea staff have developed a modus operandi that allows them to deliver fairly successfully in complementing yet detached operations."[38] The United States launched Combined Task Force 151 (CTF-151) to ensure maritime security in this region, and these diverse ventures spurred the creation of Shared Awareness and Deconfliction (SHADE) meetings, held quarterly in Bahrain to coordinate international responses to piracy in the Gulf of Aden. Overall, the numerous transnational reactions to piracy in the Gulf of Aden have demonstrated a successful model to combat piracy and to improve maritime security around Africa.

Another inimitable facet of piracy in the Gulf of Aden has been China's immersion.[39] With increased amounts of its trade navigating these waters, China became progressively concerned with piracy and maritime security in this region. China's shipping vessels more and more came under attack by pirates, prompting a vigorous response. Andrew S. Erickson and Austin M. Strange logged, "Over 1,200 Chinese merchant vessels transited the Gulf of Aden during the first eleven months of 2008, and of this number eighty-three were attacked by pirate groups," including the fishing vessel *Tianyu 8*, tanker *Zhenhua 4*, and cargo ship *Dajian*.[40] China's enlarged trade with Africa converged with a surge in piracy in the Gulf of Aden to spur an unprecedented expansion of China's naval operations in international

Maritime Forces of Djibouti prepare to board a patrol boat to increase maritime security in the waters off East Africa, western Indian Ocean island nations, and in the Gulf of Aden. February 4, 2016. (Courtesy United States Africa Command)

waters. By December 2008, China had initiated a major antipiracy deployment to the Gulf of Aden, the first of its kind for modern China. On January 6, 2009, China officially joined the international coalition combating piracy in the Gulf of Aden, sending two People's Liberation Army Navy (PLAN) destroyers, *Haikou* and *Wuhan*, and a supply ship, *Weishanhu*, to the region. China's task forces have included both destroyers and frigates, and helicopters and special operations forces have augmented these naval vessels. China's antipiracy task forces have conducted a broad spectrum of operations, including seaborne area patrols, shipping vessel escorts, and naval port visits, as well as training, coordination, and exchanges with foreign navies. These operations have increased since China's first naval engagement in the region in 2008. While coordinating and participating with foreign navies, China has ensured its autonomy. China eschewed using the IRTC, instead escorting ships on a parallel route to the north, thereby preserving its independence of action. China's antipiracy and maritime security operations have been extraordinary and have received worldwide notice as a result. Chris Rowan declared, "It marks a break in tradition for the modern Chinese navy, which usually confines itself to patrolling coastal waters."[41] Marc Lanteigne added, "China's response to the piracy threat in the Gulf of Aden, an element of the Sino-Somali relationship, has drawn much international attention due to the unprecedented deployment of Chinese People's Liberation Army (Navy) or PLA (N) vessels as part of the international anti-piracy coalition. The participation of Chinese naval forces within the coalition since January 2009 marked the first time the country's vessels have operated out of territory since the founding of the People's Republic 60 years earlier."[42]

China's economic trade with Africa and presence in the Gulf of Aden have only increased. By 2010, China eclipsed 2,000 transits through the Gulf of Aden per year by its merchant vessels.[43] As a result, China's antipiracy operations swelled. Kamerling and van der Putten observed, "By October 2011, nine consecutive taskforces had been sent from China, each one replacing its predecessor and remaining in the Gulf of Aden for about four months."[44] In addition to escorting its own vessels, China's PLAN warships have accompanied mounting numbers of foreign vessels, highlighting that its motivation has been in part economic self-interest, while other incentives have been much broader, including conducting international diplomacy, boosting China's international leadership, and augmenting its naval capabilities. As long as China's economic involvement in Africa continues, it is likely that its antipiracy actions will endure as well. China's deployment of naval forces to combat piracy in the Gulf of Aden was a significant departure from past precedent. China previously had sent forces to participate in UN peacekeeping missions, "but the naval escort mission is different in that it is not integrated into a UN-led operation (although the operations are UN-mandated) and that it involves military assets suitable for combat actions (warships and special forces)," according to Kamerling and van der Putten.[45]

Not only analysts have noticed the unparalleled engagement and expansion. Beginning on September 3, 2014, China's antipiracy efforts in the Gulf of Aden even spurred creation of an action-packed drama series for a mass audience, *In the Gulf of Aden*, on China Central Television (CCTV)-8.[46] In addition, *Operation Red Sea*, a commercial movie released in 2018, displayed the exploits of China's antipiracy role in the Gulf of Aden for theatergoers worldwide. In this fictional thriller, sailors and special operations soldiers from China's PLAN rescue hostages from presumably Somali pirates in bold and daring fashion. *Operation Red Sea* has been a commercial hit, but, more important, the film has demonstrated the increasing prominence of China's antipiracy operations.[47]

Partly as a result of the robust international response to it, piracy in the Gulf of Aden has decreased significantly. In 2016, there were only four reported incidents in this region, and they all occurred in port areas. Even though piracy in this region has diminished drastically after peaking in 2012, it has not disappeared completely. In October 2016, Somali pirates attacked the *CPO Korea*, a UK-flagged tanker off the coast of Somalia. The following year, Somali pirates on February 13, 2017, commandeered the *MV Aris 13*, a tanker, off the coast of Puntland, Somalia. This was the first successful hijacking in the Gulf of Aden since 2012. On March 24, 2017, pirates captured *Casayr 2*, a Yemini fishing vessel, off the coast of Eyl, Somalia. In 2017, the IMO issued an ominous warning: "Piracy off the coast of Somalia has not been eradicated and the underlying conditions fueling piracy have not changed."[48] Indeed.

Indicative that the threat of piracy in the Gulf of Aden has not receded entirely, 12 states in the region signed on January 12, 2017, the Jeddah Amendment to the Djibouti Code of Conduct, which "recognizes the important role of the 'blue economy' including shipping, seafaring, fisheries and tourism in supporting sustainable economic growth, food security, employment, prosperity and stability." In addition to highlighting the import of maritime security, the amendment recognized the latent danger of piracy in the region: "However, it expresses deep concern about crimes of piracy, armed robbery against ships and other illicit maritime activity, including fisheries crime, in the Western Indian Ocean and the Gulf of Aden."[49] The peril has remained real. Just past midnight on February 23, 2018, heavily armed men on a pair of pirate skiffs closed with and fired on the chemical tanker *Leopard Sun* off the coast of Somalia, which was heading south from Sohar, Oman, to Cape Town, South Africa. An embarked private security team, which is much more common than in previous years, defended the ship and repelled the brigands.[50] The attack was a potent reminder that although the threat in the Gulf of Aden has receded, it has not evaporated completely. As piracy subsided and maritime security strengthened off the coast of Somalia, another region, the Gulf of Guinea, experienced a flood in these contemporary security issues in Africa.

GULF OF GUINEA

The Gulf of Guinea represents an immense geographical area, comprising approximately 5,000 nautical miles of coastline. Although definitions of the Gulf of Guinea vary, in general it ranges from Senegal to Angola along the coast of western Africa. Economically, it involves the Economic Community of West African States (ECOWAS) and the Economic Community of Central African States (ECCAS). During the past three decades, the Gulf of Guinea has undergone a hefty multiplication in shipping traffic due to the region's vibrant economic expansion. Adeniyi Adejimi Osinowo revealed, "Indeed, container traffic in West African ports has grown 14 percent annually since 1995, the fastest of any region in Sub-Saharan Africa."[51] Related to this commercial development, attacks in this region have also risen, making piracy and maritime security critical contemporary security issues in the Gulf of Guinea.[52]

Much of this piracy has targeted Nigeria's oil industry, which boomed during the 1970s and has continued to be robust. The nation also has an extensive, and therefore difficult-to-patrol, coastline and has suffered political instability, including violent extremism and terrorism, rampant corruption, growing poverty, and heightened inequality. As a result, the Gulf of Guinea has eclipsed the Gulf of Aden as the region experiencing the most piracy attacks in Africa specifically and in the world generally. As discussed previously, since 2008, the Gulf of Aden was the region in Africa of primary concern regarding piracy and maritime security. Since 2012, however, the Gulf of Guinea has seized that dubious title: "In 2012, the Gulf of Guinea surpassed that of the Gulf of Aden (infamous for high-seas hijackings) as the region with the highest number of reported piracy attacks in the world. These attacks also tended to be more violent," observed Osinowo.[53]

In the Gulf of Guinea, piracy has escalated in the frequency of confrontations, their resulting violence, and the consequences of those assaults. Piracy in this region has resulted in oil theft, for political causes, criminal motives, or a combination thereof. The goal has not been to ransom crews but rather to steal their oil, making aggression more probable as crew safety no longer has remained as relevant as before in ransom negotiations. The Gulf of Guinea has exhibited a tendency toward oil bunkering to sell stolen cargo on illegal markets. There also have been significant operational differences in tactics used and outcomes sought by bandits operating in the Gulf of Guinea. Whereas piracy in the Gulf of Aden tended to be more economic in nature, in the Gulf of Guinea there have been overt political motivations and a demonstrated willingness to escalate violence.

Francois Vreÿ warned, "While events off the Horn of Africa lean towards criminality such as piracy and smuggling, those in West African waters (the Gulf of Guinea in particular) are often more violent and display a political-criminal link."[54] Most important, piracy has targeted the lucrative oil market in the Gulf of Guinea. Nigeria exports more oil than any country in sub-Saharan Africa and is one of the world's largest exporters, having a maximum production capacity of almost 1.9 million barrels per day and therefore ranking as the largest producer of crude oil in Africa and the sixth-largest producer in the world.[55] This prominence has attracted heightened focus on the offshore industry and oil tankers, both while they are in port and while they are in transit. The practice of bunkering has led piracy at sea toward stealing oil from vulnerable tankers and subsequently selling it on the illicit market, although there has been a recent shift toward kidnap for ransom due to lower global oil prices. The vast majority of these confrontations have occurred off the coast of Nigeria, although other incidents have transpired in the waters near the Republic of the Congo (Brazzaville), Ghana, the Democratic Republic of the Congo, Benin, Côte d'Ivoire, Guinea, Angola, and Togo, occurring both in territorial waters and in exclusive economic zones. The Gulf of Guinea also has experienced significant levels of illegal fishing.

The nature of piracy between these two regions, however, has varied. Justin V. Hastings and Sarah G. Phillips explained, "In West Africa, sophisticated piracy both preys upon and arises from the formal economy, specifically the international oil industry. As a result, piracy networks often mirror and draw from both the formal institutions in Nigeria used to regulate and protect oil production, and those engaged in oil production, processing, distribution, and transportation."[56] Therefore, the Gulf of Guinea has become a world epicenter for piracy. "Piracy attacks (and armed robbery at sea) in the Gulf of Guinea comprised a fifth of all recorded maritime incidents globally in 2013," Osinowo added.[57] Within the broader region, Nigeria has reeled from its high prevalence of piracy off its coasts. While the Gulf of Guinea accounted for approximately 20 percent of worldwide maritime assaults in 2013, Nigeria alone experienced more than 12 percent of the global total.[58]

Not only has the number of attacks in this region compounded, but so too has the level of violence associated with them: "Gulf of Guinea piracy is increasingly characterized by violent assaults against vessels and hostage takings—1,871 seafarers were victims of attacks and 279 were taken hostage in 2013. . . . Notably, Togo and Nigeria accounted for over 70 percent of the attacks and hostage taking in West Africa in 2012–2014."[59] This has developed from the modus operandi of pirates in the Gulf of Guinea. Piracy off the coast of Nigeria has grown to such an extent and demonstrated such diverse capabilities that the United Nations has characterized it as transnational organized crime.[60] Unlike in the Gulf of Aden where ransom negotiations have motivated attempts to keep hostages safe, piracy in the Gulf of Guinea has emphasized theft, resulting in less incentive for bandits to ensure the safety of a ship's crew. Unfortunately, in the warped calculus of piracy, crews have become a liability. Whereas the responses to piracy and maritime security in the Gulf of Aden have been primarily international, those in the Gulf of Guinea have been principally regional, albeit with increased worldwide concern.

There have been numerous regional maritime strategies to combat piracy in the Gulf of Guinea.[61] On July 3, 2001, Angola, Republic of the Congo (Brazzaville), Gabon, Nigeria, and São Tomé and Príncipe created the Gulf of Guinea Commission, which has sought to "constitute a framework of consultation among the countries of the Gulf of Guinea for cooperation and development, as well as for the prevention, management and resolution of conflicts that may arise from the delimitation of borders and the economic and commercial exploitation of natural resources within territorial boundaries, particularly in the overlapping Exclusive Economic Zones (EEZ) of our States." While the group has pursued cooperation between member states and focused on territorial waters, it did not originally center on piracy and maritime security.[62] In 2008, Cameroon, the Democratic Republic of the Congo, and Equatorial Guinea joined the group.[63] On October 24, 2009, leaders of ECCAS, also known by its French acronym CEEAC, met in Kinshasa, the Democratic Republic of the Congo, and established the Regional Centre for the Maritime Security of Central Africa.[64]

By late 2011, piracy in the Gulf of Guinea had become an important topic at the UN Security Council. On October 31, 2011, the Security Council adopted Resolution 2018, its first statement on piracy and maritime security in this region, and provided heightened scrutiny, *"expressing its deep concern* about the threat that piracy and armed robbery at sea in the Gulf of Guinea pose to international navigation, security and the economic development of states in the region [emphasis in the original]." The United Nations urged ECOWAS, ECCAS, and the Gulf of Guinea Commission "to develop a comprehensive strategy" to combat piracy and improve maritime security in the region.[65] Ban Ki-moon, UN secretary-general, initiated an undertaking to evaluate the situation. The secretary-general's assessment mission on piracy in the Gulf of Guinea deployed to the region from November 7 to November 24, 2011. On January 19, 2012, that delegation reported this body of water rapidly had become an epicenter for piracy in Africa. "Piracy in the Gulf of Guinea is not a new phenomenon. Since the late 1990s, the region has been facing acts of piracy targeting high-value assets, particularly oil shipments," recounted the task force. "However, since 2010, incidents of piracy and armed robbery in the area have risen significantly, making the region the second most acute piracy problem on the African continent."[66] On February 29, 2012, UN Security

Council Resolution 2039 reinforced the fact that the Gulf of Guinea had overtaken the Gulf of Aden as the most worrisome region for maritime security and expressed alarm about the escalating risk of piracy in this region, its intensifying ferocious nature, and its expanded impact on littoral countries, including "their hinterland areas and landlocked countries in the region."[67]

In 2012, Nigeria conducted Operation Pulo Shield and Operation Prosperity, a joint naval exercise between Nigeria and Benin, to improve maritime security.[68] On November 29, 2012, the Gulf of Guinea Commission signed the Luanda Declaration on Peace and Security in the Gulf of Guinea Region aimed at improving regional cooperation on piracy and maritime security.[69] On June 25, 2013, the Gulf of Guinea Commission signed at Yaoundé, Cameroon, a code of conduct for combating piracy in the region, committing to share information among member states; to increase naval capacity; and to strengthen policies, laws, and agencies responsible for maritime security in this region.[70] On August 10, 2013, José Eduardo dos Santos, Angola's president and outgoing chair of the commission, highlighted in Malabo, Equatorial Guinea, the Gulf of Guinea Commission's resolve to eradicate piracy and contribute to overall maritime security in the region and in Africa as a whole.[71] In addition, the multinational Sahara Express naval exercise has aimed to buttress maritime security in this region.[72] On March 28, 2014, leaders of ECOWAS met in Côte d'Ivoire to strategize on many issues, including maritime security. They highlighted the need to interdict and prevent the transit of illicit cargo, including drugs, arms, and humans, through the Gulf of Guinea.[73]

Even though most attention has been regional, international actors have become troubled with maritime security in the Gulf of Guinea. The EU has developed additional apprehensions, primarily due to its position as a major importer of goods, especially energy resources, from this region. On March 17, 2014, the EU crafted an official strategy to combat piracy. In it, the Council of the European Union conceded, "Europe imports about half of its energy needs, of which nearly 10% of its oil and 4% of its natural gas come from the Gulf of Guinea. Nigeria, Angola, Equatorial Guinea and Gabon are significant suppliers of crude oil, and Nigeria of natural gas."[74] There also have been private efforts led by the shipping industry, including the Maritime Trade Information Sharing Center for the Gulf of Guinea (MTISC-GOG).[75]

After decreasing slightly in 2015, piracy and armed robbery at sea in the Gulf of Guinea rose in 2016, jumping from only 35 incidents in 2015 to 62 occurrences in 2016, making it one of the areas in the world most affected by piracy and maritime security. The IMO reported that 62 of the 221 total instances worldwide in 2016 occurred in the Gulf of Guinea, making that body of water responsible for more than one-quarter of all global piracy and armed robbery at sea confrontations. Of these 62 attacks, 33 occurred in international seas, 4 arose in territorial waters, and 25 transpired in port areas, revealing the complexity of episodes and difficulty of ensuring maritime security across their spectrum.[76] Heightened maritime security has continued to be a major need in this region, especially because of its direct relationship with the region's economy. On November 24, 2016, Dakuku Peterside, director-general of the Nigerian Maritime Administration and Safety Agency (NIMASA), demanded that the elimination of piracy in the Gulf of Guinea was critical for economic growth and charged ECOWAS with its eradication.[77] With funding from the EU, 19 African countries launched on June 8, 2017, the Gulf of Guinea Interregional Network (GOGIN) to improve maritime security.[78] This was partly because the Gulf of Guinea also has been an intermediate transit point for illicit trafficking from North and South America to Europe.[79] Even so, piracy in the Gulf of Guinea has swelled, especially off the coast of Nigeria, forcing its navy to reconsider its approach to maritime security, including more partnerships with international navies. In 2018, the International Maritime Bureau characterized the waters off the coast of Nigeria as "extremely dangerous." During the first three months of that year, nearly three-quarters of all armed attacks worldwide occurred in the Gulf of Guinea.[80]

CONCLUSION

The results of piracy have been diverse and damaging. In the absence of maritime security, decreased trade, ransom payments, oil theft, and inflated insurance rates all have occurred. There have been obvious economic losses, such as the theft of oil, which Donna Nincic has estimated ranged from $300 to $400 billion in Nigeria over a five-year span.[81] In addition to oil theft, there have been other direct predicaments, including illegal fishing, kidnapping for ransom, and violence at sea. There also have been more subtle effects. Piracy has resulted in costly hikes to insurance premiums, which have been passed on to consumers worldwide. There have been extra expenses for shipboard security, including personnel, technology, and training as well as legal and ethical considerations regarding the privatization of force.[82] Other outlays of dealing with piracy have continued to climb. Oceans beyond Piracy calculated that the total costs of combating piracy in the Gulf of Guinea in 2014 amounted to between $748 and $983 billion.[83] Kidnapping, a much more pronounced phenomenon recently, has resulted in large ransom payments. There also have been stolen cargo and the impact of illicit trade on legal markets, epitomized by oil bunkering. Other indirect consequences have proliferated, including raised overheads due to rerouting shipping around problem areas or opportunity costs of certain vessels completely avoiding the region due to heightened risks. Environmental shocks have included oil spills, which in turn have hurt local fishing prospects. As a result, piracy and maritime security have emerged as major contemporary security issues in Africa. In response to the rising prevalence of piracy off the coasts of Africa, there have been continental maritime strategies to combat piracy at sea. The 2050 Africa's Integrated Maritime Strategy became effective in January 2014. In addition, representatives of more than 50 African Union countries met in Lomé, Togo, on October 15, 2016, to strategize on maritime security in Africa. The outcome was the African Charter on Maritime Security, Safety, and Development in Africa, also known as the Lomé Charter, which aimed at crafting an African maritime security agenda, and more than 30 African countries signed. In the end, successful responses to maritime security must address the myriad underlying causes of piracy.

There has been a fundamental link between weak and fragile states on land and piracy at sea, including poverty, lack of jobs, illegal markets, and the scarcity of naval capacity as demonstrated by the two case studies in this chapter. When the Siad Barre government in Somalia collapsed in 1991, chaos ensued. The anarchy was so prevalent that many observers have characterized Somalia as the archetype of a failed state, not only in Africa but also in the world. It has scored second-most fragile state of 178 countries ranked by the Fund for Peace in the Fragile States Index with a score of 113.4 out of a worst possible 120.[84] It also has ranked as one of the world's most fragile states for many years.[85] In Somalia, instability on land has transitioned to volatility at sea, which has been especially crucial because the Gulf of Aden serves as a choke point for naval passage through the Red Sea and the Suez Canal. In a related but different way, Nigeria's state stability has augured poorly for its maritime security and has presented a more nuanced case of state fragility. It has a robust economy, being Africa's largest economy and most productive oil exporter. Nigeria also historically has been relatively stable, but recent history has revealed troubling fissures. As a result, problems have brimmed in Nigeria, including extreme poverty, ubiquitous fraud, and political instability. According to the UN Development Programme, Nigeria ranked 152nd out of 188 countries, placing it near the top of the "low human development" category. This situation has held relatively consistent over much of the past decade, with the country falling one place in the index from 2010 to 2015.[86] Transparency International scored Nigeria 148th out of 180 countries on its Corruption Perceptions Index.[87] From 2007 to 2017, the nation has become increasingly fragile, situated astride the "some worsening" and "worsening" categories, illustrating a consistent decline in Nigeria's stability over the entire decade.[88] Reinforcing the close connection between conditions on land and piracy at sea, many observers have argued that efforts on land must accompany endeavors at sea, including infrastructure development efforts; legal employment opportunities, especially for youth; environmental protections, particularly for fishing;

and enforcement against illicit markets where these goods are sold, specifically regarding oil. Addressing these causes would help to remove many of the incentives that have motivated piracy in the recent past.

As a result, piracy and maritime security have been critical contemporary security issues in Africa; their importance cannot be overstated. The maritime environment is crucial to world trade, as 90 percent of commerce worldwide and nearly three-quarters of world energy supplies transit the world's oceans.[89] Maritime security has been especially important to Africa as 38 of its 54 nations possess coastlines, many of them quite lengthy. Although definitions and specificities cloud maritime security with ambiguities, one thing is clear: attacks on naval vessels, whether in international waters, territorial waters, or in ports, have been critical security problems. The causes of piracy have been diverse; weakness of state institutions on land has been primary among them. Such economic factors as illegal fishing, and such political influences as discrimination, inequality, and corruption, have fueled grievances. In addition, environmental concerns have sparked piracy, while the repercussions, especially oil bunkering, have led to environmental degradation. Two bodies of water have embodied the contemporary security issues of piracy and maritime security. First the Gulf of Aden off Somalia and more recently the Gulf of Guinea near Nigeria have demonstrated that piracy and maritime security have presented both challenges and opportunities. The Gulf of Aden acquired transnational attention as piracy surged and seemed to go unchecked. A strategic choke point for shipping transiting through the Red Sea and the Suez Canal, the Gulf of Aden experienced a great expansion of piracy, manifesting itself typically in kidnapping and hijacking for ransom. International efforts such as the IRTC, EU's Mission Atalanta, NATO's Operation Ocean Shield, and U.S. CTF-151 combated piracy in this region, including increased involvement from China's PLAN. In many ways, the Gulf of Aden has illustrated the possibilities of vigorous and concerted international initiatives to increase maritime security. In 2012, the Gulf of Guinea eclipsed the Gulf of Aden as the world's epicenter for piracy and maritime security. Ranging from the coast of Senegal in the north to the shores of Angola in the south, the Gulf of Guinea has been home to a flourishing economic boom. As a result, piracy has emerged on its horizons. Much of this scourge has targeted the region's lucrative oil industry, including offshore rigs and tankers. Most ominous, piracy in the Gulf of Guinea has been more violent, partly because the ships have not been the target; instead, pirates have coveted the cargo. Whereas international exertions battled piracy in the Gulf of Aden, regional efforts have been most prominent in the Gulf of Guinea, including the Gulf of Guinea Commission, Nigeria's Operation Pulo Shield and Operation Prosperity, and the Luanda Declaration on Peace and Security in the Gulf of Guinea Region. Piracy in the Gulf of Guinea has increased, with the frequency of attacks nearly doubling from 2015 to 2016 and representing one-quarter of all incidents worldwide.[90] While piracy and maritime security have proven crucial contemporary security issues in Africa, food security and extreme poverty have grown to vital importance for human security on the continent.

CHAPTER 7

Food Security and Extreme Poverty

OVERVIEW

Food security and extreme poverty have been critical concerns around the world; they have presented especially key contemporary security issues in Africa. The Food and Agriculture Organization (FAO), International Fund for Agricultural Development, UNICEF, World Food Programme, and World Health Organization reported, "In 2016 the number of chronically undernourished people in the world is estimated to have increased to 815 million, up from 777 million in 2015 although still down from about 900 million in 2000." This upturn was particularly troubling because the number of undernourished people globally had been declining previously. The FAO and other institutions emphasized the vital bonds between food security and violence: "Conflict is a key driver of situations of severe food crisis and recently re-emerged famines, while hunger and undernutrition are significantly worse where conflicts are prolonged and institutional capacities weak." As a result, these organizations issued "a clear warning signal" regarding the relationship between war and food security and the potential for global food security to deteriorate in violence-prone regions.[1] When analyzed worldwide, food security, or the lack thereof, has been an impediment that overwhelmingly has impaired Africa.

Food security and extreme poverty have long been setbacks for Africa. The FAO commented, "The food security situation has worsened in particular in parts of sub-Saharan Africa . . . and deteriorations have been observed most notably in situations of conflict and conflict combined with droughts or floods."[2] A mixture of such natural disasters as droughts, floods, earthquakes, desertification, and deforestation has often coalesced with such logistical shortcomings as inadequate infrastructure, insufficient distribution, and incomplete storage facilities to heighten the difficulty of achieving food security on the continent. O. P. Godwin explained, "The rate of population growth is double that of food production, thus necessitating food importation."[3] The United Nations has estimated that the population of sub-Saharan Africa has grown at nearly 3 percent per year, thereby placing additional pressure on food security and extreme poverty.[4] In addition to a burgeoning populace, food security has proven elusive for many countries in Africa. The FAO highlighted 37 countries in the world that are "in need of external assistance for food." Of these, 29 nations in Africa made the dubitable list.[5] The only non-African nations enumerated were Afghanistan, Democratic People's Republic of Korea, Haiti, Iraq, Myanmar, Pakistan, Syrian Arab Republic, and Yemen.

Analysts have assessed food security by four factors: availability, access, stability, and utilization. While much progress has been made on these variables in Africa over the past three decades, trials across these areas have persisted throughout many countries on the continent.[6] O. P. Godwin revealed, "Africa is the only region of the developing world where the regional average of food production per person has been declining over the last 40 years. In Africa as a whole, food consumption exceeded domestic production by 50 percent during the mid-1980s, when severe droughts were prevalent; in the 1990s, it exceeded domestic production by more than 30 percent."[7] Since the 1990s, food availability has risen and extreme poverty has declined across sub-Saharan Africa. The percentage of people suffering from undernourishment has lessened, but population growth has resulted in the actual number of people afflicted with malnutrition rising. Estimates have counted the number of undernourished people in Africa at approximately 243 million.[8] It is important to note that Africa also has experienced high urbanization, which has impacted food security and extreme poverty in myriad ways. From 1890 to 1990, Africa's urban population rate jumped from 5 percent to 34 percent. As a result, cities with a population of more than 1 million increased from 1 in 1900, Cairo, Egypt, to 38 by 2000, including two metropolises with more than 10 million residents, Cairo and Lagos, Nigeria.[9] The United Nations has predicted that by 2050, Africa's urban population rate will be higher than 60 percent.[10]

Even though many obstacles regarding food security and extreme poverty have persisted, sub-Saharan Africa has made laudable advances on food security over the past three decades. In September 2000, the UN Millennium Development Goals (MDGs) laid out eight areas of emphasis to achieve by 2015. The first of these goals sought to eradicate hunger and extreme poverty.[11] Specifically, MDG 1, Target 1.C pursued between 1990 and 2015 to halve the proportion of people who suffered from hunger.[12]

To implement this goal, African leaders in 2003 committed to the Comprehensive Africa Agriculture Development Programme (CAADP), which strove to enhance food security across the continent, and attained some realization in doing so. The FAO documented that "approximately one person out of four in SSA [Sub-Saharan Africa] is estimated to be undernourished today compared to a ratio of one out of three in 1990–92."[13] Within the context of improvement across the continent, however, a great deal of regional variation has existed. The FAO specified, "Advancement has been particularly remarkable in Western Africa which successfully reduced by 63 percent the proportion of its people suffering from hunger; the proportion declined from 24.2 percent in 1990–92 to 9 percent in 2014–16."[14] By comparison, during the same period central Africa swelled from 34 percent to 41 percent, representing an escalation from 24.2 million undernourished people during 1990–1992 to 58.9 million during 2014–2016.[15]

Food security and extreme poverty have been critical contemporary security issues in Africa. They also have proven interconnected because Africa imports significant, and therefore expensive, amounts of food every year. Africa has paid approximately $40 billion per year on food imports in the recent past. ReGina Jane Jere explained, "For the poorest communities, whether rural or urban, food is their main expenditure item. This applies to all countries regardless of their level of economic and agricultural development. Food insecurity is first and foremost about poverty and inequalities."[16] Part of the difficulty has been the complexity of the issue: food security has controllable factors, such as governance, corruption, and security, and far less manageable variables such as weather and environmental conditions. In addition, there often has been a direct relationship between conflict and famine, as evidenced in South Sudan. Near constant fighting has resulted in 5 million people lacking food security with 1 million of them in grave danger of starvation.[17] In contrast, drought, more than violence, negatively has obstructed food security in eastern and southern Africa where food security has ebbed and flowed with changes in weather and climate. In a detailed study of Malawi, the FAO disclosed, "Food shortages are the result of a variety of immediate factors like erratic rainfall, poor harvests, rising food prices, and the lack of resilience of the affected households and communities to withstand shocks."[18]

Leaders in Africa have attempted numerous responses to achieve food security and to overcome the scourge of extreme poverty on the continent. In 2003, African Union held a summit in Maputo, Mozambique. During the meeting, the African Union created the CAADP.[19] Also known as the Maputo Declaration, the program encouraged member states to invest a minimum of 10 percent of their annual budgets to agriculture and to grow their farming economies by at least 6 percent each successive year. The results have been less than desired. ReGina Jane Jere revealed, "But only 8 of Africa's 54 countries have kept the 10% promise, and as such the sector remains dismally underdeveloped, leading to continued food insecurity across the continent."[20]

Whereas CAADP originally focused on agriculture policy and development, recent initiatives have associated food security to nutrition in Africa. From 2008 to 2009, a global food crisis raged; world food prices skyrocketed as a result.[21] Partly in response, regional policy makers in 2010 established the Scaling Up Nutrition (SUN) network, which emphasized nutrition as one way to achieve food security. In 2011, CAADP launched the Nutrition Capacity Initiative so that countries in Africa could coordinate their agriculture and nutrition policies and improve outcomes. International programs sought to assist regional ones. In 2012, U.S. president Barack Obama led efforts at the Group of Eight (G8) Summit on the New Alliance for Food Security and Nutrition, aiming to bolster food security and reduce extreme poverty for 50 million people in sub-Saharan Africa within a decade.[22]

A major area of untapped potential to augment food security and combat extreme poverty has been to raise agricultural productivity in Africa. The African Union admitted, "Africa has 60 percent of the world's available arable land and agriculture is the source of livelihood for 70 percent of the population. Yet the continent generates only 10 percent of global agricultural output."[23] In addition to unrealized farming capacity, water security has played an increasingly vital role. The Nature Conservancy examined water security and produced in 2016 an extensive blueprint to address this dilemma in sub-Saharan Africa. This account estimated that Africa's urban population will double in the next two decades, placing extreme stress on limited water supplies, especially in burgeoning cities. Shortfalls in such water security areas as catchments, quality, conservation, and sustainability have exacerbated already-weighty difficulties of food security.[24] There also have been serious ties between food security and extreme poverty. The vast majority of Africa's population relies on agriculture for both food security and income, thereby reinforcing the connections between them. Consequently, a lack of agricultural productivity hits Africa twice, once in terms of food security and another time related to extreme poverty.

The UN Development Programme has assessed that approximately 25 percent of the world's population living in extreme poverty resides in Africa. The African Union explained, "Food security and human development are inextricably linked with mediating factors such as productivity, nutrition, resilience and empowerment."[25] Women have played a critical function in overcoming these contemporary security issues in Africa. The African Union has calculated that women account for around 60 percent of all agricultural production across the continent.[26] In response, some observers have advocated for nutritious and affordable pulse crops, which

Women watering their crops in Nianing, Senegal. February 27, 2016. (Courtesy United States Africa Command)

include pigeon pea, cowpea, lentil, and chickpea. Lisa F. Clark remarked, "Increasingly, there is a global consensus that pulse crops can help address ongoing nutrition and food security challenges in sub-Saharan Africa. Evidence shows that scaling-up production and consumption of pulses grown in sub-Saharan Africa has the potential to make positive contributions to socioeconomic and environmental sustainability."[27]

On January 25, 2018, José Graziano da Silva, FAO director-general, in his address to the 30th African Union summit gathered in Addis Ababa, Ethiopia, remarked, "Achieving zero hunger in our lifetime is still possible." Graziano admitted, however, that it "will require a redoubling of current efforts and a push for political commitment and timely concrete actions such as never seen before."[28] Two nations in Africa that have demonstrated the hindrances of food security and extreme poverty the most during the past three decades have been Ethiopia and Malawi.

ETHIOPIA

The Federal Democratic Republic of Ethiopia is a landlocked eastern African nation comprising more than 1,100,000 square kilometers and bordering Djibouti, Eritrea, Kenya, Somalia, South Sudan, and Sudan. With its capital at Addis Ababa, it is the only African nation without a colonial legacy, having been an independent monarchy throughout its lengthy past, which some histories date back 2,000 years to the Aksumite Kingdom. The lone exception was the Italian occupation from 1936 to 1941.[29] Its dominant terrain features include a high plateau with a central mountain range divided by the Great Rift Valley, which is prone to severe drought, devastating earthquakes, and volcanic eruptions. Ethiopia is home to more than 105 million people, making it the most populous landlocked country in the world and the second-most crowded country in Africa. Nearly two-thirds of Ethiopia's population is under the age of 25. The majority of Ethiopians are Christians, including more than 43 percent Ethiopian Orthodox and nearly 19 percent Protestant, while roughly one-third of Ethiopia's population is Muslim. Its diverse population includes a range of ethnic groups; most numerous among these are the Oromo and Amhara.

Emperor Haile Selassie ruled Ethiopia from 1930 to 1974, when the Derg overthrew him in a coup d'état and established a socialist state.[30] In turn, another uprising led by the Ethiopian People's Revolutionary Democratic Front seized power in 1991, leading to a constitution in 1994 and elections in 1995. A war with Eritrea erupted in 1998 over disputed borders, resulting in a tenuous peace treaty in 2000, and Ethiopia invaded Somalia in 2006 in response to the rise of the Union of Islamic Courts (UIC) in Mogadishu. War in the region has inflicted a heavy price on Ethiopia, with refugees

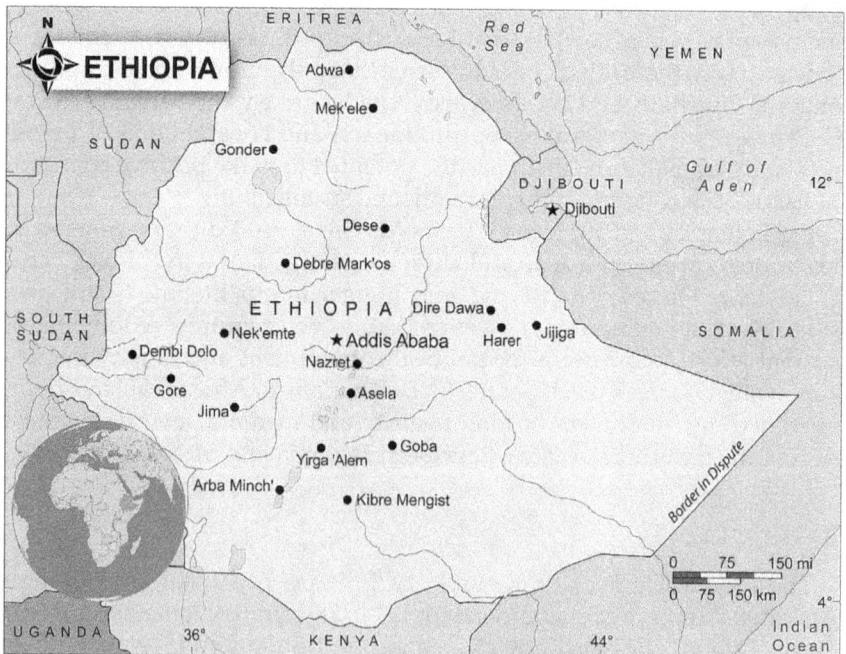

from Eritrea, Somalia, South Sudan, Sudan, and Yemen numbering nearly 1 million people, while Ethiopia has more than 1.7 million internally displaced persons (IDPs), mostly as a result of its border clash with Eritrea and ongoing ethnic and separatist fighting. Elections brought President Mulatu Teshome Wirtu to power on October 7, 2013. The vast majority of its economy relies on agriculture, including cereals, pulses, and oilseeds, although natural and man-made problems have resulted in widespread and persistent starvation and famine, making Ethiopia one of the world's poorest and most food-insecure nations. Most Ethiopians farm and raise livestock, producing diverse crops of coffee, cotton, sugarcane, and khat, a local plant used as a stimulant, while herding cattle, sheep, and goats. Ethiopia has the most abundant livestock population in Africa, while the country's major export is coffee.[31]

In many ways, Ethiopia has embodied the complications of food insecurity and extreme poverty for Africa for much of the past three decades. Ethiopia has been subject to severe climate trials, including the ironic yet devastating combination of droughts and floods. This dual threat has depleted soils, thereby increasing its long-term ramifications for food security and extreme poverty. Aggravating its food security ordeals, Ethiopia also has been one of the region's poorest countries.[32] Due to the severity of the impediments there, the FAO has conducted more than 100 projects in Ethiopia over the past 10 years focused on food security and extreme poverty. As a result and indicative of its importance to these issues in Africa, the FAO-Ethiopia office in Addis Ababa also has served as the FAO Sub-Regional Office for Eastern Africa and the FAO representation to the African Union.[33]

This is partly due to Ethiopia's lengthy struggle with food security and extreme poverty and to a certain extent owing to some of its successes in combating them. In 1984, Ethiopia faced one of the greatest famines in modern history.[34] Since 1995, Ethiopia has improved food security and reduced extreme poverty, although significant hurdles have endured. For much of the past decade, Ethiopia's economy has experienced "strong, broad-based growth," averaging 10.5 percent annually from 2006 to 2016, which has been nearly double the regional average.[35] Ethiopia also has boosted its agricultural productivity. Two critical factors in its economy are agriculture and livestock. Agriculture contributes 44 percent of Ethiopia's gross domestic product (GDP), occupies 80 percent of its labor pool, and delivers 70 percent of its earnings from exports.[36] Historically, maize has been the most important crop in terms of food security, particularly for those policy makers focused on agricultural productivity. Livestock also has been vital because it provides multiple benefits in Ethiopia, including food, income, power, and fertilizer. This dynamic has been especially true at the household level for both food security and income; some observers have estimated that livestock contributes approximately 85 percent of farm cash income.[37] Livestock accounts for between one-third and one-half of agricultural GDP and more than 15 percent of national GDP.[38]

Ethiopia has made significant strides in several categories. From 1995 to 2011, Ethiopia reduced extreme poverty throughout the country by 49 percent. From 2003 to 2010, the nation dedicated approximately 15.2 percent of its annual budget to agriculture.[39] After declining from 1990 to 1992 and remaining relatively flat from 1992 to 2003, Ethiopia's GDP has risen significantly and steadily from 2003.[40] The results have been remarkable. The prevalence of underweight children under 5 years of age dropped from 34.6 percent in 2005 to 29.2 percent in 2011, stunting fell from 50.7 percent in 2006 to 44.2 percent in 2011, and wasting declined from 12.3 percent in 2005 to 10.1 percent in 2011.[41] As a result, the World Bank praised the outcomes: "Ethiopia has proven resilient. Over the past two decades, there has been significant progress in key human development indicators: primary school enrollment has quadrupled, child mortality been cut in half, and the number of people with access to clean water has more than doubled. These gains, together with more recent moves to strengthen the fight against malaria and HIV/AIDS, paint a picture of more well-being in Ethiopia."[42] One extensive study on food security in Ethiopia from 1996 to 2011 revealed, "We find that average quantities and calorie consumption per adult equivalent have consistently and considerably improved

General Samora Yunis, Chief of Staff Ethiopian National Defense Force, and Siraj Fergessa, Ethiopian Minister of Defense, host a traditional Ethiopian coffee ceremony. March 31, 2016. (Courtesy United States Africa Command)

over the last 15 years." The report continued: "Also, the content of the diet is changing with a gradual shift toward high-value foods such as animal products, fruits and vegetables, and processed foods. While the quantities of cereals slightly increased over the last decade, we see a shift away from lower-priced cereals (e.g., sorghum and maize) to more expensive ones (e.g., teff). These changes in diets seem shaped by improvements in household income levels."[43]

There have been, however, exceptions to this laudable progress over the past three decades. Roughly one-third of Ethiopia's population has continued undernourished. A major drought in Ethiopia in 2000 severely hurt the country, with over 10 million people suffering.[44] In addition to drought and flooding, land degradation and deforestation have stayed perennial hurdles for Ethiopia. There also have been important bonds between availability and nutrition for food security. In 2005, the World Bank and Ethiopia created the Productive Safety Nets Program (PSNP), which has provided money and food in exchange for employment on public works projects. The program has been large, benefiting approximately 8 million people in 318 of Ethiopia's most food-insecure districts.[45] In 2008, Ethiopia created a National Nutrition Strategy (NNS), while in 2012, Ethiopia created a Policy and Investment Framework (PIF) focused on the agriculture sector, which sought to make Ethiopia a food-secure middle-income country by 2020.[46] The PIF is a "strategic framework" meant to improve Ethiopia's agricultural productivity from 2010 to 2020. It is also intended to implement the goals previously outlined in the CAADP.[47] In 2012, Ethiopia crafted the National Social Protection Strategy to cover social support programs from 2014 to 2019.[48] In 2013, the FAO, African Union, and Lula Institute, a nongovernmental organization established by Luiz Inácio Lula da Silva, Brazil's former president, agreed to tackle the impediments of food security and extreme poverty, setting ambitious goals toward ending hunger and malnutrition, and the result was the Renewed Partnership to End Hunger in Africa by 2025.[49] This organization chose four countries to pilot the broader program, including Ethiopia. As a result, Ethiopia received approximately $2 million in 2014 "for enhancing livelihoods and reducing poverty through economic diversification and decent work opportunities for rural communities."[50]

From June 26 to June 27, 2014, the African Union devoted its 23rd session to food security and extreme poverty. Leaders signed the Malabo Declaration on Accelerated Agricultural Growth and Transformation for Shared Prosperity and Improved Livelihoods. This comprehensive agreement reinforced and reaffirmed the African Union's goal to end hunger in Africa by 2025 by doubling agricultural productivity levels, halving losses after harvest, protecting vulnerable social groups, and improving nutrition, especially among children.[51] The Malabo Declaration also coupled food security and extreme poverty: while seeking to eliminate hunger in

Africa by 2025, it hoped to halve privation during the same time period, largely through agricultural growth.[52]

Even with some progress, however, Ethiopia's prospects for food security have stayed problematic. The three pillars of the Country Programing Framework all have momentous trials ahead. Ethiopia's crop productivity has stayed consistently "very low," while postharvest losses from insects and disease have been as high as 30 percent.[53] The country's livestock sector also has faced substantial strains: "Critical shortages of the required quality and quantity of livestock feed, incidence and distribution of livestock diseases and lack of capacity to meet international safety and sanitary standards are major bottlenecks."[54] Regarding sustainable natural resource management, the FAO and Ethiopia's government cautioned, "Land, forest and range resources degradation, inefficient agricultural water management and productivity are prevalent."[55] The FAO has reported that widespread drought persists, especially in the south and southeastern portions of the country, resulting in approximately 8.5 million people in those regions becoming food insecure. Regional variations have reached even higher proportions, as the Somali Region of the country had 42 percent of its population food insecure in September 2017.[56]

The issue of seeds in Ethiopia has been substantial. There has been a prevalence of depleted soils in Ethiopia, which when combined with the lack of improved seeds has lessened crop productivity. Therefore, seeds have been a decisive component for Ethiopia regarding food security and extreme poverty. Boaz Blackie Keizire observed, "For example, the type of seeds to be developed or multiplied must be those seeds that have the greatest impact on food security and poverty. The choice cannot be made by scientists alone: stakeholders, the private sector, the farmers and civil society must also play their part."[57] Beginning in 2000, Ethiopia's government dictated a series of stringent regulations to the seed sector, but the results were negligible. On January 24, 2013, Ethiopia moved toward public-private partnerships "aimed at increased inspection and certification, genetic consistency and greater seed supply," with the hopes that cooperation with the seed industry would yield better results.[58]

The future prospects for food security and extreme poverty in Ethiopia have been tenuous at best. Numerous obstacles related to infrastructure have lingered unresolved. Lisa F. Clark signaled, "For Ethiopia (and many other SSA countries), infrastructural challenges (transportation networks, water access, reliable energy sources) also need to be included in food and nutrition security strategies and assessments of needs. Otherwise, broad-based strategies will continue to face implementation problems due to lack of institutional and human capacity on the ground."[59] In addition, urban and rural differences have produced starkly separate hurdles. Commenting on the increasing urbanization rates and changing diets in Ethiopia, I. W. Hassen, Mekdim Dereje, Bart Minten, and Kalle Hirvonen warned that "the next decade will see Ethiopia battling with high under-nutrition in rural areas and increasing overweight and obesity rates in the cities."[60] Other issues have included sustainable forestry, and the Reducing Emissions from Deforestation and Forest Degradation Programme (REDD+) established a Nationwide Forestry Inventory in Ethiopia.[61] To address these impediments moving forward, Ethiopia in 2017 partnered with the FAO to craft the Country Programming Framework (CPF) as a five-year strategy to chart policies addressing improving food security and reducing poverty from 2016 to 2020. The goal has been to promote farming, especially commercial agriculture. The strategy has focused on three pillars: "crop, livestock and sustainable natural resources management and resilience."[62] In addition, social unrest in the country increased in 2018.[63]

As a result, Ethiopia has symbolized the dual trials of food security and extreme poverty in Africa, evidenced by the fact that approximately one-quarter of all global food aid to sub-Saharan Africa has gone to Ethiopia.[64] Although the nation has seen its human development metrics improve, much more work needs to be done: the UN Human Development Index classified Ethiopia 174th out of 188 countries.[65] In addition, the International Food Policy Research Institute rated Ethiopia 104th out of 119 countries that it tracks.[66] Domestic unrest has complicated the food security situation. On February 14, 2018, Hailemariam Desalegn, Ethiopia's prime minister, unexpectedly resigned amid protests by the nation's two largest ethnic groups, the Oromo and Amhara.[67] In addition, Ethiopia has faced disproportionate shocks to food security from weather. Mitiku Kassa, commissioner of the National Disaster Management Commission, remarked, "Ethiopia's geographical location and its diverse agro-ecology makes it vulnerable to climate-induced disaster mainly to drought and floods." Indeed. As a result, Ethiopia has nearly 8 million people in dire need of food aid.[68]

MALAWI

The Republic of Malawi is a landlocked country that rests between Mozambique, Tanzania, and Zambia in southern Africa, and its capital is Lilongwe. Malawi encompasses a total area of 118,484 square kilometers and is home to Lake Malawi, one of Africa's largest lakes. In addition, Lake Nyasa, approximately 580 kilometers long, harbors the most fish species of any lake around the globe. Malawi claims some natural resources, including arable land producing rice, maize, and cassava, as well as limestone, uranium, coal, bauxite, and gemstones, among others, although most of these natural resources have gone untapped. Malawi is home to approximately 19 million people, the vast majority of whom are Christian, and the country suffers from strong land pressure, high population density, and widespread rampant poverty, especially in its southern region. The UN Human Development Index ranked Malawi 170th out of 188 countries, placing it near the bottom of the "low human development" category. This situation has existed for much of the past decade, as Malawi increased its score by only one position from 2010 to 2015.[69] Related to low development, Malawi is one of the world's poorest countries, with more than half of its population living in extreme poverty.[70] In addition, poverty rates in Malawi have swollen over much of the past two decades. In 2004, 17.8 percent of Malawi's households were poor, whereas in 2010, that number had risen to 18.9 percent. This was especially true in rural areas, where 21.4 percent of households were poor in 2010. In addition to the heightened percentage of poor households in Malawi, the depth of their poverty also plunged during this time frame, from an average of 8.0 percent below the poverty line in 2004 to 9.3 percent beneath the poverty line in 2010.[71] More than two-thirds of Malawians are younger than 25 years old. HIV/AIDS also has been a perennial scourge, with approximately 9 percent of its adult population suffering from this disease since 1990, receding from the peak of 15.2 percent in 2000. In addition, Malawi has nearly 500,000 orphans as a result of HIV/AIDS.[72]

Formerly the British protectorate of Nyasaland, Malawi gained independence in 1964. President Hastings Kamuzu Banda ruled Malawi until

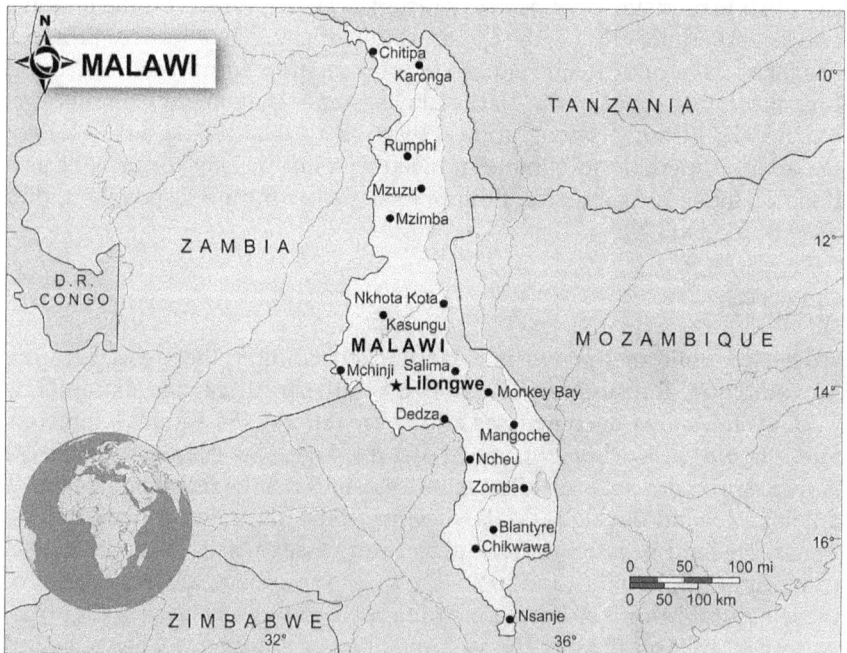

1994, and voters in May 2004 elected President Bingu wa Mutharika, who died on April 5, 2012. As a result, Joyce Banda became president two days later. Corruption has been a persistent problem in Malawi. In October 2013, a government scandal emerged, colloquially referred to as "Cashgate," triggering a freeze in foreign investment. Perceptions of vice have remained high in Malawi; Transparency International ranked the country 122nd out of 180 countries around the world.[73] Voters in May 2014 elected Peter Mutharika president, who is the brother of the former president.

Since independence, Malawi has made agriculture the main pillar of its economy. In 1986, the FAO established representation in Malawi, focusing on food security and improved nutrition throughout the country. Agriculture contributes nearly one-third of national GDP, employs more than two-thirds of the population, and results in three-fourths of foreign exchange earnings.[74] Agriculture, especially maize, dominates the country. The nation benefits from some exports, with tobacco being the largest. Farmers also grow cotton as a cash crop, especially in the south of the country. Extensive agriculture, however, has not achieved food security or alleviated widespread poverty in Malawi. In 2002, the nation suffered a crisis, which "has drawn stark attention to the failures of development policies over the last forty years to create wealth and develop a robust economy, or the markets on which such an economy must depend."[75] The lack of large tracts of farmland, a rapidly expanding population, and extensive use of nonirrigated methods in a country facing repeated and persistent droughts all have hampered the productivity of agriculture in Malawi.[76]

In addition to environmental constraints, Malawi has faced significant infrastructure limitations, including inadequate transportation and communication networks, which hinder agricultural production and diversification efforts. Such shortcomings have made Malawi highly susceptible to shocks, both market-driven ones due to prices and environmental ones resulting from its climate. Andrew Dorward and Jonathan Kydd maintained, "Low levels of financial and physical capital, together with reliance on agriculture and natural resources, make poor rural economies and livelihoods particularly exposed and vulnerable to *risks of natural shocks*. These may arise from adverse weather (affecting crop yields or damaging physical assets); human, crop or animal disease; or physical insecurity (as a result of crime, political violence or conflict)."[77] In Malawi's case, many of these trials have stemmed from low agricultural productivity, lack of diversification, and the environment, especially drought. In addition, the country has faced numerous environmental challenges, including widespread deforestation, land degradation, and water pollution, among others.[78]

In 2006, Malawi launched Operation Dongosolo, which removed street vendors from such cities as Lilongwe, Blantyre, and Zomba. Liam Riley explained, "*Dongosolo* changed how low-income households could earn a living in the informal sector to buy food, and it changed the places where food was available, in some cases making it less physically accessible."[79] The consequences were considerable, as many people in Malawi's cities relied on vending for both food and income. The repercussions, however, extended much farther. Liam Riley clarified, "*Dongosolo* was played out in the core areas of Malawi's cities and yet had consequences for the country as a whole, for both rural households who relied on occasional vending in town as well as those urban households no longer able to earn a living through street vending."[80]

There has been a recent shift in Malawi toward extractive industries. Beginning around 2009, the Karonga District in the northern part of the country became a hub of mining activity, including coal and uranium. Much of the uranium production has come from the Kayelekera mine located in Karonga, which is Malawi's largest quarry.[81] The increase in mining has produced detrimental results for many Malawians and has aggravated food security and extreme poverty in the country. Commercial mining has led to the forced relocation of farmers, disruption of water supplies, contamination of water and crops, and rampant pollution. Human Rights Watch advised, "Over the past 10 years, Malawi's government has promoted private investment in mining and resource extraction as a way to diversify its economy, which previously centered on agricultural production."[82] Much of this activity has revolved around Lake Malawi, and this mining has impacted women disproportionately. Human Rights Watch feared that "concerns about water pollution compelled many women and girls to walk longer distances to fetch water from what they believed was a less contaminated source, further away from the mines. This exposed them to dangers and left them with less time to attend school, earn money, and rest."[83] In 2015, Malawi joined the Extractive Industries Transparency Initiative, but this new development has degraded Malawi's environmental security, resulting in deforestation, water pollution, and industrial waste.[84]

In addition to commercial mining, there also has been a shift toward artisanal and small-scale mining (ASM), especially focused on gemstones and limestone, which can provide a source of income to augment subsistence farming. Paul Justice Kamlongera related the two: "All signs point to the diminished viability of agriculture being an underlying cause of this poverty: in areas where there are accessible mineral deposits, therefore, many smallholder farmers are turning to ASM [artisan and small-scale mining] for supplementary income. The sector is unique because its low barriers to entry mean that smallholders only require a pick and shovel to start working."[85] In 2010, the FAO and the Malawi government crafted the National Medium-Term Priority Framework (NMTPF), focusing on food security, nutrition, natural resources management, and rural development.[86] In

2014, the FAO crafted a new Country Programme Framework (CPF) for Malawi. In it, the FAO noted that nearly half of children under the age of five in the country evidenced malnutrition and stunted growth, and "micronutrient deficiencies in both adults and children remain high."[87]

On May 20, 2014, voters elected Peter Mutharika for a five-year term in a disputed election where Mutharika won slightly more than one-third of ballots cast.[88] Malawi has made some gains regarding food security and extreme poverty, but much more progress needs to be accomplished. The climate has been a major difficulty for Malawi, especially drought and flooding. In 2015, devastating floods ravaged Malawi, destroying agriculture and crippling the economy.[89] Inflation ran rampant, reaching nearly 30 percent and remaining at 19.5 percent throughout the following year, thereby aggravating food security and extreme poverty through skyrocketing food prices.[90] Malawi's GDP growth rate slowed to 2.5 percent in 2016 but increased to 4.5 percent in 2017. Reducing inflation helped: it fell from 22.8 percent in August 2016 to 9.3 percent in August 2017. As a result, food prices dropped at the same time that agricultural productivity improved. The World Bank augured, "Improved weather patterns with increased rainfall in 2017 are expected to result in higher levels of agricultural output than were recorded in 2015 and 2016."[91] An extensive study of Malawi's development recorded, "Despite decades of development efforts supported by significant amounts of foreign aid, Malawi has experienced weak and volatile economic growth over a sustained period of time and has fallen behind its peers. . . . Given that several important factors have been working in Malawi's favor, the lack of progress in growth and poverty reduction is puzzling."[92]

The World Bank cautioned that "poverty and inequality remain stubbornly high in Malawi. Rural poverty persists with one in two people still poor, driven by poor performance of the agriculture sector, volatile economic growth, population growth, and limited opportunities in non-farm activities."[93] Malawi increasingly has undergone urbanization. In 2017, roughly 16 percent of Malawi's population lived in urban areas, which is not surprising given that Malawi has only 4 major cities and 27 urban centers. Further urbanization presents not only such promises as economic growth but also such impediments as inadequate infrastructure and strained social services.[94] Inflation, although appreciably better, has lingered as a threat to food security and extreme poverty because of the potential for food prices to rise in this overwhelmingly poor nation. Inflation in Malawi has been volatile and has remained high for much of the past three decades, eclipsing 80 percent in 1995, 45 percent in 1999, and 25 percent in 2013. From 1980 to 2015, it remained near 10 percent at its lowest levels and exhibited major unpredictability.[95] In 2018, the FAO highlighted Malawi as one of the countries in the world most needing external food assistance.[96] In addition, Fall Armyworm, a persistent pest that ravages cereal crops, emerged to decimate Malawi's harvest, provoking a national disaster. David Phiri, FAO subregional coordinator for southern Africa, advised, "It is equally important to draw lessons from previous experiences and implement resilience-building interventions such as prepositioning water infrastructure, supplementary feeds and disease surveillance for livestock."[97] The result has been precarious food security at best. Saulos Chilima, Malawi's vice president, stated, "The 2017 food security assessment report by the Malawi Vulnerability Assessment Committee projected about one million people as requiring relief food assistance during the lean season, from December 2017 to March 2018."[98] Overall, Malawi has exhibited the trials of food security and extreme poverty in Africa, even in the absence of prolonged conflict.

CONCLUSION

Food security and extreme poverty have been critical contemporary security issues in Africa. While some improvements have been made in these areas during the past three decades, both in Africa and around the world, the continent still needs to overcome more obstacles. In 2015, there were 777 undernourished people around the world, and that total increased to 815 million in 2016.[99] Africa has suffered disproportionately from these contemporary security issues. A burgeoning population, much of it under the age of 25, has combined with such significant environmental challenges as droughts, floods, desertification, and deforestation, to lessen food security and to increase extreme poverty on the continent. Of the 37 countries around the globe most in need of improvements to food security, 29 have been in Africa.[100] Of the more than 815 million food-insecure people around the globe, more than one out of every four of them have resided in Africa.[101] Complicating this difficulty, Africa also has undergone significant urbanization. Regional and international efforts have tackled these contemporary security issues of food security and extreme poverty. The UN MDGs and the CAADP have aspired to improve food security and reduce extreme poverty across Africa. Recent programs have reinforced nutrition's vital importance to food security, including the SUN network, the Nutrition Capacity Initiative, and the New Alliance for Food Security and Nutrition. These endeavors have hinged on improving agricultural productivity in Africa, empowering women to play a vital role in doing so, and leveraging the potential of pulse crops.

Two countries have embodied the contemporary security issues of food security and extreme poverty in Africa: Ethiopia and Malawi. For the past three decades, Ethiopia has exemplified these dual tribulations; it has suffered terrible famines, often triggered by devastating droughts, damaging floods, or both. In addition, Ethiopia has stayed one of the world's poorest countries. It has proven resilient, however, in the face of tremendous hurdles and has made some progress on improving food security and alleviating extreme poverty. The nation has averaged 10.5 percent economic growth from 2006 to 2016 and has boosted its agricultural productivity.[102] The country also halved its extreme poverty from 1995 to 2011.[103] While Ethiopia has made certain gains, much progress awaits, especially improving the nation's infrastructure and resiliency to shocks.

In a distinct way, Malawi has characterized the problems of food security and extreme poverty in Africa. Ranked as one of the world's least developed and poorest countries, Malawi has suffered from food insecurity.[104] Agriculture has represented a significant part of its economy, but the country has endured low productivity, infrastructure shortcomings, and recurrent droughts. In addition, problems in Malawi's few urban areas, exemplified by Operation Dongosolo, have illustrated difficulties in that realm. The emerging mining industry in Malawi has complicated matters, lessening agricultural productivity, polluting crops and water, and adversely impacting the livelihoods of many Malawians. Artisanal and small-scale mining have held some promise for additional income, although inflation has dwarfed other factors in lessening food security and aggravating extreme poverty through ever-higher food prices. Ethiopia and Malawi have demonstrated the importance and persistence of food security and extreme poverty as critical contemporary security issues in Africa. At the same time, international actors have increased their engagement with Africa during the past three decades, including the distinctive approaches of the United States and China vis-à-vis Africa.

CHAPTER 8

International Responses

OVERVIEW

Over the past several decades, Africa has risen in prominence in international affairs and has increased engagement with many international actors.[1] Countries in Africa have created significant commercial growth and have become some of the most flourishing economies globally. Of the 10 fastest growing economies in the world in 2018, 6 were in Africa, including Ghana (8.3 percent), Ethiopia (8.2 percent), Côte d'Ivoire (7.2 percent), Djibouti (7.0 percent), Senegal (6.9 percent), and Tanzania (6.8 percent).[2] Some estimates have predicted that Africa's economy will near $30 trillion by 2050.[3]

Globalization has driven some of these developments. Isaac Fokuo discerned, "Far from holding Africa back, the drive towards insularity in the developed world could actually help to accelerate economic growth on the continent."[4] Since 2003, the World Bank has produced an annual report entitled "Doing Business," which charts regulations that help or hinder business activity in 190 countries around the world. The methodology measures many dynamics, including regulating labor markets, dealing with construction permits, providing electricity, registering property, getting credit, protecting minority investors, trading across borders, paying taxes, enforcing contracts, resolving insolvency, and starting a business.[5] For the past several years, several countries in Africa have been among the 10 most improved nations for business activity, including Djibouti, Malawi, Nigeria, and Zambia.[6]

The emergence of BRICS (Brazil, Russia, India, China, and South Africa) and MINT (Mexico, Indonesia, Nigeria, and Turkey) as common rubrics for the dynamic growth of emerging markets has illustrated Africa's amplified interaction and augmented leadership in the world economy.[7] It also has opened the possibility of nations in Africa pursuing multilateral relations with these countries.[8] For example, Kenya has made substantial reforms for the past several years, resulting in it climbing more than 30 rankings in 2016 and another 12 spots in 2017 to reach 80th out of 190 countries.[9]

Of course, obstacles have persisted. Paul D. Williams cautioned, "Although often depicted as the marginalized continent that globalization forgot, Africa and Africans are not immune from the wider processes driving world politics. Indeed, not only has politics on the continent been shaped by its interactions with outsiders for centuries, but its recent wars have exemplified what might be termed the dark side of liberal globalization."[10] Public debt has endured as a major concern in many countries. In sub-Saharan Africa, it increased from 40 percent of GDP in 2013 to 56 percent of GDP in 2017, including significant accumulations in oil-dependent countries.[11] In addition to public debt, significant disparities have appeared across Africa as a whole. The World Bank characterized sub-Saharan Africa as having "the widest variation" of world regions: Mauritius ranked 25th out of 190 countries around the world for doing business, while Somalia ranked last at 190th.[12]

Africa has played an ever more major role in the world economy, and many nations have responded with enhanced interaction on the continent. Singapore has boosted activity in Africa, especially with Rwanda and Tanzania. Maliki Osman, senior minister of state at Singapore's Ministry of Foreign Affairs, revealed, "We see Africa as a bright spot because there's so much potential."[13] Some observers have regarded Singapore as a precedent for Africa given Singapore's rise from a meager economy with few natural resources to one of the world's leading business centers after little more than 50 years.[14] This "Singapore model" has rested on three pillars: effective central government, foreign direct investment, and robust enforcement against corruption. Of course, problems have continued. Osman highlighted Singapore's difficulty convincing its citizens to leave the country's development behind for opportunities abroad and advised, "From our own experience Africa will have to provide the necessary infrastructure, not just physical but economic, that ensures investors that their investments will be worthwhile."[15]

Brazil also has fostered dealings with Africa over the past three decades. *African Business* reported, "Brazil and Africa relations have witnessed something of a renaissance over the last decade especially since the previous Lula administration made the continent a core focus of its foreign relations and also trade relations strategy."[16] Contracta, a Brazilian company, has pursued substantial development projects in Accra and Kumasi, Ghana, "specifically large-scale projects that can benefit a large population with regards to infrastructure."[17] Brazil has planned to replicate such initiatives and to strengthen its relations with Africa.

Likewise, Turkey has boosted liaisons with Africa over the past three decades and has benefited from an absence of colonial history on the continent.[18] Michael Asiedu explained that "Turkey's foreign policy has progressively evolved to include a key focus on Sub-Saharan Africa in terms of development and humanitarian assistance."[19] Turkey crafted in 1998 its Opening to Africa Action Plan and joined the African Development Bank as a nonregional member. In November 2014, Turkey held the Turkey–Africa Partnership Summit in Malabo, Equatorial Guinea.[20] There have been numerous signs of Turkey's strengthened associations with Africa: Turkey has had significant economic development projects in many countries in Africa, including Burkina Faso, the Democratic Republic of the Congo (DRC), Gambia, Mauritania, Senegal, and Sudan. Turkey maintained 12 embassies in Africa in 2009, but that number had more than tripled by 2016, and its bilateral trade with countries in Africa went from a modest $742 million in 2000 to nearly $6 billion by 2008. By 2015, Turkey–Africa trade had eclipsed $17.5 billion.[21]

Within the setting of Africa's heightened importance and augmented position in international relations, two major powers, the United States and China, have bolstered their dealings in Africa over the past three decades for myriad reasons. Grant T. Harris explained how a host of concerns, including intercontinental dangers, commercial prospects, global politics, and humanitarian crises, has necessitated U.S. policy makers' amplified attention toward Africa. Harris concluded, "A review of Africa's importance to US national security emphasizes two key messages: first, that the United States ignores Africa—replete with vexing transnational threats as well as massive economic opportunity—at its peril; and second, that Africa's geopolitical and economic importance will only grow over time."[22] José de Arimatéia Da Cruz and Laura K. Stephens elucidated, "Apart from the long-standing humanitarian interest in the region, the U.S. is now expanding its foreign policy scope and giving the African continent a place of greater importance in its national security calculations."[23] China also has enlarged its involvement with Africa over the past three decades, demonstrated by more than 1 million workers from China who currently reside in Africa. *African Business* documented, "Chinese investments in Africa have risen sharply in recent years, from $7bn in 2008 to $26bn in 2013. By July 2016 Chinese investments had increased by 515% from full-year 2015 figures."[24] China's strengthened association with Africa not only has been economic but also has involved political influence, as well as more and more military presence.[25] Sophie Harman and William Brown perceived, "Much attention has focused on the economic aspects of China's growing importance in international politics; Africa provides ample evidence and cases for exploration with regard to

China's growing political role."[26] As a result, the United States and China have represented international responses to contemporary security issues in Africa, albeit in unique ways with distinctive differences.

UNITED STATES

The United States has amplified relations with Africa over the past three decades, most visibly with the creation in 2007 of U.S. Africa Command (AFRICOM).[27] Many factors spurred this momentous development.[28] The end of the Cold War removed the bipolar order that had dominated much of international affairs since World War II. Another reason was the worrisome prevalence of weak and fragile states, especially in Africa, and U.S. concerns regarding their repercussions for international security and U.S. national interests. Likewise, the rise of international terrorism, especially prominent attacks in Africa, created distress about the spread of violent extremism on the continent.[29] The 1998 bombings of U.S. embassies in Nairobi, Kenya, and Dar es Salaam, Tanzania, were potent reminders of these festering threats. Africa's abundant natural resources, especially oil, increased economic interactions, as Nigeria became the largest supplier in Africa of oil to the United States. In addition, trepidation over China's increased position prompted renewed focus on the continent for many U.S. analysts and policy makers.[30] China's augmented investments in Africa, much of it related to natural resources, including its receipt of approximately one-third of its total oil from Africa, have caused angst among U.S. policy makers.[31] A recent posture statement by AFRICOM revealed, "Africa's sustained economic growth, improved social development, and growing entrepreneur class are unlocking the continent's potential for international investment and trade, raising its geostrategic importance to the U.S. while also attracting international competition for access, influence, and trade."[32]

On February 6, 2007, President George W. Bush created U.S. AFRICOM, and Robert Gates, U.S. secretary of defense, announced the decision to the public.[33] On October 17, 2008, the command became active at a ceremony in Stuttgart, Germany.[34] Prior to the establishment of AFRICOM, three unified commands addressed U.S. national interests in Africa, including European Command (Africa's mainland), Central Command (Djibouti, Egypt, Eritrea, Ethiopia, Kenya, Somalia, and Sudan), and Pacific Command (Madagascar, Seychelles, and Africa's Indian Ocean coast). More recently, U.S. initiatives on Africa had existed as a subunified component of U.S. European Command (EUCOM).

AFRICOM monitors the entire continent except Egypt, which still falls under U.S. Central Command. U.S. army general William E. "Kip" Ward, commander of the organization, explained, "Within AFRICOM's mission in helping to bring stability to Africa, there are two sides to peace operations and those two sides are mutually supported. One is the restoration of peace. . . . The other is the sustainment of peace."[35] AFRICOM maintains its headquarters in Stuttgart, Germany, and oversees six component forces: U.S. Naval Forces Africa headquartered in Naples, Italy; U.S. Air Forces Africa headquartered in Ramstein, Germany; U.S. Marine Corps Forces Africa headquartered in Stuttgart, Germany; U.S. Army Forces Africa headquartered in Vicenza, Italy; Special Operations Command Africa headquartered in Stuttgart, Germany; and Combined Joint Task Force–Horn of Africa headquartered at Camp Lemonnier, Djibouti. The first three of these, U.S. Naval Forces Africa, U.S. Air Forces Africa, and U.S. Marine Corps Forces Africa, provide the same role for EUCOM.

Therefore, AFRICOM has been an economy of force operation. Michael G. Kamas, David W. Pope, and Ryan N. Propst clarified, "Although USAFRICOM covers a large continent and is engaged in over 15 named operations, it is an economy of force command with limited assigned forces that relies on force allocation and force sharing agreements with U.S. European Command (USEUCOM) to execute its mission."[36] Brian J. Dunn explained, "The establishment of USAFRICOM reflects America's need to engage Africa in a sustained shaping fashion rather than in

Brigadier General Donald C. Bolduc, Special Operations Command Africa commander, inspects troops with his Senegalese counterpart Brigadier General Amadou Kane in Thies, Senegal. February 8, 2016. (Courtesy United States Africa Command)

a reactive crisis mode."[37] AFRICOM can respond to emergencies, however, with support from the Special Purpose Marine Air Ground Task Force–Crisis Response based at Moron Air Base, Spain; U.S. Special Operations Force–Crisis Response Force based in Baumholder, Germany; and the East Africa Response Force based in Djibouti.

AFRICOM's stated goals have demonstrated that Africa has risen in prominence in the U.S. security framework: "The United States Africa Command in concert with other US government agencies and international partners conducts sustained security engagement through military-to-military programmes, military-sponsored activities and other military operations as directed to promote a stable and secure African environment in support of US foreign policy."[38] The primary goal has been to promote stability on the continent; to do this AFRICOM has sought to build security capacity among African partner nations. Other aims have included combating violent extremist organizations (VEOs); defense institution building; improving maritime security; peace support operations; humanitarian and disaster response; and combating illegal trafficking of humans, drugs, and weapons.[39]

Michael E. Hess, a senior administrator with the U.S. Agency for International Development (USAID), explained that AFRICOM has employed a multifaceted approach, using "defense, diplomacy and development."[40] Peter A. Dumbuya added, "It also includes conflict prevention or what some in the Pentagon call 'phase zero.'"[41] Costas M. Constantinou and Sam Okoth Opondo elucidated, "Given its broad mandate, AFRICOM is now concerned with 'Phase Zero' operations, which include duties and activities that were previously the concern of non-military US agencies, NGOs and local communities—from building schools and digging wells, to HIV/AIDS research/advocacy, dental work and veterinary immunization exercises."[42]

This development has not been without critics.[43] Costas M. Constantinou and Sam Okoth Opondo revealed, "These moves by the military participating in 'Operations Other than War' have been considered an attempt to 'demilitarize the military', while others view such activities as the militarization of civilian practice."[44] AFRICOM has supported other initiatives, such as the U.S. Department of State's Africa Contingency Operations Training Assistance (ACOTA) program, in which more than 20 African nations have taken part. In addition, the command has partnered with the U.S. Department of State on the Security Governance Initiative (SGI), which has worked to improve capacity and oversight to the security sector in partner nations in Africa, including Ghana, Kenya, Mali, Niger, Nigeria, and Tunisia.[45] Other examples have included the International Military Education and Training (IMET) program and the Foreign Military Sales (FMS) program. Even civilian observers have commented on AFRICOM's novel emphasis, training the military forces of U.S. allies in

Africa with a purpose of improving overall stability rather than projecting a broad American presence onto the continent. Roger Kaplan remarked, "The long-term strategy of our Africa Command (AFRICOM) is to render African militaries more effective and professional—meaning concerned with security and humanitarian missions, not with political power."[46]

As a result, AFRICOM has manifested an amplified U.S. focus on Africa. Ward concluded, "No longer is Africa the second or third priority for three other geographic Unified Commands. It is our first priority."[47] The creation of AFRICOM also has engendered robust debate, creating both supporters and detractors of the novel organization. "Those in favor of AFRICOM argue that the new strategic interest in Africa is mutually beneficial to Africa and the United States since the U.S. will be collaborating in African states to curtail instability and secure peace—the conditions necessary to maximize democracy and minimize the potential for terrorism," explicated Jahi Issa and Salim Faraji. "Those who oppose AFRICOM argue that to a very large extent United States military policies do not measure up to Africa's needs and could in all likelihood amount to U.S. imperialistic control over Africa and its people," Jahi Issa and Salim Faraji concluded.[48]

In 2015, AFRICOM crafted a theater campaign plan. This strategic road map highlighted five main lines of effort, including combating al-Shabaab and supporting African Union Mission in Somalia (AMISOM); fighting VEOs in the Sahel and Maghreb; stopping Boko Haram in Nigeria; interdicting illicit activity in the Gulf of Guinea and central Africa; and building African partner capacity in peacekeeping, humanitarian assistance, and disaster relief.[49] To accomplish its goals, AFRICOM has conducted annual exercises, including African Endeavor.[50] In its long-term theater strategy, the unit highlighted security force assistance "as the decisive effort of our strategy."[51]

While there has been some praise of AFRICOM, there has been considerable concern about and criticism of the new organization. First among these apprehensions was the considerable difficulty involved in locating the new command due to apprehensions about its perceptions in light of Africa's colonial legacy; as a result, AFRICOM has maintained its headquarters in Germany.[52] Some critics have argued that the group has militarized relations between the United States and African nations.[53] José de Arimatéia Da Cruz and Laura K. Stephens cautioned, "Most African states harbor extensive fears that hosting the AFRICOM headquarters will increase militarization, terrorism, the 'scramble' for natural resources and decrease regional influence."[54] There also have been complications related to any potential Status-of-Forces Agreement (SOFA), especially concerning an Article 98 arrangement.[55] Some commentators have contended that the U.S. emphasis on diplomacy, defense, and development, colloquially referred to as the 3Ds, has amalgamated three distinct activities into one ambiguous whole. Costas M. Constantinou and Sam Okoth Opondo advised, "The most troubling implication of this merging has been the blunt definition of underdevelopment as a danger, a condition that breeds insecurity in both the domestic and international spheres, thus legitimating the peace and war interventions of neoliberal governmentality and the contemplation of transforming entire societies."[56]

Maintaining its same five lines of effort, AFRICOM in 2017 identified violent extremism and terrorism in Africa as "the greatest threat to U.S. interests emanating from Africa."[57] U.S. Marine Corps general Thomas D. Waldhauser, commander of AFRICOM, testified before the U.S. Congress, "Africa remains an enduring interest for the U.S." and hoped that his command's "efforts, in coordination with the efforts of our allies and partners, will have a lasting impact on the security and stability of the African continent."[58] In 2018, Waldhauser characterized AFRICOM's approach as "by, with and through" U.S. allies on the continent. At the same time, however, he acknowledged that military power alone would not answer many of the most pressing contemporary security issues in Africa. "Very few—if any—of the challenges on the continent can be resolved through the use of military force. . . . Africom's first strategic tenet stresses the military activities are designed to support and enable U.S. diplomatic and development efforts."[59] The United States, however, has not been the only major power in international affairs to intensify dealings with Africa during the past three decades. China has done so as well but with important contrasts.

CHINA

China has compounded its activity in Africa, exceeding that of the United States, so much so that one observer characterized China–Africa relations as "one of the most critical developments in international affairs" in the past decade.[60] China does not have a legacy of colonialism in Africa, which affords it what some observers consider "common ground" with many nations on the continent.[61] China has had, however, a lengthy history of involvement in Africa, maintaining some presence in Africa since the creation of the People's Republic of China (PRC) on October 1, 1949.[62] Over the first three decades of the PRC's existence, Mao Zedong, chair of the Communist Party of China, fostered China's engagement with Africa. In 1954, China launched a foreign policy known as the Five Principles of Peaceful Coexistence, which included noninterference in internal affairs, peaceful coexistence, equality and mutual benefit, nonaggression, and mutual respect for territory.[63] Donovan C. Chau traced Maoist China's involvement in Algeria, Ghana, and Tanzania from 1955 to 1976, which was quite extensive.[64]

From this historical context, many analysts have observed a significant intensification of China's immersion in Africa over the past three decades.[65] It is important to note that China's relationship with Africa has not been static but rather has changed over time in response to fluctuations in both Africa and China. Emmanuel Obuah explained, "These relations have undergone metamorphosis from one based on support for socialism and political liberation to one dictated and driven by economic opportunism and resource needs of an expanding Chinese economy."[66] China's enlarged activities in Africa have been part of a broader trend of redoubled commitment by many countries, including Brazil, India, Russia, and Turkey, among others.[67]

During the late spring and early summer of 1989, students in Beijing led massive protests at Tiananmen Square, sparking what many international observers characterized as the 1989 Democracy Movement in China. In response to the demonstrations, the communist government declared martial law and deployed military forces to suppress the rallies in Tiananmen Square, although the antigovernment campaign eventually spread to hundreds of other cities throughout China. In the process, soldiers killed hundreds of demonstrators and imprisoned innumerable others. Many countries around the world condemned the brutal repression of the protests, and some nations imposed harsh economic sanctions on China as a result.[68] Since that pivotal moment, China has sought to amplify its leadership in the international community, including expanding its relations with Africa.

Chris Rowan demonstrated "three essential roots" of China's contemporary engagement with Africa: a growing role in international relations in the aftermath of Tiananmen Square, a booming trade with Africa beginning in the 1990s, and an interest in gaining allies from Africa in the United Nations, especially in support of its One China policy regarding Taiwan.[69] Therefore, China has wielded "soft power" in Africa, focusing on economic and diplomatic instruments of national power to sustain its presence on the continent and, by extension, its leadership role in international affairs.[70] Other aspects of soft power have included China's extensive information operations, including training journalists and funding media operations; China has leveraged extensive broadcasting outlets in Africa, including StarTimes, CCTV, China Radio International, Xinhua News Agency, *China Daily*, and *ChinAfrica*.[71] Marc Lanteigne divulged, "From the turn of the century, China has expanded its international interests and policies at an ever-quickening pace in an effort to incorporate regional engagement well beyond the Asia-Pacific region. This cross-regional diplomacy has been most keenly felt in the developing world, and it is in sub-Saharan Africa where Beijing's diplomatic reach has been most carefully scrutinized in recent years."[72] Much of this activity has been in nations in Africa with abundant natural resources, including Angola and Sudan.

China has maintained specific goals in Africa that have formed an important part of its overall grand strategic framework, including economic, political, and even military elements. First among these has been to foster support for its One China policy, especially backing from countries in Africa represented at the United Nations. In addition, China has pursued economic development predicated on its "no strings attached" approach, which divorces economic concerns from such other issues as human rights.[73] As a result, natural resources and raw materials in Africa, especially oil from Angola, Nigeria, and Sudan, have formed a key aspect of China's augmented presence on the continent. Sophie Harman and William Brown explained, "In this way, debates over China's role in Africa draw us into classic international relations problems of competition over resources, and the balance between relative and absolute gains from mutual cooperation, all of which are involved in this aspect of Africa's international relations."[74]

In order to accomplish its objectives, China has taken numerous actions during the past three decades vis-à-vis Africa. In October 2000, China created the multilateral Forum on China-Africa Cooperation (FOCAC).[75] Almost 80 ministers and numerous senior officials attended from more than 40 countries in Africa, creating a significant diplomatic and economic bond between China and Africa. Much of this trend has focused on the twin pillars of noninterference and state sovereignty. The forum has continued to meet annually and to hold a summit every three years. The results have been staggering. By the end of 2000, China had nearly 500 companies doing business in Africa.[76] One outcome has been a steady influx of professionals, managers, and executives from China into Africa, which has provoked some backlash.[77] In 2002, China formalized its "go out" policy, which produced as many as 50 leading strategic state-owned enterprises.[78] In 2003, China created special economic zones (SEZs) to foster economic development projects and to lessen trade barriers.[79] The Africa Partnership Forum held its fourth meeting in 2005, where the China–Africa relationship was a central topic.[80] In 2006, China crafted an Africa White Paper, outlining a comprehensive grand strategy agenda for its increased engagement on the continent.[81] China produced in 2015 a second Africa policy paper, revealing its consistent vision of engagement in Africa for the future. Xi Jinping, China's president, publicized the updated policy at FOCAC's second summit held in South Africa that same year.[82]

These policies have achieved a meteoric growth in trade between China and Africa. China–Africa trade in 1995 amounted to less than $5 billion, exceeded $10 billion by 2000, and skyrocketed to $107 billion by 2008.[83] Bruce Guenther elucidated, "In particular, China's increasing thirst for hard commodities has led to a growth of commodity exports from certain Sub-Saharan African countries, particularly oil from Sudan (41% of total exports) and Angola (23% of total exports) and base metals from the DRC. . . . Between 1995 and 2005, the combined share of oil, iron ore, cotton, diamonds and timber exports from Sub-Saharan Africa to China grew from 50% to more than 80%."[84]

In addition to ascending trade, China boosted investments in Africa. In March 2004, China extended Angola a credit of $2 billion, which gained worldwide notice.[85] Two years later, more than two dozen Chinese companies launched a chamber of commerce in Angola's capital, Luanda, and China provided Angola another $1 billion in credit.[86] Trade between China and Africa continued to rise steeply, reaching $9 billion in 2000, $40 billion in 2005, and $70 billion in 2007, making it Africa's second-largest trading partner. By 2008, trade between China and Africa exceeded $100 billion, rendering China Africa's first-largest trading partner and eclipsing the United States and European Union for the first time. By 2010, trade between China and Africa reached $115 billion.[87]

In large part due to this amplified interaction with Africa, China in 2010 also became the second-largest economy in the world based on purchasing power parity behind only the United States.[88] Such enlarged trade also has led to other responses, including expanded contacts between leaders from China and Africa. On March 21, 2005, Hu Jintao, China's president, met with Joseph Kabila, president of the DRC, to enhance cooperation between the two countries and to promote their "long-term stable friendship." Much of this commitment has stemmed from China's requirement for mineral resources, which the DRC has in abundance.[89] China also has pursued a heightened presence in other resource-rich countries in Africa, including Angola, Ghana, and South Sudan.

China has maintained numerous large investment projects throughout Africa. In Kenya, China has funded the Standard Gauge Railway (SGR), and China has invested $6 billion in Sudan, mostly in the nation's expansive oil industry.[90] In addition to money, China has sent a staggering number of workers to Africa. By one estimate, there were over 1 million migrants from China living in Africa by 2014, most of them with connections to various economic development projects on the continent.[91] Diplomatic contacts have also multiplied. Ngari Gituku explained, "Over the last couple of years, a tradition has emerged in which Beijing's Foreign Minister pays a number of African nations a visit at the beginning of every year. This annual ritual seems to be the 'forum' where tweaked Sino-Africa relations policies are communicated devoid of elaborate fanfare yet brimming with significance nonetheless."[92] On May 10, 2007, China appointed Liu Guijin, former ambassador to South Africa and Zimbabwe, as special representative for African affairs, raising the profile of its diplomacy on the continent.[93] Three days later, the China Development Bank created the China–Africa Development Fund, initially financing it with $1 billion and then growing it to $5 billion.[94] That same year, China pledged $10 million for humanitarian aid in Darfur, although China's arms sales to Sudan and vested interest in oil counterbalanced its benevolent rhetoric.[95]

Tang Xiaoyang reported, "China's imports from Africa have grown from US$5.43 billion in 2002 to US$113.2 billion in 2012; this means a 20-fold increase within a decade."[96] Jonathan Holslag added, "As an export market, China outweighs the European Union in eight countries. Especially in Sudan, the Democratic Republic of the Congo (DRC) and Angola, exports to China have expanded dramatically."[97]

Much of this economic activity has involved oil, especially from Angola and Sudan. In the case of Angola, the cessation of conflict there benefited China and allowed a shift in Angola's trade toward China and India, two countries that economists have referred to as the "Asian Drivers." Renato Aguilar and Andrea Goldstein explained, "The Asian Drivers' expansion in Angola is possibly happening faster than elsewhere as it is taking place after traditional partners have disengaged from the country during the civil war and during a period of rapid growth and structural change. Although Sudan has received more attention, Angola is possibly the clearest example of increasing Chinese involvement in African economic and political affairs."[98] China's historical approach to Africa has focused on specific bilateral economic issues without addressing internal conditions within any particular state in Africa. There is some recent indication that this precedent might have shifted, especially in the case of Sudan. Many critics have argued that China's lack of conditionality profits powerful elites in African nations without ensuring meaningful reforms to improve living conditions within those countries. "Chinese and Indian aid and financing have no policy or value-based conditionality. Thus, there is less pressure on the government for designing and implementing better policy, improving governance and transparency, reducing poverty and fighting corruption," lambasted one such appraisal.[99] Other observers have taken this censure one step further: "Links with China are now so valuable that African countries cannot afford to upset Beijing" on a host of issues, including the One China policy, democracy, human rights, or even parity of advantage in development projects.[100] Some occurrences have indicated that this trend may change. Ngari Gituku pointed out, "The interest in the cessation of hostilities in South Sudan is an important indicator that in coming days China is likely to act arbiter in situations caught up in civil strife across Africa."[101]

On December 4, 2015, Xi Jinping, China's president, boasted, "China-Africa relations have today reached a stage of growth unmatched in history."[102] Xi also promised to continue the advance through 10 specific plans, including training 200,000 technicians in Africa, allowing 40,000 migrants from Africa to train in China, and providing 30,000 scholarships to youth in Africa.[103] Analysts have reacted in myriad ways to these enhancements. Sifudein Adem characterized three major responses: optimism that China's immersion will transform Africa, pessimism that China's engrossment profits only itself, and pragmatism that China's engagement furthers the interests of both China and Africa, albeit with more advantages accruing to China.[104]

There has been extensive denunciation of China's augmented interaction with Africa. Even though many commentators have held positive views of China's enlarged position in Africa, others have decried the move for various reasons. One criticism has been the extensive lack of employment for workers in Africa due to such large numbers of migrant laborers from China. Another consideration has been widespread environmental degradation associated with some of China's economic development projects. Jonathan Holslag revealed, "Popular criticism of China's investments in Africa stems from low environmental standards, labour safety, harsh working conditions, dumping and a lack of investment outside the mining and oil sectors."[105]

More recently, there have been concerns regarding China's reinforced military presence in Africa because China's entanglement with security in Africa has grown. The nation's augmented participation in UN peacekeeping operations has had positive and negative implications. Saferworld estimated that China has deployed mounting numbers of troops with UN peacekeeping forces in Africa, beginning in 2003 with less than 500, reaching 1,500 in 2006, and surpassing 2,000 in 2009.[106] Most of these peacekeepers have been engineers, police, medical, and transportation specialists. As China's trade, personnel, and investment in Africa have amplified, so too has China's emphasis on military presence on the continent.

As previously discussed, China has participated in antipiracy operations in the Gulf of Aden, which the UN Security Council mandated. Andrew S. Erickson and Austin M. Strange explained that "since 2008 China's antipiracy escorts have provided important soft-power benefits for Beijing on a truly international stage. For the first time in its modern history China has deployed naval forces operationally beyond its immediate maritime periphery for extended durations, to protect merchant vessels from pirates in the Gulf of Aden."[107] As a result, China's interest in Africa has extended beyond growing economics, augmented trade, and amplified diplomacy, to include participation in UN operations, thereby bolstering China's military readiness and proficiency. Some analysts have interpreted this dynamic as a newfound willingness on the part of Beijing to project military power to protect its interests in Africa.[108] China's widespread partaking in antipiracy operations in the Gulf of Aden also has allowed it to develop its naval capabilities through repeated deployments and continual operations. Andrew S. Erickson and Austin M. Strange disclosed, "More broadly, the persistent threat of piracy in international waters has enabled China to expand its far-seas security operations under the umbrella of benign international cooperation."[109]

Other critics have pointed to China's willingness to supply arms to nations in Africa. Arms shipments from China to Zimbabwe in April 2008 created serious international dismay.[110] China has provided arms to other nations in Africa, including Ethiopia, Eritrea, and Sudan. China's association with security in Africa has multiplied over time. Near the end of 2015, President Xi pledged $60 million to the African Union's African Standby Force and the African Capacity for the Immediate Response to Crisis.[111] In March 2018, China's parliament voted to suspend presidential term limits, thereby extending Xi Jinping's presidency. As a result, China's heightened involvement in Africa has continued undiminished. In addition, Xi's signature policies vis-à-vis Africa, including the Belt and Road initiative, UN reform, and an expanded military role, have gained momentum from his augmented power.[112] Meanwhile, trade between China and Africa has continued to swell, with bullish estimates that it could eclipse several hundred billion dollars in the near future.[113]

CONCLUSION

Africa has elevated its importance in international affairs during the past three decades. Many of the world's fastest growing economies have been in Africa, including 6 of the top 10.[114] As a result, many international actors have intensified their activity on the continent. Globalization has had both positive and negative effects for Africa, but the emergence of BRICS and MINT has illustrated Africa's growing leadership in world politics and the global economy. Such countries as Singapore, Brazil, and Turkey all have fostered relationships in Africa.

The two countries that have symbolized intensified interactions in Africa the most, however, have been the United States and China. The United States has emphasized Africa in its strategic outlook, demonstrated most forcefully by its creation in 2007 of AFRICOM. As a result, the novel organization has come to represent Africa's heightened importance to Washington and an avenue through which the United States has sought to address its security concerns on the continent. With AFRICOM, the United States has hoped to improve African partner nations' capacity and thereby reduce instability. Other determinations have included combating VEOs; improving maritime security; providing humanitarian and disaster response; and interdicting illegal trafficking of humans, drugs, and weapons.

In contrast, China has amplified engagement with Africa in a more tangible and nuanced fashion. China has placed Africa at the forefront of its grand strategic framework during the past three decades, including economic trade, diplomatic engagement, and military operations. Ever since the Tiananmen Square incident in 1989, China has sought an enlarged leadership role in international relations, has ramped up trade with Africa, and has courted allies in the United Nations, especially those from Africa. Whereas the United States has focused on hard power in the form of AFRICOM, China has wielded considerable soft power in Africa, including economic, informational, and diplomatic influence. China's goals in Africa have been threefold: to gain support for its One China policy from nations in Africa, to ensure its access to Africa's abundant natural resources, and to elevate its leadership and prestige in international affairs. China has taken numerous actions to accomplish these ambitions, including creating FOCAC, designating SEZs, and crafting multiple Africa white papers outlining the continent's elevated place within its global outlook. The results have been astounding. China's trade with Africa exploded from less than $5 billion in 1995 to more than $100 billion by 2008.[115] It peaked in 2014 at around $213 billion but fell in 2016 to roughly $125 billion.[116] China also has funded numerous investment projects on the continent, including Kenya's Standard Gauge Railway and substantial outlays in Angola and Sudan's oil industries. Concerns over China's approach have been numerous, however, focusing on China's "no strings attached" approach, which, critics have argued, benefits wealthy elites, fuels rampant corruption, and funds arms purchases.[117] In addition, China has wielded significant military presence in Africa.

These two international responses have proven intertwined. Peter A. Dumbuya explained, "Some analysts view AFRICOM as an American response to increasing Chinese economic influence in Africa."[118] Jahi Issa and Salim Faraji clarified, "It is obvious that Africa is strategic to United States interest. Africans want the United States to engage in equal trade, buttressed by their increasing young population, oil and other natural resources exports, and an increasing middle class. If we continue to have a myopic vision concerning Africa, we risk the chance of engaging Africa unilaterally, and increasing China's and other emerging powers continuing influence on the continent."[119] While the United States and China have demonstrated Africa's growing importance in international affairs, the presence of the many contemporary security issues in Africa analyzed in this book has demonstrated that Africa is a critical region of the world. Even so, these matters have not existed within a vacuum. Understanding the important linkages between them and their implications for Africa's future prospects has become more important than ever before.

CHAPTER 9

Linkages and Future Prospects

OVERVIEW

When Aisha, the young woman abducted by the Nigerian militant group Boko Haram, reunited with her parents on January 30, 2018, in Borno State after six long years as a captive of the violent extremist organization, the painful yet joyous occasion highlighted the prevalence of contemporary security issues in Africa. The incident also provided hope that with an informed understanding and constant vigilance, things could improve for a brighter tomorrow. The prevalence of weak and fragile states in Africa has been pronounced, with 33 of the world's 50 most fragile governments on the continent.[1] The Central African Republic (CAR) has portended the dangers of perennially fragile states, while Mali has demonstrated that even historically stable governments can succumb rapidly to weakness as a result of violence. Likewise, ethnic conflict and civil war have been no strangers to Africa. At least 20 civil wars have occurred on the continent during the past three decades.[2] Uganda's devastating experience with the Lord's Resistance Army (LRA) has illustrated how ethno-religious conflict can ravage a country and spill over to neighboring countries, including the CAR, the Democratic Republic of the Congo (DRC), and South Sudan. It also has proven that such scourges can be defeated with coordinated efforts and steady perseverance. In a different vein, Sudan has proven that civil war can beget civil war. The conflict that engulfed Sudan for more than two decades eventually bore South Sudan on July 9, 2011, which then devolved into its own civil war on December 15, 2013, with significant consequences. As those two nations' recurrent fighting over oil has attested, natural resources have prolonged discord in Africa, if not sparked it, while environmental security has become victim to such struggles. Angola's vast oil resources and the war that plagued it for nearly three decades have proved the point, while the DRC's more recent experiences have illustrated that abundant natural resources have not always guaranteed benefits for the broader population but instead have encouraged looting, even attracting instigators from outside the country. Violent extremism and terrorism have been significant challenges throughout much of Africa. Al-Shabaab has stayed a scourge on Somalia while also extending its violence to neighboring countries in the region, including Uganda but especially Kenya. Boko Haram has ravaged Nigeria, becoming the world's most deadly terrorist group in 2014 and overturning that nation's political structure by influencing Goodluck Jonathan's presidential defeat in 2015. Unrest on land has spilt over to the maritime environment, where security against piracy has vexed many nations in Africa. In the Gulf of Aden, piracy escalated, garnered international attention, and became a model of successful efforts to counteract it. In the Gulf of Guinea, however, the tide turned as piracy in that region has become more prevalent, especially violent, and further complicated than its predecessor to the east. Food security and extreme poverty have lingered as perennial impediments for many countries in Africa. More than three-quarters of the world's most food-insecure nations in the recent past have been on the continent.[3] Ethiopia has confirmed that policy changes have helped improve food security, while certain elements such as drought have remained largely intractable. Likewise, Malawi has proven how food security and extreme poverty have been inextricably linked. Africa's role in global affairs has grown, making engagement with the international community more frequent. The United States has focused on ensuring stability on the continent through building the capacity of its allies in Africa, most tangibly with the creation and expansion of AFRICOM. Pursuing a different tack, China has concentrated on compounded trade and economic development, albeit with a heightened position in counterpiracy operations and expanded diplomacy. Contemporary security issues in Africa have seen much improvement over the past three decades. Even so, many obstacles have persisted. The African Union has characterized the new millennium as an "African turning point," with a "renewed determination" to eradicate contemporary security issues in Africa.[4] In fact, the African Union's grand strategic blueprint for the continent during the next five decades has articulated eight aspirations involving prosperity, integration, governance, security, culture, people, and leadership. Most relevant to this book has been the fourth ambition: "A peaceful and secure Africa."[5] As the preceding chapters have shown, however, there has remained much more work to be done.

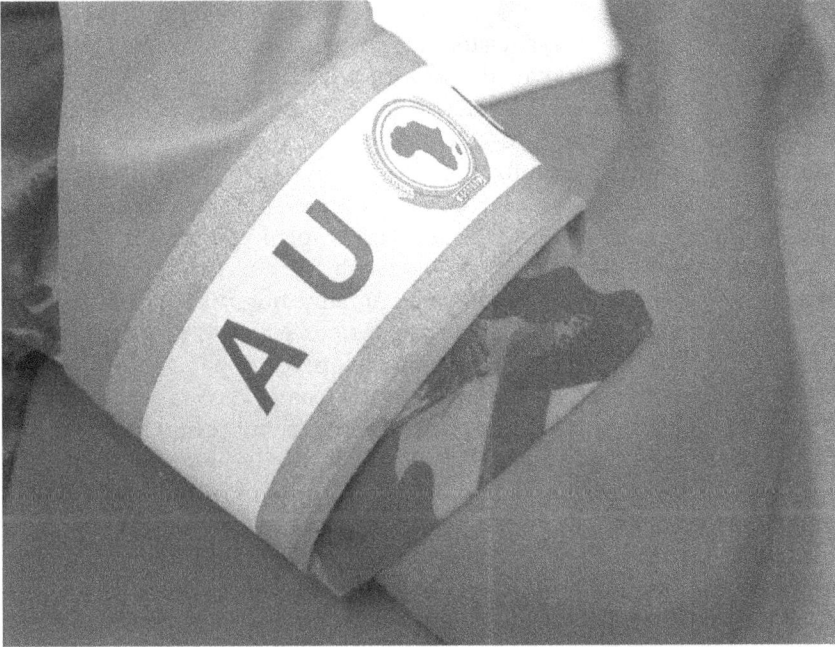

Military and civilian officials from more than nine countries gathered at Camp Lemonnier, Djibouti. November 3, 2015. (Courtesy United States Africa Command)

LINKAGES

This book has covered a wide array of contemporary security issues in Africa, including weak and fragile states, ethno-religious conflict and civil wars, natural resources and environmental security, violent extremism and terrorism, piracy and maritime security, food security and extreme poverty, and international responses. These trials, however, have not existed in isolation; they have influenced each other in myriad ways. What follows are some considerations of the secondary repercussions of contemporary security issues in Africa that build upon and expand on the overviews and case studies presented thus far in this volume, which all focused on their primary effects.

As noted in Chapter 2 of this volume, the prevalence of weak and fragile states has been a significant contemporary security issue in Africa. In addition to the critical effects of weak and fragile states discussed earlier, the implications of this quandary have influenced other vital areas. Weak and fragile states have erupted into ethno-religious conflict and civil wars. This especially has been the case when nations have had a diverse, multiethnic population and have allowed, or worse have encouraged, ethnic or religious discrimination, thereby stoking into outright flames the embers of ethno-religious tension over the lack of equitable access to power and resources within an underdeveloped state. Clement Mweyang Aapengnuo perceived, "In many cases, the political choices made by states lay the foundation for ethnic mobilization."[6] The prevalence of weak and fragile states in Africa also has had second-order effects on natural resources and environmental security. The CAR has ample innate assets, including timber, uranium, diamonds, and gold, with some individual mines generating millions of dollars in revenue annually, but militant groups have syphoned off many of these resources. Various leaders and factions have used these lucrative means to purchase weapons, to pay soldiers, and to extend conflict. Therefore, natural resources have become an accelerant that fuels and sustains fighting, creating underlying instability and further undermining the country. This dynamic also has worked in reverse, as evidenced by the DRC. In its case, the abundance of natural resources has attracted outside actors, including militant groups from Rwanda and Uganda. The intervention of fighters across the DRC's borders in search of plunder has undercut its strength. There also has been a tangible connection between weak and fragile states and violent extremism and terrorism. Mali, a former paragon of stability and democracy, quickly degenerated into chaos. The jihadist group Ansar al-Dine hastily seized direction of the resulting insurgency from the nonsectarian and separatist Tuareg groups organized under the banner of the National Movement for the Liberation of Azawad (MNLA). The chaos resulted in tangible gains in clout and abilities by terrorist groups. The infusion of weapons and availability of training, first in Libya and then in Mali, fomented Ansar al-Dine's intent and reinforced its proficiencies. This trend was not unique to Mali. François Heisbourg cautioned, "The threat level in West Africa has risen greatly during the last decade, with well-armed jihadist groups from Algeria and the Sahel benefitting from the ready availability of weapons and money, while sub-Saharan terrorism, notably in Nigeria, becomes ever more violent and deeply entrenched in densely populated countries."[7] The crisis in Mali strengthened al-Qaeda in the Islamic Maghreb (AQIM), as it profited from the anarchy and increased its illegal trafficking in drugs, weapons, and humans to fund its violent extremist operations. Endemic exploitation, as one critical characteristic of a fragile state, also has played a significant role in terrorism. Oluwakemi Okenyodo elucidated, "Corruption within the bodies responsible for enforcing the law shapes expectations and tolerance of corruption in a society more generally. In such contexts, citizens are more likely to challenge the symbols of authority. Violent crime and conflict are more likely to result."[8]

There also have been weighty connections between ethno-religious conflict and civil wars and several other issues discussed in this volume. The

LRA moved from Uganda into the CAR, specifically the southeast area of that country. This repositioning further destabilized the CAR by adding another armed group to an already-violent and anarchic struggle. While not unique to this nation, political leaders exacerbated ethnic and religious tensions to accumulate power and resources. Regarding religion in the CAR, Adama Dieng, UN special adviser on the prevention of genocide and former registrar of the International Criminal Tribunal for Rwanda, feared, "Religion is being manipulated by parties with vested interests, who stand to gain by fueling hostility and hatred between people of different faiths, and who sometimes even incite and commit acts that may constitute atrocity crimes. This violence, and the failure to hold accountable those responsible, shatters societies."[9] In addition, ethno-religious conflict and civil wars in Sudan resulted in the independence of South Sudan, which itself degenerated into ethnic conflict and civil war, albeit with a less intense religious dimension than the former struggle with Sudan. As a result of near-constant war since its inception, South Sudan's displaced population exploded from approximately 125,000 in December 2013 to nearly 4,000,000 by October 2017, including 1,870,000 internally displaced persons (IDPs) within South Sudan. The Africa Center for Strategic Studies warned, "A population movement of this magnitude, with majorities of some ethnic groups displaced, has the potential to cause massive and lasting damage to the country's social fabric, as well as its viability as a sovereign state."[10] Persistent ethnic conflict and civil war in South Sudan have undermined public trust in the government, have created large-scale population movements, and have provided little hope of resolution; they also have transformed the promising birth of the world's youngest country into the newest embodiment of a weak and fragile state, teetering on the brink of total collapse. Kate Almquist Knopf regretted, "After nearly three years of civil war, South Sudan has ceased to perform even the minimal functions and responsibilities of a sovereign state. It exercises no monopoly over coercive power, and its ability to deliver public services, provide basic security, and administer justice is virtually nonexistent."[11] Ethnic conflict and civil war in South Sudan have resulted in a marked escalation in violent extremism and terrorism in that nation. The Global Terrorism Index documented, "Both Boko Haram and al-Shabaab have been active since 2008 while the Sudan People's Liberation Movement in Opposition (SPLM-IO) commenced their terror campaign only in 2014. Yet SPLM-IO is responsible for the fifth highest number of fatalities over the last fifteen years."[12] Such a situation has indicated that the rise in violent extremism and terrorism will likely remain high for some time. Ethno-religious conflict and civil war in South Sudan have impacted its neighbors throughout the region: more than half of the total displaced population has fled to other countries. Confronted with constant violence, South Sudan's population understandably has escaped to every surrounding country, including 1,034,106 to Uganda, 447,287 to Sudan, 416,886 to Ethiopia, 110,377 to Kenya, 85,426 to DRC, and 2,057 to CAR. Such massive population shifts have placed severe strains on neighboring countries, which have possessed limited capacity to handle them and thereby have become mired in conflict themselves, as has been the case with the DRC and CAR. As a result of persistent fighting in South Sudan, the Bidi Bidi refugee settlement in Uganda has become the world's largest, claiming 285,000 refugees.[13]

Land has been one of the most abundant natural resources in Africa. It also has presented a source of both opportunity and tension. Jeffrey Herbst has shown how copious territory has influenced weak and fragile states in Africa because vast but sparsely populated terrain has proven a perennial difficulty, ensuring that states have consolidated their strength in capitals with significant declines in outlying regions.[14] In addition, land has become the critical feature in interaction between ethnic groups and the state in Africa. Tore Wig explained, "Indeed, one of the most common issues that ethnic groups and governments bargain over in Africa is land."[15] When tensions over territory have intensified, they often have erupted into ethno-religious conflict and civil wars, as has been the case in Uganda and Sudan. In addition, natural resources and environmental security have exhibited critical linkages to food security and extreme poverty. Paul D. Williams cautioned, "Of particular concern is the continuing destruction of ecosystems and the inability of people (both foreigners and locals) to stop a variety of processes such as climate change, deforestation, desertification and land degradation (affecting both cropland and pasture), as well as increasing water and food scarcity."[16] Even more prominent, natural resources have related to international responses. China's amplified interaction in Africa has derived from its focus on resource-rich nations on the continent. In 2010, Angola became the primary provider of crude oil to China, replacing Saudi Arabia.[17] China's interactions with Africa have exhibited strong connections to the continent's abundant natural resources, especially oil from Angola and Sudan and minerals from the DRC.

There also have been vital connections between violent extremism and terrorism and weak and fragile states. Somalia, the quintessence of a failed state, created conditions out of which al-Shabaab emerged. In the ensuing anarchy, state failure and violent extremism have contributed to food insecurity, not only for Somalia but also for neighboring countries. One million refugees have migrated from Somalia to surrounding nations, including Kenya, exacerbating food security challenges in the region, as refugee camps have lacked adequate supplies for such large influxes.[18] Likewise, Mali's weakened central government has proven unable to stem the growth of Islamist groups such as Ansar al-Dine and Movement for Unity and Jihad in West Africa (MUJWA), creating a vicious cycle that further has undermined state institutions and political legitimacy. This dynamic also has worked in the reverse direction. Nigeria historically has been a stable nation, but the recent emergence of Boko Haram ominously has degraded steadiness in the country in two distinct ways. First, violent extremism and terrorism have exacerbated ethno-religious fault lines and have prompted heavy-handed government responses that have targeted civilians of certain ethnic and religious groups as well as perpetrators. Second, violent extremism and terrorism have triggered a series of reprisals. Chris Kwaja delineated, "Each outbreak of violence worsens suspicions and renders communal reconciliation more difficult, deepening the cycle and further incentivizing polarization."[19] Therefore, as ethno-religious conflict has persisted, it has debilitated the country. Since 2015, Nigeria has deteriorated as a weak and fragile state, falling to the 13th worst ranking on the Fragile States Index and residing in the "high alert" category. As with other weak and fragile states, Nigeria's woes have impacted its neighbors, including Cameroon, Chad, and Niger. The Fund for Peace has attributed much of this deterioration to Boko Haram.[20]

Piracy and maritime security also have exhibited second-order effects. There has been a vital connection between illegal fishing and food security. The precipitous decline in fisheries around the world and especially near Africa has elicited swells in piracy, as evidenced in the Gulf of Aden. The massive coastline of the continent and the critical dependence of a large proportion of its population on the maritime environment have meant that many Africans depend on fish in their daily diets. In addition, there has been an essential nexus between piracy and maritime security and violent extremism and terrorism. The threat of piracy in the Gulf of Aden has contributed to, and even has combined with, al-Shabaab in Somalia. Likewise, the threat of piracy in the Gulf of Guinea has aided and even coalesced with Boko Haram in Nigeria. The correlations between piracy and maritime security and food security and extreme poverty have been numerous and significant. Somali pirates have interrupted food relief efforts by the UN World Food Programme to alleviate starvation in Somalia. In addition, piracy and maritime security have evidenced important linkages with international responses. Both the United States and China have participated in the transnational reactions to piracy and maritime security, especially in the Gulf of Aden. The U.S. effort has included Combined Task Force 151 (CTF-151), while China's exertions have included its most significant military deployment outside its borders in modern history. Andrew S. Erickson and Austin M. Strange divulged, "Over a six-year span beginning in December 2008, China has contributed over ten thousand navy personnel in nearly twenty task forces. In nearly eight hundred groups, these forces have escorted over six thousand Chinese and foreign commercial vessels."[21] China's antipiracy efforts in the Gulf of Aden have been noteworthy, not only as a precedent for increased international involvement away from China but also unparalleled in size and scope. As a result, there have been signs of the United States' cautious acceptance of China as an international navy, including China's first participation in Rim of the Pacific (RIMPAC), the largest U.S.-led naval exercise in the world, during July and August 2014 where the People's Liberation Army Navy (PLAN) provided vessels and more than 1,000 sailors.[22] Tensions between the two major powers have flared, however, as the United States in 2018 disinvited China from further participation in the exercise, largely due to China's continued militarization of the South China Sea.[23]

There always has been a crucial relationship between food security and extreme poverty and many of the contemporary security issues in Africa examined throughout this book. On January 25, 2018, Antonio Guterres, UN secretary-general, noted at the 30th African Union summit in Addis Ababa, Ethiopia, "The majority of undernourished people in Africa live in countries affected by conflict. Hunger is almost twice as high in conflict-affected countries with a protracted crisis. Stronger commitment by governments, the African Union and the United Nations is needed to promote peace, human rights and sustainable development."[24] Food security and extreme poverty have been more prevalent in weak and fragile states. In Mali, the dismal economic conditions, rampant corruption, and overall feeble governance have caused more than 350,000 IDPs and triggered a food security crisis throughout the country. In the CAR, inadequate authority has combined with conflict and IDPs to place severe strains on food security. The Food and Agriculture Organization (FAO) reported that in the CAR momentous buildups in IDPs meant that over 1 million people, nearly one-third of the population, have been "in need of urgent assistance for food."[25] In Nigeria, the destruction wrought by the violent extremist organization Boko Haram has resulted in unimaginable population displacement and food insecurity. The UN High Commissioner for Refugees estimated that by October 2014, the violence had occasioned 1.4 million IDPs and more than 4.5 million people have faced food insecurity, including roughly 1.5 million malnourished children and pregnant women.[26] In Nigeria, even excellent food production has not counteracted the downturn in food security created by fighting. The FAO lamented, "In spite of two consecutive years of bumper harvests and the positive prospects for 2017 aggregate production, the humanitarian situation remains critical in many countries of the subregion, mainly due to the continuing civil conflict in northern Nigeria, which has resulted in large population displacements, both internally and in the neighbouring countries of Cameroon, Chad and Niger."[27] In Mali, unrest has exacerbated food security and worsened conditions, especially in the northern part of the country. The U.S. Agency for International Development has estimated that the fighting has resulted in roughly 601,000 Malians requiring immediate food assistance, with more than half of these people located in the war-ridden north.[28] Of course, not all food security challenges have stemmed from violence, as a regional food crisis occurred at around the same time, but nonetheless, the upheaval has worsened food security throughout the country.[29] In South Sudan, near-constant civil war since 2013 has resulted in 4.5 million IDPs and refugees and gravely has aggravated its food security trials. One detailed study on the humanitarian impact of the ethnic conflict and civil war documented that in October 2013, "only a scattering of counties faced famine and only for certain months of the year." In stark contrast, in early 2018 nearly two-thirds of counties in South Sudan have experienced "acute levels of food insecurity [that] are persisting throughout the year." As a result, ethnic conflict and civil war in South Sudan have created a food security catastrophe throughout the young nation.[30] Other reports have indicated that every state in the country "is experiencing crisis or emergency levels of food insecurity," and that people often go days without food.[31] In some countries, however, food security and extreme poverty problems have existed in the absence of protracted fighting. One extensive study of Malawi's economic development commented, "Malawi's low and volatile growth performance relative to that of its peers is particularly striking given that Malawi has stayed politically stable and free of conflicts and has suffered no more weather-related or other external shocks than other countries in the region." The report continued, "Some countries such as Mozambique and Rwanda have faced even more difficult conditions, needing to rebuild their nations after violent conflict, yet still have managed to achieve higher and more sustained growth than Malawi."[32]

There also have been vital linkages between international responses and other contemporary security issues examined in this volume, including natural resources and environmental security. China's construction boom has led to increased demand for innate materials, especially minerals. *African Business* reported, "China continues to grow rapidly. Since it consumes 40% of the world's copper and around half of its iron ore, cement and coal, its performance is key to the commodities outlook."[33] Therefore, much of China's increased activity in Africa has centered on natural resources. Some observers have critiqued its heightened involvement in Africa due to China's "no strings attached" policy. Isaac Fokuo cautioned, "Chinese investments come largely unencumbered with conditions. These seemingly open-ended arrangements have been controversial because some claim the relationships are emboldening corrupt and despotic leaders, and that Chinese investors are indifferent to the rule of law."[34] Augmented interaction in Africa by international actors has led to heightened contention among them, impacting security at the country, regional, and even international levels. In its annual posture statement, AFRICOM explained, "Just as the U.S. pursues strategic interests in Africa, international competitors, including China and Russia, are doing the same. Whether with trade, natural resource exploitation, or weapons sales, we continue to see international competitors engage with African partners in a manner contrary to the international norms of transparency and good governance."[35]

FUTURE PROSPECTS

Africa has emerged as an important region and significant influence in worldwide affairs. As a result, contemporary security issues in Africa matter more than ever before, not only for the continent but also for the international system. Africa's robust economic developments, the Africa Integrated High Speed Train Network for example, have combined with its burgeoning and predominately young population to make Africa a region of great potential. One extensive study on trends in Africa's development predicted, "The demographic size of Africa in the world has grown from 9 per cent of the total in 1960 to 15 per cent in 2010. By 2050, its share of global population will reach 23 per cent and it will be considerably larger than either China or India."[36]

In addition to a flourishing populace, Africa has an extremely young population. This situation augurs well for the continent's future. In many African nations, approximately two-thirds of the population is younger than 25 years old; the continent has an overall median age of 18. UNICEF recorded, "Demographics are key to Africa's increasing centrality to the global development and growth agenda. In particular, the demographics of Africa's children are experiencing a shift on a scale perhaps unprecedented in human history." Such a projection is not just hyperbole. The report concluded that "on current trends, almost 2 billion babies will be born in Africa in the next 35 years. Over the same period Africa's under-18 population will increase by two thirds, reaching almost 1 billion by mid-century; and close to half of the world population of children will be African by the end of the 21st century."[37] Such a massive demographic shift toward adolescence has significant implications. Jakkie Cilliers, Barry Hughes, and Jonathan Moyer revealed, "The youthful momentum of Africa's growing population means that, by 2050, almost one in four of the world's people will live in Africa."[38] As a result, some cogent observers have argued that policy responses to contemporary security issues in Africa should encourage youth engagement as one way to leverage demographic trends toward improving the political structure and security environment in Africa.[39]

Urbanization has been another major trend. Africa's urbanization rate stood at less than 20 percent in 1960. By 1990, it was 32 percent; by 2000, it was 38 percent; by 2010, it was 42 percent; and some observers project that it will be 56 percent by 2050.[40] The rise of the world's leading emerging markets, Brazil, Russia, India, China, and South Africa, as well as Mexico,

Indonesia, Nigeria, and Turkey, will continue to impact Africa, providing it additional leverage and economic opportunity, especially with China and India. Other issues have portended less positive occurrences. Climate change has already disproportionately impacted Africa and will continue to do so, including negative repercussions on the continent's food security and water availability. The UN Environment Programme warned, "No continent will be struck as severely by the impacts of climate change as Africa." Such an ominous admonition has presaged momentous shocks to food security and water availability; the same report estimated that upward of 250 million people in Africa "are projected to be exposed to increased water stress due to climate change" by 2020.[41]

The African Union's "Agenda 2063" has illuminated future prospects for the continent and has articulated a comprehensive vision to achieve "the realization of the 21st Century as the African Century." The outlook has enunciated economic, social, and security aspirations for the continent to accomplish during the next fifty years. The ultimate goal is "an integrated, prosperous and peaceful Africa, driven by its own citizens and representing a dynamic force in the international arena."[42] Many of the goals of "Agenda 2063" will require determinations that address the vital contemporary security issues in Africa presented in this book, as well as considering climate change, eradicating poverty, modernizing agriculture, protecting resources, eliminating hunger, and ending conflict. The last goal is especially relevant. The African Union has made a bold commitment: "Silence the guns by 2020, through enhanced dialogue-centered conflict prevention and resolution, to make peace a reality for all our people. We pledge not to bequeath the burden of conflicts to the next generation of Africans by ending all wars in Africa by 2020."[43] The African Union has made steady strides to make this ambition a reality, establishing an African Human Security Index to ensure improvement.[44] As a result, the African Union pledged, "Africa shall be a strong, united, resilient, peaceful and influential global player and partner with a significant role in world affairs."[45] This change has already started to occur and likely will continue in the future. Its ultimate achievement, however, will only ensue within the context of improved security on the continent. An informed understanding of contemporary security issues in Africa is an important first step toward overcoming these obstacles. Solving them will require coordinated national, regional, and international efforts. Their accomplishment, however, will ensure a safe and secure environment within which necessary political, economic, and social reforms can occur in order to ensure that the 21st century is indeed the African Century.

Chronology

December 10, 1982	United Nations crafted the UN Convention on the Law of the Sea (UNCLOS)
January 22, 1986	Yoweri Museveni led National Resistance Army and over-ran Kampala, Uganda
August 6, 1986	Alice Lakwena created the Holy Spirit Movement
January 26, 1991	Siad Barre's rule ended in Somalia
October 10, 2000	China created the multilateral Forum on China-Africa Cooperation (FOCAC)
March 2002	Uganda's government launched Operation Iron Fist against the Lord's Resistance Army (LRA)
April 4, 2002	National Union for the Total Independence of Angola (UNITA) reached a cease-fire and peace agreement with Angola's government
July 11, 2003	Maputo Declaration
April 7, 2004	United Nations created an action plan to prevent genocide
January 9, 2005	Khartoum and Sudan People's Liberation Army (SPLA) signed the Comprehensive Peace Agreement, which temporarily halted the civil war and opened a path toward independence for South Sudan
July 30, 2005	John Garang, SPLA leader, Sudan's vice president, and presumptive future president of South Sudan, died in a helicopter crash

December 29, 2006	Ethiopia's occupation of Mogadishu began
February 6, 2007	U.S. president George W. Bush created U.S. Africa Command (AFRICOM)
June 2, 2008	UN Security Council Resolution 1816 emphasized international cooperation against piracy off the coast of Somalia
June 20, 2008	Leaders signed the Libreville Comprehensive Peace Agreement
October 1, 2008	U.S. leaders activated AFRICOM at a ceremony in Stuttgart, Germany
January 6, 2009	China sent People's Liberation Army Navy (PLAN) task force to combat piracy in the Gulf of Aden
January 30, 2009	Ethiopia's occupation of Mogadishu ended
July 11, 2010	Al-Shabaab bombed a crowded restaurant in Kampala, Uganda
July 26, 2010	African Union leaders reaffirmed the 1994 African Maritime Transport Charter
January 9–15, 2011	South Sudan became the world's newest country after 98.83 percent of voters chose independence
July 9, 2011	South Sudan celebrated independence
January 16, 2012	Tuareg rebellion erupted in Mali
February 9, 2012	Al-Shabaab joined al-Qaeda
March 21–22, 2012	Military coup overthrew President Amadou Toumani Touré in Mali
April 6, 2012	National Movement for the Liberation of Azawad (MNLA) declared Azawad an independent state
May 26, 2012	MNLA and Ansar al-Dine joined forces in Mali
September 11–12, 2012	Attack on U.S. embassy in Benghazi, Libya
January 8, 2013	Islamist fighters advanced toward airport near Mopti, Mali
January 11, 2013	African and French intervention in Mali began
March 25, 2013	Seleka leader Michel Djotodia declared himself president of the Central African Republic
July 19, 2013	African Union and United Nations established the Mission Internationale de Soutien à la Centrafrique sous conduite Africaine (MISCA), also known as International Support Mission to the Central African Republic

September 4, 2013	Voters elected Ibrahim Boubacar Keïta as president of Mali
September 21, 2013	Al-Shabaab attacked Westgate Mall in Nairobi, Kenya
November 12, 2013	UN Security Council Resolution 2124
November 13, 2013	United States declared Boko Haram a terrorist organization
December 15, 2013	Civil war erupted in South Sudan
April 10, 2014	UN Security Council Resolution 2149 created UN Multi-dimensional Integrated Stabilization Mission in the CAR (MINUSCA)
April 14–15, 2014	Boko Haram kidnapped 276 schoolgirls from the town of Chibok, Borno State, Nigeria
March 28, 2015	Goodluck Jonathan lost presidential reelection largely due to his administration's inability to defeat the Boko Haram insurgency
April 19, 2017	Uganda halted its search for Joseph Kony, leader of the LRA
August 23, 2017	Voters elected João Lourenço, Angola's former defense minister, as the nation's third president
February 19, 2018	Boko Haram abducted 110 girls from the Government Science and Technical College in Dapchi, Yobe State, Nigeria

Notes

CHAPTER 1

1. Olatunji Omirin, "50 Boko Haram Abductees Reunited with Parents," *Daily Trust (Abuja, Nigeria)*, January 30, 2018.

2. "Disagreement in North over Ultimatum to Jonathan," *Nigerian Tribune (Oyo State, Nigeria)*, August 13, 2014.

3. "Chibok Schoolgirls: Jonathan Plotted to Remove Me—Governor Shettima," *Nigerian Tribune (Oyo State, Nigeria)*, November 30, 2017.

4. "Boko Haram—881 Killed, 376 Injured in 100 Days," Africa News Service, September 7, 2015.

5. Hamza Idris and Hamisu Kabir Matazu, "Fleeing Boko Haram Insurgents Lurk in Borno, Yobe Villages," *Daily Trust (Abuja, Nigeria)*, January 30, 2018.

6. "Military Rescues 30,000 Women, Children from Boko Haram in 2 Years Dan-Ali," *Nigerian Tribune (Oyo State, Nigeria)*, February 5, 2018.

7. "Large Number of Girls May Have Been Abducted by Boko Haram," *Nigerian Tribune (Oyo State, Nigeria)*, February 21, 2018.

8. Paul Obi, "Troops Rescue 1,000 Hostages from Boko Haram," Africa News Service, May 8, 2018.

9. On security in Africa, see Olayiwola Abegunrin, ed., *Africa in the New World Order: Peace and Security Challenges in the Twenty-First Century* (Plymouth: Lexington Books, 2014); James J. Hentz, ed., *Routledge Handbook of African Security* (Abingdon: Routledge, 2014); Paul D. Williams, *War and Conflict in Africa* (Cambridge: Polity, 2011); Toyin Falola and Adebayo O. Oyebade, *Hot Spot: Sub-Saharan Africa* (Santa Barbara, CA: Greenwood, 2010).

10. The literature on colonialism in Africa and its legacy is vast. For a representative sample, see Lawrence James, *Empires in the Sun: The Struggle for the Mastery of Africa* (New York: Pegasus, 2017); Martin Meredith, *The Fortunes of Africa: A 5000-Year History of Wealth, Greed, and Endeavour* (New York: PublicAffairs, 2014);

Toyin Falola, ed., *The Dark Webs: Perspectives on Colonialism in Africa* (Durham, NC: Carolina Academic, 2005); Mahmood Mamdani, *Citizen and Subject: Contemporary Africa and the Legacy of Late Colonialism* (Princeton, NJ: Princeton University Press, 1996); Andrew Roberts, ed., *The Colonial Moment in Africa: Essays on the Movement of Minds and Materials, 1900–1940* (Cambridge: Cambridge University Press, 1990). On postcolonial Africa, see Martin Meredith, *The Fate of Africa: A History of the Continent since Independence* (New York: PublicAffairs, 2005).

11. O. P. Godwin, "Embracing the Challenges for Africa," *Environment* 44, no. 4 (May 2002): 13.

12. UN Development Programme, "Human Development Report 2016: Human Development for Everyone," 2016, p. 27, available at http://hdr.undp.org/sites/default/files/2016_human_development_report.pdf (accessed March 17, 2018). See especially Figure 1.1, "Regional Trends in Human Development Index Values."

13. Ibid., 200–201. The only country in the bottom 20 not in Africa was Afghanistan, which ranked 169th out of 188 countries and above the 19 most underdeveloped countries in Africa.

14. Freedom House, "Freedom in the World 2018: Democracy in Crisis," 2018, available at https://freedomhouse.org/sites/default/files/FH_FITW_Report_2018_Final_SinglePage.pdf (accessed March 3, 2018). On Freedom House's methodology, see Freedom House, "Freedom in the World 2018: Methodology," 2018, pp. 1–17, available at https://freedomhouse.org/report/methodology-freedom-world-2018 (accessed March 3, 2018).

15. Freedom House, "Freedom in the World 2018," pp. 6–7, 10, 18.

16. Paul D. Williams, "Thinking about Security in Africa," *International Affairs* 83, no. 6 (November 2007): 1021.

17. Uppsala University Uppsala Conflict Data Program, "UCDP Conflict Encyclopedia," 2018, available at http://ucdp.uu.se/?id=1 (accessed March 4, 2018). For definitions, see Uppsala University Uppsala Conflict Data Program, "Definitions," 2018, available at http://www.pcr.uu.se/research/ucdp/definitions/ (accessed March 4, 2018).

18. Uppsala University Uppsala Conflict Data Program, "Armed Conflict by Region, 1946–2016," 2017, available at http://www.pcr.uu.se/digitalAssets/667/c_667494-l_1-k_armed-conflict-by-region--1946-2016.pdf (accessed March 4, 2018).

19. Paul D. Williams, "The African Union's Peace Operations: A Comparative Analysis," *African Security* 2, no. 2/3 (November 2009): 97–118.

20. On human security, see Derek S. Reveron and Kathleen A. Mahoney-Norris, *Human Security in a Borderless World* (Boulder, CO: Westview Press, 2011).

21. Fund for Peace, "Fragile States Index 2017: Annual Report," May 14, 2017, pp. 6–7, available at http://fundforpeace.org/fsi/2017/05/14/fragile-states-index-2017-annual-report/ (accessed March 28, 2018).

CHAPTER 2

1. On weak and fragile states, see Robert I. Rotberg, ed., *When States Fail: Causes and Consequences* (Princeton, NJ: Princeton University Press, 2004); Robert D. Kaplan, "The Coming Anarchy: How Scarcity, Crime, Overpopulation,

Tribalism, and Disease Are Rapidly Destroying the Social Fabric of Our Planet," *Atlantic* 273, no. 2 (February 1994): 44–77.

2. On the methodology behind the Fragile States Index and a full listing of the 12 indicators and more than 100 subindicators, see Fund for Peace, "Fragile States Index 2017: Annual Report," May 14, 2017, pp. 24–33, available at http://fund forpeace.org/fsi/2017/05/14/fragile-states-index-2017-annual-report/ (accessed March 28, 2018).

3. Ibid., 6–7.

4. Ibid., 40–41.

5. Jeffrey Herbst, *States and Power in Africa: Comparative Lessons in Authority and Control*, 2nd ed. (Princeton, NJ: Princeton University Press, 2014), 3.

6. Tore Wig, "Peace from the Past: Pre-Colonial Political Institutions and Civil Wars in Africa," *Journal of Peace Research* 53, no. 4 (July 2016): 510.

7. Noel Anderson, "Peacekeepers Fighting a Counterinsurgency Campaign: A Net Assessment of the African Union Mission in Somalia," *Studies in Conflict and Terrorism* 37, no. 11 (November 2014): 936.

8. Oscar Gakuo Mwangi, "State Collapse, *Al-Shabaab*, Islamism, and Legitimacy in Somalia," *Politics, Religion, and Ideology* 13, no. 4 (December 2012): 523.

9. Transparency International, "Our Organisation," 2018, available at https://www.transparency.org/whoweare/organisation (accessed May 16, 2018).

10. Transparency International, "Corruption Perceptions Index 2016," January 25, 2017, available at https://www.transparency.org/whatwedo/publica tion/corruption_perceptions_index_2016 (accessed January 22, 2018).

11. Transparency International, "What Are the Costs of Corruption," 2018, available at https://www.transparency.org/what-is-corruption#costs-of-corrup tion (accessed May 16, 2018).

12. On Somalia, see Andrew Harding, *The Mayor of Mogadishu: A Story of Chaos and Redemption in the Ruins of Somalia* (New York: St. Martin's Press, 2016); James Fergusson, *The World's Most Dangerous Place: Inside the Outlaw State of Somalia* (Boston, MA: Da Capo Press, 2013); Bronwyn Bruton, "Somalia: A New Approach," Council on Foreign Relations Center for Preventative Action Council Special Report No. 52, March 2010.

13. Marielle Debos, "Fluid Loyalties in a Regional Crisis: Chadian 'Ex-Liberators' in the Central African Republic," *African Affairs* 107, no. 427 (April 2008): 225–241.

14. Amnesty International, "The Central African Republic's Human Rights Crisis," April 9, 2014, p. 1, available at https://www.amnesty.org/en/latest/news/2014/04/qa-central-african-republic-s-human-rights-crisis/ (accessed January 14, 2018).

15. "Central African Republic's UN Protection Force Approved," BBC News, October 30, 2013, available at http://bbc.com/news/world-africa-24744757 (accessed January 15, 2018).

16. "Central African Republic—Fleeing Bossangoa," All Africa, February 3, 2014.

17. Human Rights Watch, "Central African Republic: Muslims Forced to Flee," February 12, 2014, p. 2, available at https://www.hrw.org/news/2014/02/12/central-african-republic-muslims-forced-flee (accessed January 14, 2018).

18. Amnesty International, "The Central African Republic's Human Rights Crisis," p. 3. On ethnic cleansing, see Amnesty International, "Ethnic Cleansing and Sectarian Killings in the Central African Republic," February 12, 2014,

pp. 1–32, available at https://s3-eu-west-1.amazonaws.com/alfrescotemporary/ AI_CAR+report_Feb2014.pdf (accessed January 14, 2018).

19. Human Rights Watch, "Central African Republic: Muslims Forced to Flee," p. 2.

20. Abjurrahim Sıradağ, "Explaining the Conflict in Central African Republic: Causes and Dynamics," *Epiphany: Journal of Transdisciplinary Studies* 9, no. 3 (2016): 86–103.

21. Human Rights Watch, "Central African Republic: Muslims Forced to Flee," p. 9.

22. Emizet F. Kisangani, "Social Cleavages and Politics of Exclusion: Instability in the Central African Republic," *International Journal on World Peace* 32, no. 1 (March 2015): 33–59.

23. Institute for Justice and Reconciliation, "Central African Republic: A Conflict Misunderstood," Occasional Paper 22, May 12, 2017, pp. 1–21, available at http://www.ijr.org.za/home/wp-content/uploads/2012/07/CAR-Report-.pdf (accessed May 4, 2018).

24. Louisa Lombard and Sylvain Batianga-Kinzi, "Violence, Popular Punishment, and War in the Central African Republic," *African Affairs* 114, no. 454 (January 2015): 61.

25. UN Security Council, "Central African Republic: Monthly Forecast," November 2017, p. 1, available at http://www.securitycouncilreport.org/ monthly-forecast/2017-11/central_african_republic_23.php (accessed January 15, 2018).

26. Central Intelligence Agency, "Central African Republic," in *The World Factbook* (Washington, DC: Central Intelligence Agency, 2018), available at https:// www.cia.gov/library/publications/the-world-factbook/ (accessed May 9, 2018).

27. Peter Gwin, "The Burning Heart of Africa," *National Geographic* 231, no. 5 (May 2017): 61.

28. Rama Venkatasawmy, "Ethnic Conflict in Africa: A Short Critical Discussion," *Transcience* 6, no. 2 (2015): 33.

29. Paul D. Williams and Arthur Boutellis, "Partnership Peacekeeping: Challenges and Opportunities in the United Nations–African Union Relationship," *African Affairs* 113, no. 451 (April 2014): 254–278. On European Union and African Union's security cooperation, see African Union, "Joint Communiqué by Federica Mogherini, EU High Representative and Vice-President; Neven Mimica, EU Commissioner for International Cooperation and Development; and Smail Chergui, AU Commissioner for Peace and Security," August 1, 2016, p. 1, available at http://www.peaceau.org/uploads/joint-communique-eng.pdf (accessed February 24, 2018).

30. "Central African Republic's UN Protection Force Approved."

31. UN Security Council, "Resolution 2127 (2013)," December 5, 2013, pp. 1–12, available at http://www.un.org/en/ga/search/view_doc.asp?symbol=S/RES/21 27(2013) (accessed January 15, 2018).

32. Martin Welz, "Briefing: Crisis in the Central African Republic and the International Response," *African Affairs* 113, no. 453 (October 2014): 606.

33. UN Security Council, "Resolution 2387 (2017)," November 15, 2017, p. 8, available at http://www.un.org/en/ga/search/view_doc.asp?symbol=S/RES/23 87(2017) (accessed February 7, 2018).

34. Ibid., 14.

35. Harriet Sherwood and Margaux Benn, "Pope Francis Arrives in Central African Republic in Historic War Zone Visit," *Guardian*, November 29, 2015.

36. Elizabeth Murray and Fiona Mangan, "The 2015–2016 CAR Elections, A Look Back: Peaceful Process Belies Serious Risks," U.S. Institute of Peace Special Report 403, May 2017, pp. 4, 6, available at https://www.usip.org/sites/default/files/2017-05/sr403-2015-2016-car-elections-a-look-back-peaceful-process-belies-serious-risks.pdf (accessed January 15, 2018).

37. International Monetary Fund, "Standing with the Central African Republic," January 25, 2017, p. 2, available at https://www.imf.org/en/News/Articles/2017/01/25/SP012517-Standing-with-Central-African-Republic (accessed January 14, 2018).

38. Conciliation Resources, "Analysis of Conflict and Peacebuilding in the Central African Republic," 2015, p. 7.

39. Murray and Mangan, "The 2015–2016 CAR Elections, A Look Back," p. 9.

40. UN Security Council, "Resolution 2339 (2017)," January 27, 2017, pp. 1–12, available at http://www.un.org/en/ga/search/view_doc.asp?symbol=S/RES/2339(2017) (accessed January 15, 2018).

41. "Central African Republic—Bangui Hit by Violence, Pastor Killed," Africa News Service, May 2, 2018.

42. Central Intelligence Agency, "Mali," in *The World Factbook* (Washington, DC: Central Intelligence Agency, 2018), available at https://www.cia.gov/library/publications/the-world-factbook/ (accessed May 9, 2018).

43. François Heisbourg, "A Surprising Little War: First Lessons of Mali," *Survival* 55, no. 2 (April–May 2013): 7.

44. Zachary Devlin-Foltz, "Africa's Fragile States: Empowering Extremists, Exporting Terrorism," *Africa Security Brief: A Publication of the Africa Center for Strategic Studies*, no. 6 (August 2010): 5.

45. Roger Kaplan, "Losing Mali: The Administration Will Not Avoid Further Involvement in an African Tribal War," *American Spectator* 45, no. 10 (December 2012/January 2013): 34.

46. Alexis Arieff, "Crisis in Mali," Congressional Research Service Report Prepared for Members and Committees of Congress, January 14, 2013, p. 7.

47. Martin van Vliet, "Weak Legislatures, Failing MPs, and the Collapse of Democracy in Mali," *African Affairs* 113, no. 450 (January 2014): 46.

48. Tuareg communities also have inhabited Algeria, Burkina Faso, Libya, Mali, and Niger. On the Tuareg, see Andrew Alesbury, "A Society in Motion: The Tuareg from the Pre-Colonial Era to Today," *Nomadic Peoples* 17, no. 1 (Summer 2013): 106–125.

49. Robert B. Lloyd, "Ungoverned Spaces and Regional Insecurity: The Case of Mali," *School of Advanced International Studies Review of International Affairs* 36, no. 1 (Winter/Spring 2016): 137.

50. Ralph A. Austen, *Trans-Saharan Africa in World History* (Oxford: Oxford University Press, 2010), 23–48.

51. Morten Bøås and Liv Elin Torheim, "The Trouble in Mali—Corruption, Collusion, Resistance," *Third World Quarterly* 34, no. 7 (2013): 1281.

52. Jean Ping, "The Crisis in Mali: Outline the Course to Peace and Stability," *Harvard International Review* 35, no. 3 (Winter 2014): 22.

53. Heisbourg, "A Surprising Little War," 8.

54. Lloyd, "Ungoverned Spaces and Regional Insecurity," 133.

55. "Algeria, Tunisia Unrest Exposes Frustrations," *Daily News Egypt*, January 7, 2011. On the Arab Spring, see Asef Bayat, *Revolution without Revolutionaries: Making Sense of the Arab Spring* (Stanford, CA: Stanford University Press, 2017); Mark L. Haas and David W. Lesch, eds., *The Arab Spring: The Hope and Reality of the Uprisings* (Boulder, CO: Westview Press, 2017); Jason Brownlee, Tarek Masoud, and Andrew Reynolds, *The Arab Spring: Pathways of Repression and Reform* (Oxford: Oxford University Press, 2015).

56. On the connection between terrorism and political instability, see Institute for Economics and Peace, "Global Terrorism Index 2017: Measuring and Understanding the Impact of Terrorism," November 2017, p. 39, available at http://vi sionofhumanity.org/app/uploads/2017/11/Global-Terrorism-Index-2017.pdf (accessed March 18, 2018). See especially Table 2.1, "Deaths from Terrorism in Arab Spring Countries, 2009–2016."

57. UN Security Council, "Resolution 1973 (2011)," March 17, 2011, pp. 1–8, available at http://www.un.org/en/ga/search/view_doc.asp?symbol=S/RES/ 1973(2011) (accessed January 9, 2018).

58. On Libya and Gaddafi's rise to power, see Dirk Vandewalle, *A History of Modern Libya*, 2nd ed. (Cambridge: Cambridge University Press, 2012). On Gaddafi's downfall, see Andrei Netto, *Bringing Down Gaddafi: On the Ground with the Libyan Rebels*, trans. Michael Marsden (New York: St. Martin's Press, 2014); Ethan Chorin, *Exit the Colonel: The Hidden History of the Libyan Revolution* (New York: PublicAffairs, 2012). On Libya after Gaddafi, see Olajide Akanji, "A Critical Analysis of the Security Crisis in Post-Gaddafi Libya," *Africa Insight* 45, no. 2 (September 2015): 11–26; Francis Nguendi Ikome, "After Gaddafi and Mubarak: A New North African Role in the African Union," *Africa Insight* 42, no. 3 (December 2012): 68–90.

59. Ping, "The Crisis in Mali," 23.

60. Van Vliet, "Weak Legislatures, Failing MPs, and the Collapse of Democracy in Mali," 55.

61. Arieff, "Crisis in Mali," p. 7.

62. "Great Timbuktu Rescue Mission," *Weekend Argus (South Africa)*, June 2, 2013. On Timbuktu's history, see Elias N. Saad, *Social History of Timbuktu: The Role of Muslim Scholars and Notables, 1400–1900* (Cambridge: Cambridge University Press, 1983).

63. Roland Marchal, "Briefing: Military (Mis)adventures in Mali," *African Affairs* 112, no. 448 (July 2013): 494.

64. Terje Østebø, "Islamic Militancy in Africa," *Africa Security Brief: A Publication of the Africa Center for Strategic Studies*, no. 23 (November 2012): 6.

65. UN Security Council, "Resolution 2056 (2012)," July 5, 2012, pp. 1–6, available at http://www.un.org/en/ga/search/view_doc.asp?symbol=S/RES/ 2056(2012) (accessed January 15, 2018).

66. UN Security Council, "Resolution 2071 (2012)," October 12, 2012, pp. 1–4, available at http://www.un.org/en/ga/search/view_doc.asp?symbol=S/RES/ 2071(2012) (accessed January 15, 2018).

67. UN Security Council, "Resolution 2085 (2012)," December 20, 2012, pp. 1–7, available at http://www.un.org/en/ga/search/view_doc.asp?symbol=S/RES/ 2085(2012) (accessed November 18, 2017).

68. ECOWAS member nations include Benin, Burkina Faso, Cape Verde, Côte d'Ivoire, Gambia, Ghana, Guinea, Guinea Bissau, Liberia, Mali, Niger, Nigeria, Senegal, Sierra Leone, and Togo. On the community, see Economic Community of West African States, "History," 2018, available at http://www.ecowas.int/about-ecowas/history/ (accessed May 17, 2018).

69. On the French intervention, see Christopher S. Chivvis, *The French War on Al Qa'ida in Africa* (Cambridge: Cambridge University Press, 2016).

70. "France Confirms Death of Al-Qaeda Leader in Mali," Agency Tunis Afrique Presse, March 23, 2013.

71. Jemal Oumar, "Al-Qaeda Affiliate AQIM Names New Field Leader to Replace Slain Abou Zeid," Africa News Service, March 28, 2013.

72. UN Security Council, "Resolution 2100 (2013)," April 25, 2013, pp. 1–11, available at http://www.un.org/en/ga/search/view_doc.asp?symbol=S/RES/2100(2013) (accessed January 10, 2018).

73. UN Peacekeeping, "MINUSMA Fact Sheet," 2018, pp. 1–2, available at https://peacekeeping.un.org/en/mission/minusma (accessed May 22, 2018).

74. Van Vliet, "Weak Legislatures, Failing MPs, and the Collapse of Democracy in Mali," 66.

75. Costas M. Constantinou and Sam Okoth Opondo, "Engaging the 'Ungoverned': The Merging of Diplomacy, Defence and Development," *Cooperation and Conflict* 51, no. 3 (September 2016): 318.

76. Lloyd, "Ungoverned Spaces and Regional Insecurity," 137. In addition to Mali, this concept has applied to other African nations. On ungoverned spaces and the Democratic Republic of the Congo, see Theo Neethling, "The Lord's Resistance Army in the DRC: The Problem of Ungoverned Spaces and Related Regional Insecurity," *Africa Insight* 43, no. 1 (June 2013): 32–44.

77. Constantinou and Opondo, "Engaging the 'Ungoverned,'" 318.

78. Bøås and Torheim, "The Trouble in Mali—Corruption, Collusion, Resistance," 1281.

79. "Malians Pick Up the Pieces after Hotel Attack," All Africa, November 23, 2015.

80. Fund for Peace, "Fragile States Index 2017," pp. 11, 36, 40–41. The other three states were Libya, Syria, and Yemen, while Mali ranked 31st worst in 2017 and 4th worst from 2007 to 2017.

81. Marchal, "Briefing: Military (Mis)adventures in Mali," 496.

82. UN Security Council, "Report of the Secretary-General on the Situation in Mali," June 11, 2015, pp. 1–21, available at http://www.un.org/en/ga/search/view_doc.asp?symbol=S/2015/426 (accessed March 11, 2018).

83. "West Africa—Hollande Announces New Military Operation in West Africa," France 24, July 19, 2014.

84. African Union Peace and Security Council, "Report on Mali and the Sahel and the Activities of the African Union Mission for Mali and the Sahel," August 11, 2014, pp. 1–7, available at http://www.peaceau.org/uploads/psc.rpt.449.mali-sahel.11.08.2014.pdf (accessed February 24, 2018).

85. UN Peacekeeping, "MINUSMA Fact Sheet," pp. 1–2.

86. Bøås and Torheim, "The Trouble in Mali—Corruption, Collusion, Resistance," 1279.

87. "Security Situation in Mali Is Getting Worse," Targeted News Service, May 1, 2018.

88. Fund for Peace, "Fragile States Index 2017," pp. 6–7.

89. Transparency International, "Corruption Perceptions Index 2016," pp. 1–12.

CHAPTER 3

1. Rama Venkatasawmy, "Ethnic Conflict in Africa: A Short Critical Discussion," *Transcience* 6, no. 2 (2015): 26.

2. Robert Picciotto, "Conflict Prevention and Development Co-Operation in Africa: An Introduction," *Conflict, Security, and Development* 10, no. 1 (March 2010): 2.

3. On ethnicity in Africa, see Daniel N. Posner, *Institutions and Ethnic Politics in Africa* (Cambridge: Cambridge University Press, 2005).

4. Jan Angstrom, "The Sociology of Studies of Ethnic Conflict: Explaining the Causal Status of Development," *Civil Wars* 3, no. 3 (Autumn 2000): 25.

5. Donald L. Horowitz, *Ethnic Groups in Conflict*, 2nd ed. (Berkeley: University of California Press, 2000), 3–5, 17, 23, 29–34, 173, 198–199, 233–235, 303, 339–340, 433, 485–499, 558, 590, 656.

6. Jean Ping, "The Crisis in Mali: Outline the Course to Peace and Stability," *Harvard International Review* 35, no. 3 (Winter 2014): 23.

7. Pade Badru, "Ethnic Conflict and State Formation in Post-Colonial Africa: A Comparative Study of Ethnic Genocide in the Congo, Liberia, Nigeria, and Rwanda-Burundi," *Journal of Third World Studies* 27, no. 2 (Fall 2010): 149–169; Julie Kaye and Daniel Béland, "The Politics of Ethnicity and Post-Conflict Reconstruction: The Case of Northern Ghana," *Journal of Contemporary African Studies* 27, no. 2 (April 2009): 177–200.

8. United Nations, "Convention on the Prevention and Punishment of the Crime of Genocide," December 9, 1948, p. 278, available at https://treaties.un.org/doc/publication/unts/volume%2078/volume-78-i-1021-english.pdf (accessed February 28, 2018).

9. Ibid., 280.

10. UN Security Council, "Resolution 955 (1994)," November 8, 1994, pp. 1–15, available at http://www.unmict.org/specials/ictr-remembers/docs/res955-1994_en.pdf?q=ictr-remembers/docs/res955-1994_en.pdf (accessed March 25, 2018). On the ICTR, see UN Mechanism for International Criminal Tribunals, "The ICTR in Brief," 2018, pp. 1–2, available at http://unictr.unmict.org/en/tribunal (accessed May 22, 2018). The UN Security Council also created the International Criminal Tribunal for the former Yugoslavia after the Balkan conflict. The ICTR closed on December 31, 2015.

11. Adama Dieng, "Protecting Vulnerable Populations from Genocide," *UN Chronicle* 53, no. 4 (December 2016): 10.

12. UN Secretary-General, "Action Plan to Prevent Genocide," April 7, 2004, pp. 1–4, available at http://www.un.org/en/genocideprevention/documents/about-us/Doc.2_Press%20Release_SG%20Plan%20of%20Action.pdf (accessed March 25, 2018).

13. Dieng, "Protecting Vulnerable Populations from Genocide," 11.

14. Clement Mweyang Aapengnuo, "Misinterpreting Ethnic Conflicts in Africa," *Africa Security Brief: A Publication of the Africa Center for Strategic Studies*, no. 4 (April 2010): 1.

15. Chris Kwaja, "Nigeria's Pernicious Drivers of Ethno-Religious Conflict," *Africa Security Brief: A Publication of the Africa Center for Strategic Studies*, no. 14 (July 2011): 1–8. On ethno-religious violence in Jos, also see Adam Higazi, "The Jos Crisis: A Recurrent Nigerian Tragedy," Friedrich-Ebert-Stiftung (FES) Nigeria Discussion Paper no. 2, January 2011, pp. 1–34, available at http://library.fes.de/pdf-files/bueros/nigeria/07812.pdf (accessed March 1, 2018).

16. Jana Krause, "A Deadly Cycle: Ethno-Religious Conflict in Jos, Plateau State, Nigeria," Geneva Declaration Secretariat Working Paper, 2011, pp. 1–70, available at https://reliefweb.int/sites/reliefweb.int/files/resources/GD-WP-Jos-deadly-cycle.pdf (accessed March 25, 2018).

17. Human Rights Watch, "'They Do Not Own This Place': Government Discrimination against 'Non-Indigenes' in Nigeria," April 2006, pp. 1–64, available at https://www.hrw.org/sites/default/files/reports/nigeria0406webwcover.pdf (accessed March 1, 2018).

18. Kwaja, "Nigeria's Pernicious Drivers of Ethno-Religious Conflict," 1. On violence in Nigeria's northeast, see Chapter 5 of this volume.

19. Ransford Ocansey, "CHRAJ Not a Toothless Bulldog—Commissioner," Africa News Service, July 10, 2004; Lindsey Hilsum, "Hutu Ideology Justifies Genocide of Tutsis as Preventative Ethnic Medicine: Officials Have Fostered the Belief That It Was the Minority's Fault They Were Killed," *Guardian*, July 11, 1994.

20. Aapengnuo, "Misinterpreting Ethnic Conflicts in Africa," 1.

21. On Sierra Leone, see David Keen, *Useful Enemies: When Waging Wars Is More Important Than Winning Them* (New Haven, CT: Yale University Press, 2012), 1–6, 33–34, 198–206, 223–227; Paul Richards, *Fighting for the Rain Forest: War, Youth, and Resources in Sierra Leone* (Oxford: James Currey, 1996); William Reno, *Corruption and State Politics in Sierra Leone* (Cambridge: Cambridge University Press, 1995).

22. Rachel Glennerster, Edward Miguel, and Alexander D. Rothenberg, "Collective Action in Diverse Sierra Leone Communities," *Economic Journal* 123, no. 568 (May 2013): 287.

23. Human Rights Watch, "Even a 'Big Man' Must Face Justice: Lessons from the Trial of Charles Taylor," July 2012, pp. 1–20, available at https://www.hrw.org/sites/default/files/reports/sierraLeone0712ForUpload_0.pdf (accessed March 25, 2018).

24. Tore Wig, "Peace from the Past: Pre-Colonial Political Institutions and Civil Wars in Africa," *Journal of Peace Research* 53, no. 4 (July 2016): 509.

25. Ping, "The Crisis in Mali," 24.

26. Yomi Kazeem, "What Is a Coup? These 40 African Countries Could Help Explain," Quartz Africa, November 16, 2017, available at https://qz.com/1130009/what-is-coup-zimbabwe-joins-40-african-countries-that-have-had-coups/ (accessed January 5, 2018).

27. Teodardo Calles, "The International Year of Pulses: What Are They and Why Are They Important?" Food and Agriculture Organization of the United Nations Article 7, pp. 1–3, available at http://www.fao.org/3/a-bl797e.pdf (accessed January 15, 2018).

28. Central Intelligence Agency, "Uganda," in *The World Factbook* (Washington, DC: Central Intelligence Agency, 2018), available at https://www.cia.gov/library/publications/the-world-factbook/ (accessed May 9, 2018).

29. On the Buganda, see Cathrine Johannessen, "Kingship in Uganda: The Role of the Buganda Kingdom in Ugandan Politics," Christian Michelsen Institute (CMI) Working Paper no. 8, 2006, pp. 1–14, available at https://www.cmi.no/publications/file/2176-kingship-in-uganda.pdf (accessed March 2, 2018).

30. Wig, "Peace from the Past," 513.

31. Central Intelligence Agency, "Uganda."

32. On Amin, see Alicia C. Decker, *In Idi Amin's Shadow: Women, Gender, and Militarism in Uganda* (Athens: Ohio University Press, 2014).

33. On atrocities, see Andrew Rice, *The Teeth May Smile but the Heart Does Not Forget* (New York: Metropolitan, 2009).

34. "Besigye Vows Not to Surrender 'Election Win' to Museveni," Africa News Service, April 5, 2016.

35. Central Intelligence Agency, "Uganda."

36. On the LRA, see Adam Dolnik and Herman Butime, *Understanding the Lord's Resistance Army Insurgency* (Hackensack, NJ: World Scientific, 2017); Evelyn Amony, *I Am Evelyn Amony: Reclaiming My Life from the Lord's Resistance Army*, edited with an Introduction by Erin Baines (Madison: University of Wisconsin Press, 2015); Lawrence E. Cline, *The Lord's Resistance Army* (Santa Barbara, CA: Praeger, 2013); Alexis Arieff and Lauren Ploch, "The Lord's Resistance Army: The U.S. Response," Congressional Research Service Report Prepared for Members and Committees of Congress, April 11, 2012; Tim Allen and Koen Vlassenroot, eds., *The Lord's Resistance Army: Myth and Reality* (London: Zed, 2010).

37. On syncretism in sub-Saharan Africa, see Linda E. Thomas, "South African Independent Churches, Syncretism, and Black Theology," *Journal of Religious Thought* 53, no. 2/1 (January 1997): 39–50.

38. On the connection between the spirit world and power in Africa, see Stephen Ellis and Gerrie ter Haar, "Religion and Politics: Taking African Epistemologies Seriously," *Journal of Modern African Studies* 45, no. 3 (September 2007): 385–401.

39. Juliys Barigaba, "How an Army Armed with Sticks and Stones Nearly Overran Kampala," *EastAfrican*, January 29, 2007, available at http://www.theeastafrican.co.ke/magazine/434746-252998-c6gb9y/index.html (accessed January 13, 2018).

40. Kony's group first claimed the title the Lord's Army and later seized the title of the Lord's Resistance Army (LRA). On Joseph Kony, see Ledio Cakaj, *When the Walking Defeats You: One Man's Journey as Joseph Kony's Bodyguard* (London: Zed, 2016); Opiyo Oloya, *Child to Soldier: Stories from Joseph Kony's Lord's Resistance Army* (Toronto: University of Toronto Press, 2013); Alexis Arieff, Rhoda Margesson, Marjorie Ann Browne, and Matthew C. Weed, "International Criminal Court Cases in Africa: Status and Policy Issues," Congressional Research Service Report Prepared for Members and Committees of Congress, July 22, 2011; Adam Branch, *Displacing Human Rights: War and Intervention in Northern Uganda* (Oxford: Oxford University Press, 2011); Sverker Finnström, *Living with Bad Surroundings: War, History and Everyday Moments in Northern Uganda* (Durham, NC: Duke University Press, 2008).

41. Theo Neethling, "The Lord's Resistance Army in the DRC: The Problem of Ungoverned Spaces and Related Regional Insecurity," *Africa Insight* 43, no. 1 (June 2013): 33.

42. Richard Dowden, "A Convenient War: Uganda's President Has Ensured That the West Is Dependent on Him," *Prospect*, no. 222 (September 2014): 46.

43. On the LRA and child soldiers, see Oloya, *Child to Soldier*; Peter Eichstaedt, *First Kill Your Family: Child Soldiers of Uganda and the Lord's Resistance Army* (Chicago: Lawrence Hill, 2009).

44. Vera Achvarina and Simon F. Reich, "No Place to Hide: Refugees, Displaced Persons, and the Recruitment of Child Soldiers," *International Security* 31, no. 1 (Summer 2006): 127–164.

45. James Bevan, "The Myth of Madness: Cold Rationality and 'Resource' Plunder by the Lord's Resistance Army," *Civil Wars* 9, no. 4 (December 2007): 343.

46. UN Peacekeeping, "MONUC: United Nations Organization Mission in the Democratic Republic of the Congo," 2018, p. 1, available at http://peacekeeping .un.org/sites/default/files/past/monuc/index.shtml (accessed May 22, 2018).

47. U.S. Congress, "Public Law 111–172, Lord's Resistance Army Disarmament and Northern Uganda Recovery Act of 2009," May 24, 2010, available at https:// www.congress.gov/111/plaws/publ172/PLAW-111publ172.pdf (accessed January 29, 2018).

48. African Union Peace and Security Council, "Report of the Chairperson of the Commission on the Implementation of the African Union-Led Regional Cooperation Initiative for the Elimination of the Lord's Resistance Army," June 17, 2013, pp. 1–6, available at http://www.peaceau.org/uploads/psc-rpt-lra-380-17-06-2013-2-.pdf (accessed February 24, 2018).

49. African Union, "The African Union Appoints a New Special Envoy for the Issue of the Lord's Resistance Army," July 10, 2014, p. 1, available at http://www .peaceau.org/uploads/auc-com-lra-10-07-2014.pdf (accessed February 24, 2018).

50. "Dominic Ongwen's ICC Trial Starts in December," *Daily Monitor, Uganda (Kampala, Uganda)*, May 31, 2016.

51. "U.S. Says It's Still 'Working Closely' with Uganda to Eliminate LRA," *Daily Monitor, Uganda (Kampala, Uganda)*, June 13, 2016.

52. "Uganda Ends Anti-LRA Military Operation in Central African Republic," *Sudan Tribune*, April 20, 2017.

53. "LRA Continues to Operate in Three African Countries: AU Report," *Sudan Tribune*, June 7, 2017.

54. "Moroccan Peacekeepers Rescue 15 Hostages of Resistance Army in Central African Republic," *Morocco World News*, April 7, 2018.

55. Freedom House, "Freedom in the World 2018: Democracy in Crisis," 2018, p. 18, available at https://freedomhouse.org/sites/default/files/FH_FITW_Report_2018_Final_SinglePage.pdf (accessed March 3, 2018).

56. Haggai Matsiko, "Museveni Wants Seven Year Term," Africa News Service, April 30, 2018.

57. Central Intelligence Agency, "Sudan," in *The World Factbook* (Washington, DC: Central Intelligence Agency, 2018), available at https://www.cia.gov/ library/publications/the-world-factbook/ (accessed May 9, 2018).

58. Eric Reeves, "Oil Crisis: Extortion and Misappropriation Are Not 'Negotiations,'" Africa News Service, January 30, 2012.

59. Central Intelligence Agency, "South Sudan," in *The World Factbook* (Washington, DC: Central Intelligence Agency, 2018), available at https://www.cia.gov/ library/publications/the-world-factbook/ (accessed May 9, 2018).

60. On the Mahdi, see Dominic Green, *Three Empires on the Nile: The Victorian Jihad, 1869–1899* (New York: Free Press, 2007). On the contemporary relevance of

the Mahdi, see Timothy R. Furnish, *Holiest Wars: Islamic Mahdis, Their Jihads, and Osama bin Laden* (Westport, CT: Praeger, 2005).

61. Kenneth Omeje and Nicodemus Minde, "The SPLM Government and the Challenges of Conflict Settlement, State-Building and Peace-Building in South Sudan," *Africa Insight* 45, no. 1 (June 2015): 54.

62. On the Lost Boys, see John Bul Dau with Michael S. Sweeney, *God Grew Tired of Us* (Washington, DC: National Geographic, 2007); Alephonsion Deng, Benson Deng, and Benjamin Ajak with Judy A. Bernstein, *They Poured Fire on Us from the Sky: The True Story of Three Lost Boys from Sudan* (New York: PublicAffairs, 2005).

63. James Schofield, "Civilians Slaughtered as Rebel Army Runs Amok," *Sunday Age*, December 15, 1991.

64. On international responses to Darfur, see Don Cheadle and John Prendergast, *Not on Our Watch: The Mission to End Genocide in Darfur and Beyond* (New York: Hyperion, 2007). On human rights abuses, see Gérard Prunier, *Darfur: A 21st Century Genocide* (Ithaca, NY: Cornell University Press, 2005).

65. United Nations, "UNAMID: African Union/United Nations Hybrid Operation in Darfur," 2018, pp. 1–2, available at https://peacekeeping.un.org/en/mission/unamid (accessed June 1, 2018).

66. Thomas G. Weiss and Martin Welz, "The UN and the African Union in Mali and Beyond: A Shotgun Wedding?" *International Affairs* 90, no 4 (July 2014): 894.

67. James Harkin, "The Stillborn State: The Creation of South Sudan Has Brought War Not Peace—Those Who Would Divide Syria Should Take Note," *Prospect*, no. 246 (September 2016): 60. The voting lasted from January 9 to January 15, 2011, and the exact tally of southern Sudanese supporting independence was 98.83 percent.

68. Michael S. Sweeney, "The Spoiling of the World: In South Sudan Decades of Civil War Led to Independence—And Yet More War," *Military History Quarterly: Quarterly Journal of Military History* 29, no. 1 (Autumn 2016): 84. From 2012 to 2013, the Khartoum government denied South Sudan's access to the pipeline in an attempt to increase fees associated with its usage.

69. Ole Frahm, "Making Borders and Identities in South Sudan," *Journal of Contemporary African Studies* 33, no. 2 (April 2015): 251–267.

70. Omeje and Minde, "The SPLM Government and the Challenges of Conflict Settlement, State-Building and Peace-Building in South Sudan," 52.

71. Harkin, "The Stillborn State," 59.

72. Sweeney, "The Spoiling of the World," 78.

73. Alex de Waal, "When Kleptocracy Becomes Insolvent: Brute Causes of the Civil War in South Sudan," *African Affairs* 113, no. 452 (July 2014): 347–369.

74. "Abyei Talks to Resume This Month in Addis Ababa," *Sudan Tribune*, November 1, 2017; "Abyei Remains Contested Area between Sudan and South Sudan, Says SPLM Official," *Sudan Tribune*, September 18, 2011; "Abyei Arbitration: What Next," *Sudan Tribune*, May 11, 2009.

75. Tesfa-Alem Tekle, "South Sudanese in Ethiopia Welcome Peace Deal Signed by President Kiir," *Sudan Tribune*, August 27, 2015.

76. On the power-sharing agreement, see Kate Almquist Knopf, "Ending South Sudan's Civil War," Council on Foreign Relations Special Report no. 77, November 2016, pp. 6–7, available at https://cfrd8-files.cfr.org/sites/default/files/pdf/2016/11/CSR77_Knopf_South%20Sudan.pdf (accessed February 8, 2018).

77. "Opposition Replaces Missing Leader Machar," Africa News Service, July 24, 2016.

78. Knopf, "Ending South Sudan's Civil War," pp. vii—viii. Advocates of such an approach have pointed to the use of international administrations to transition Cambodia, East Timor, and Kosovo out of conflict.

79. Anup Phayal, Prabin B. Khadka, and Clayton L. Thyne, "What Makes an Ex-Combatant Happy? A Micro-Analysis of Disarmament, Demobilization, and Reintegration in South Sudan," *International Studies Quarterly* 59, no. 4 (December 2015): 654–668.

80. Jenik Radon and Sarah Logan, "South Sudan: Governance Arrangements, War, and Peace," *Journal of International Affairs* 68, no. 1 (Fall/Winter 2014): 149–167.

81. Human Rights Watch, "They Burned It All: Destruction of Villages, Killings, and Sexual Violence in Unity State, South Sudan," July 2015, pp. 1–42, available at https://www.hrw.org/sites/default/files/report_pdf/southsudan0715_web_0 .pdf (accessed January 14, 2018).

82. Africa Center for Strategic Studies, "Humanitarian Costs of South Sudan Conflict Continue to Escalate," January 29, 2018, p. 1, available at https://africa center.org/wp-content/uploads/2018/01/Food-Insecurity-in-South-Sudan-2013- v-Feb-May-2018-.pdf (accessed February 5, 2018).

83. "South Sudan: Peace Process under Threat as Violence Surges across Country, Warns UN Mission," *Premium Official News*, April 30, 2018.

84. Picciotto, "Conflict Prevention and Development Co-Operation in Africa," 2.

85. Knopf, "Ending South Sudan's Civil War," p. 3.

CHAPTER 4

1. Richard M. Auty, *Sustaining Development in Mineral Economies: The Resource Curse Thesis* (Abingdon: Routledge, 1993).

2. Dominik Kopiński, Andrzej Polus, and Wojciech Tycholiz, "Resource Curse or Resource Disease? Oil in Ghana," *African Affairs* 112, no. 449 (October 2013): 584.

3. M. J. Morgan, "Making the Most of Africa's Resources," *African Business* 46, no. 382 (January 2012): 32. On the Dutch disease, see Jonas B. Bunte, "Wage Bargaining, Inequality, and the Dutch Disease," *International Studies Quarterly* 60, no. 4 (December 2016): 677–692; Emmanuel K. K. Lartey, "Financial Openness and the Dutch Disease," *Review of Development Economics* 15, no. 3 (August 2011): 556–568. On the Dutch disease in Africa, see Emmanuel Owusu-Sekyere, Reneé van Eyden, and Francis M. Kemegue, "Remittances and the Dutch Disease in Sub-Saharan Africa: A Dynamic Panel Approach," *Contemporary Economics* 8, no. 3 (September 2014): 289–298; Ismail O. Fasanya, Adegbemi B. O. Onakoya, and Misbaudeen A. Adabanija, "Oil Discovery and Sectoral Performance in Nigeria: An Appraisal of the Dutch Disease," *IUP Journal of Applied Economics* 12, no. 2 (April 2013): 25–40; Pedro M. G. Martins, "Do Large Capital Inflows Hinder Competitiveness? The Dutch Disease in Ethiopia," *Applied Economics* 45, no. 8 (March 2013): 1075–1088; Hazel M. McFerson, "Extractive Industries and African Democracy: Can the 'Resource Curse' Be Exorcised?" *International Studies Perspectives* 11, no. 4 (November 2010): 335–353.

4. Mick Moore, "The Development of Political Underdevelopment," in *Global Encounters: International Political Economy, Development and Globalization*, ed. Graham Harrison (London: Palgrave Macmillan, 2005), 34.

5. Jessica Moody, "Senegal's Gas Discoveries—Gift or Curse," *African Business* 51, no. 438 (February 2017): 62.

6. Philippe Le Billon, "Angola's Political Economy of War: The Role of Oil and Diamonds, 1975–2000," *African Affairs* 100, no. 398 (January 2001): 56.

7. On ratification, see UN Secretariat, "Convention to Combat Desertification: Update on Ratification of the UNCCD," December 21, 2016, p. 1, available at http://www2.unccd.int/sites/default/files/relevant-links/2017-07/Ratification%20list%20Dec2016.pdf (accessed November 14, 2017).

8. United Nations, "United Nations Convention to Combat Desertification," 1994, p. 4, available at http://www2.unccd.int/sites/default/files/relevant-links/2017-01/UNCCD_Convention_ENG_0.pdf (accessed November 14, 2017).

9. Ibid., 2.

10. On food security in Africa, see Chapter 7 of this volume.

11. O. P. Godwin, "Embracing the Challenges for Africa," *Environment* 44, no. 4 (May 2002): 10.

12. On climate change and Africa, see Elizabeth Thomas-Hope, ed., *Climate Change and Food Security: Africa and the Caribbean* (Abingdon: Routledge, 2017).

13. African Union, "Agenda 2063: The Africa We Want," final ed., April 2015, pp. 3–4, available at http://www.un.org/en/africa/osaa/pdf/au/agenda2063.pdf (accessed February 4, 2018).

14. Food and Agriculture Organization, "Global Forest Resources Assessment 2015: How Are the World's Forests Changing?" 2nd ed., 2016, pp. 1–44, available at http://www.fao.org/3/a-i4793e.pdf (accessed March 25, 2018).

15. Kenneth Omeje and Nicodemus Minde, "The SPLM Government and the Challenges of Conflict Settlement, State-Building and Peace-Building in South Sudan," *Africa Insight* 45, no. 1 (June 2015): 65.

16. Morgan, "Making the Most of Africa's Resources," 32.

17. On oil in Africa, see Nicholas Shaxson, *Poisoned Wells: The Dirty Politics of African Oil* (Basingstoke: Palgrave, 2007).

18. Matthew Green, "Crude Realities: Can Ghana Escape Africa's Oil Curse," *Financial Times*, August 28, 2008.

19. Kopiński, Polus, and Tycholiz, "Resource Curse or Resource Disease?" 585.

20. Ibid., 601.

21. Moody, "Senegal's Gas Discoveries—Gift or Curse," 63.

22. Ibid., 62.

23. On Cabinda, see Victor Ojakorotu, "Nature's Gift, Man's Curse: Natural Resources and Civil Conflicts in the Niger Delta and Cabinda," *Africa Insight* 41, no. 3 (December 2011): 111–126.

24. Food and Agriculture Organization, "Increasing Agricultural Production in Angola," July 2014, pp. 1–2, available at http://www.fao.org/3/a-bt830e.pdf (accessed January 6, 2018).

25. Ibid.

26. Le Billon, "Angola's Political Economy of War," 56.

27. UN Development Programme, "Human Development Report 2016: Human Development for Everyone," 2016, p. 200, available at http://hdr.undp.org/sites/default/files/2016_human_development_report.pdf (accessed March 17, 2018).

28. Ibid., 204.

29. Trading Economics, "Crude Oil Production: Africa," March 2018, p. 1, available at https://tradingeconomics.com/country-list/crude-oil-production?continent=africa (accessed May 2, 2018).

30. Organisation for Economic Co-Operation and Development, "Angola," 2007, p. 109, available at https://www.oecd.org/countries/angola/38561655.pdf (accessed May 2, 2018).

31. Jedrzej George Frynas and Geoffrey Wood, "Patrimonialism and Petro-Diamond Capitalism: Peace, Geopolitics and the Economics of War in Angola," *Review of African Political Economy* 28, no. 90 (December 2001): 590.

32. Renato Aguilar and Andrea Goldstein, "The Chinisation of Africa: The Case of Angola," *World Economy* 32, no. 11 (November 2009): 1549.

33. Ibid., 1547.

34. "Angola Displaces Nigeria to Become Africa's Top Oil Producer—OPEC," Africa News, February 14, 2017, available at http://www.africanews.com/2017/02/14/angola-displaces-nigeria-to-become-africa-s-top-oil-producer-opec// (accessed May 2, 2018).

35. Energy Information Administration, "Country Analysis Brief: Angola," May 18, 2016, pp. 1–15, available at https://www.eia.gov/beta/international/analysis_includes/countries_long/Angola/angola.pdf (accessed February 8, 2018).

36. UN Development Programme, "Human Development Report 2016," p. 271.

37. On the Cold War and Africa, see Elizabeth Schmidt, *Foreign Intervention in Africa: From the Cold War to the War on Terror* (Cambridge: Cambridge University Press, 2013); Lise Namikas, *Battleground Africa: Cold War in the Congo, 1960–1965* (Stanford, CA: Stanford University Press, 2013); Sergey Mazov, *A Distant Front in the Cold War: The USSR in West Africa and the Congo, 1956–1964* (Stanford, CA: Stanford University Press, 2010).

38. Herbert M. Howe, "Private Security Forces and African Stability: The Case of Executive Outcomes," *Journal of Modern African Studies* 36, no. 2 (June 1998): 307–331.

39. Aguilar and Goldstein, "The Chinisation of Africa," 1545–1546. On mines, see "Over 400,000 Square Meters of Land Cleared from Landmines," Africa News Service, December 18, 2017; Jean-Louis Arcand, Aude-Sophie Rodella-Boitreaud, and Matthias Rieger, "The Impact of Land Mines on Child Health: Evidence from Angola," *Economic Development and Cultural Change* 63, no. 2 (January 2015): 249–279.

40. Charles Chisala, "Jonas Savimbi: Who Was He?" Africa News Service, February 27, 2002. On Savimbi, see Alec Russell, "The Cold War Crooner," in *Big Men, Little People: The Leaders Who Defined Africa* (New York: New York University Press, 2000), 95–126.

41. "The Angolan Peace Accord," Africa News Service, April 24, 2002.

42. Christopher Thompson and Marshall van Valen, "France's Elite in 'Angolagate' Trial," *Financial Times*, October 6, 2008.

43. Central Intelligence Agency, "Angola," in *The World Factbook* (Washington, DC: Central Intelligence Agency, 2018), available at https://www.cia.gov/library/publications/the-world-factbook/ (accessed May 9, 2018).

44. Frynas and Wood, "Patrimonialism and Petro-Diamond Capitalism: Peace, Geopolitics and the Economics of War in Angola," 594.

45. Anver Versi, "A Future Full of Light," *African Business* 49, no. 417 (March 2015): 77.

46. Danai Majaha, "Lourenço to Become Angola's Third President," Africa News Service, September 11, 2017. The exact percentages were 61.1 percent for MPLA and 26.7 percent for UNITA.

47. "Angola's First New President in 38 Years Is a Product of Even Older Politics," Quartz Africa, available at https://qz.com/1063009/angola-elections-who-is-angolas-new-president-joao-lourenco/ (accessed January 19, 2018).

48. Kimber Kraus, "Poverty in Angola: Causes, Updates and Statistics," Borgen Project, February 19, 2016, p. 1, available at https://borgenproject.org/poverty-angola-causes-updates-statistics/ (accessed March 13, 2018).

49. Sigfrido Burgos and Sophal Ear, "China's Oil Hunger in Angola: History and Perspective," *Journal of Contemporary China* 21, no. 74 (March 2012): 351–367.

50. Rafael Marques de Morais, "The New Imperialism: China in Angola," *World Affairs* 173, no. 6 (March/April 2011): 69–70.

51. Marcus Power, "Angola 2025: The Future of the 'World's Richest Poor Country' as Seen through a Chinese Rear-View Mirror," *Antipode* 44, no. 3 (June 2012): 993.

52. De Morais, "The New Imperialism," 72.

53. Freedom House, "Freedom in the World 2018: Democracy in Crisis," 2018, p. 9, available at https://freedomhouse.org/sites/default/files/FH_FITW_Report_2018_Final_SinglePage.pdf (accessed March 3, 2018).

54. "Nigeria Upstages Angola in Crude Oil Production," All Africa, April 4, 2018.

55. "Angola at Crossroads as New Broom Sweeps Economy," *National (Abu Dhabi, United Arab Emirates)*, May 7, 2018.

56. On Leopold, see Adam Hochschild, *King Leopold's Ghost: A Story of Greed, Terror, and Heroism in Colonial Africa* (New York: Houghton Mifflin Harcourt, 1998).

57. On Sese Seko, see Michela Wrong, *In the Footsteps of Mr. Kurtz: Living on the Brink of Disaster in Mobutu's Congo* (New York: HarperCollins, 2001).

58. On Rwanda, see Jean Hatzfeld, *Machete Season: The Killers in Rwanda Speak* (New York: Farrar, Straus and Giroux, 2005); Roméo Dallaire, *Shake Hands with the Devil: The Failure of Humanity in Rwanda* (New York: Carroll & Graf, 2003); Philip Gourevitch, *We Wish to Inform You That Tomorrow We Will Be Killed with Our Families: Stories from Rwanda* (London: Picador, 1998).

59. On the Democratic Republic of the Congo, see Georges Nzongola-Ntalaja, *The Congo: From Leopold to Kabila, A People's History* (London: Zed, 2002).

60. On blood diamonds, see Greg Campbell, *Blood Diamonds: Tracing the Deadly Path of the World's Most Precious Stones* (New York: Basic Books, 2004).

61. Ingrid Samset, "Conflict of Interests or Interests in Conflict? Diamonds and War in the DRC," *Review of African Political Economy* 29, no. 93/94 (September–December 2002): 463–480.

62. Pelin Ekmen, "From Riches to Rags—the Paradox of Plenty and Its Linkage to Violent Conflict," *Goettingen Journal of International Law* 3, no. 2 (2011): 481.

63. Ibid., 478–479.

64. Christopher W. Mullins and Dawn L. Rothe, "Gold, Diamonds, and Blood: International State-Corporate Crime in the Democratic Republic of the Congo," *Contemporary Justice Review* 11, no. 2 (June 2008): 93.

65. UN Security Council, "Resolution 143 (1960)," July 14, 1960, p. 1, available at http://www.un.org/en/ga/search/view_doc.asp?symbol=S/RES/143(1960) (accessed March 24, 2018).

66. United Nations, "Republic of the Congo-ONUC Background," 2018, pp. 1–2, available at https://peacekeeping.un.org/en/mission/past/onucB.htm (accessed May 22, 2018). On Hammarskjöld, see Susan Williams, *Who Killed Hammarskjöld? The UN, the Cold War and White Supremacy in Africa* (Oxford: Oxford University Press, 2014).

67. UN Security Council, "Resolution 1279 (1999)," November 30, 1999, pp. 1–3, available at http://www.un.org/en/ga/search/view_doc.asp?symbol=S/RES/12 79%281999%29 (accessed March 24, 2018).

68. United Nations, "MONUC Background," 2018, p. 1, available at https://peace-keeping.un.org/en/mission/past/monuc/background.shtml (accessed May 22, 2018).

69. UN Security Council, "Resolution 1925 (2010)," May 28, 2010, pp. 1–8, available at http://www.un.org/en/ga/search/view_doc.asp?symbol=S/RES/1925(2010) (accessed March 24, 2018).

70. United Nations, "MONUSCO Fact Sheet," 2018, pp. 1–2, available at https://peacekeeping.un.org/en/mission/monusco (accessed May 22, 2018).

71. Ibid. Of the 15,424 peacekeeping troops, Pakistan contributed 3,462, India provided 2,625, and Bangladesh furnished 1,704.

72. Bruce Guenther, "The Asian Drivers and the Resource Curse in Sub-Saharan Africa: The Potential Impacts of Rising Commodity Prices for Conflict and Governance in the DRC," *European Journal of Development Research* 20, no. 2 (June 2008): 347–348.

73. Central Intelligence Agency, "Democratic Republic of the Congo," in *The World Factbook* (Washington, DC: Central Intelligence Agency, 2018), available at https://www.cia.gov/library/publications/the-world-factbook/ (accessed May 9, 2018).

74. UN Security Council, "Resolution 1698 (2006)," July 31, 2006, pp. 1–5, available at http://www.un.org/en/ga/search/view_doc.asp?symbol=S/RES/1698(2006) (accessed November 20, 2017).

75. Nicolas Cook, "Conflict Minerals in Central Africa: U.S. and International Responses," Congressional Research Service Report Prepared for Members and Committees of Congress, July 20, 2012, p. 1.

76. For statistics on conflict, see International Rescue Committee, "Mortality in the Democratic Republic of Congo: An Ongoing Crisis," May 1, 2007, pp. 1–21, available at https://www.rescue.org/sites/default/files/document/661 /2006-7congomortalitysurvey.pdf (accessed March 25, 2018).

77. Cook, "Conflict Minerals in Central Africa," p. 6. On the organization, see Organisation for Economic Co-Operation and Development, "History," 2018,

p. 1, available at http://www.oecd.org/about/ (accessed March 13, 2018). On conflict minerals, see Organisation for Economic Co-Operation and Development, "Due Diligence Guidance for Responsible Supply Chains of Minerals from Conflict-Affected and High-Risk Areas," 2016, available at http://www.oecd.org/daf/inv/mne/OECD-Due-Diligence-Guidance-Minerals-Edition3.pdf (accessed March 13, 2018).

78. Ekmen, "From Riches to Rags—the Paradox of Plenty and Its Linkage to Violent Conflict," 489.

79. Cook, "Conflict Minerals in Central Africa," p. 1.

80. Morgan, "Making the Most of Africa's Resources," 33.

81. "Anti-Kabila Protests Turn Deadly in Democratic Republic of Congo," All Africa, January 21, 2018.

82. Guenther, "The Asian Drivers and the Resource Curse in Sub-Saharan Africa," 354.

83. Human Rights Watch, "DR Congo: Human Rights Watch Submission to the African Commission on Human and Peoples' Rights," November 1, 2017, pp. 1–4, available at https://www.hrw.org/print/310992 (accessed January 16, 2018).

84. Leo Charles Zulu, "Neoliberalization, Decentralization and Community-Based Natural Resources Management in Malawi: The First Sixteen Years and Looking Ahead," *Progress in Development Studies* 12, no. 2/3 (April 2012): 193. It is important to note that in his comprehensive study of Malawi, Zulu found CBNRM "producing more challenges than opportunities."

85. African Union, "Agenda 2063," p. 15.

86. "Violence Is Roiling the Democratic Republic of Congo," *Gulf News (United Arab Emirates)*, April 15, 2018.

CHAPTER 5

1. Institute for Economics and Peace, "Global Terrorism Index 2017: Measuring and Understanding the Impact of Terrorism," November 2017, pp. 2, 14, available at http://visionofhumanity.org/app/uploads/2017/11/Global-Terrorism-Index-2017.pdf (accessed March 18, 2018).

2. Ibid., 10–13, 16, 19, 43, 46. Nations in Africa ranking in the top 10 worldwide have included Nigeria (3rd), Somalia (7th), Libya (10th), Egypt (11th), Democratic Republic of the Congo (13th), South Sudan (14th), Cameroon (15th), Sudan (18th), Central African Republic (19th), and Niger (20th).

3. Analysts and policy makers alternatively have referred to ISIL as Islamic State of Iraq and the Levant (ISIL), Islamic State of Iraq and Syria (ISIS), Islamic State (IS), or Daesh in Arabic. For consistency, the author has used ISIL throughout this volume.

4. Institute for Economics and Peace, "Global Terrorism Index 2017," p. 46. ISIL has been by far the world's deadly terrorist group, claiming 1,132 attacks, 9,132 deaths, and 7,723 injuries in 2016. On ISIL, see p. 73.

5. Africa Center for Strategic Studies, "More Activity but Fewer Fatalities Linked to African Militant Islamist Groups in 2017," January 26, 2018, pp. 1–2, available at https://africacenter.org/spotlight/activity-fewer-fatalities-linked-african-militant-islamist-groups-2017/ (accessed February 5, 2018).

6. Zachary Devlin-Foltz, "Africa's Fragile States: Empowering Extremists, Exporting Terrorism," *Africa Security Brief: A Publication of the Africa Center for Strategic Studies*, no. 6 (August 2010): 2.

7. Terje Østebø, "Islamic Militancy in Africa," *Africa Security Brief: A Publication of the Africa Center for Strategic Studies*, no. 23 (November 2012): 1.

8. Institute for Economics and Peace, "Global Terrorism Index 2017," p. 46.

9. Noel Anderson, "Peacekeepers Fighting a Counterinsurgency Campaign: A Net Assessment of the African Union Mission in Somalia," *Studies in Conflict and Terrorism* 37, no. 11 (November 2014): 936.

10. Central Intelligence Agency, "Somalia," in *The World Factbook* (Washington, DC: Central Intelligence Agency, 2018), available at https://www.cia.gov/library/publications/the-world-factbook/ (accessed May 9, 2018).

11. On Barre's rule and its implications for Somalia, see Mohamed Haji Ingiriis, "How Somalia Works: Mimicry and the Making of Mohamed Siad Barre's Regime in Mogadishu," *Africa Today* 63, no. 1 (Fall 2016): 57–82.

12. On clan violence, see Lidwien Kapteijns, *Clan Cleansing in Somalia: The Ruinous Legacy of 1991* (Philadelphia: University of Pennsylvania Press, 2013).

13. On the UN humanitarian intervention, see Walter Clarke and Jeffrey Herbst, eds., *Learning from Somalia: The Lessons of Armed Humanitarian Intervention* (Boulder, CO: Westview Press, 1997).

14. Ken Menkhaus, "The Crisis in Somalia: Tragedy in Five Acts," *African Affairs* 106, no. 204 (July 2007): 357–390.

15. On al-Shabaab, see Stig Jarle Hansen, *Al-Shabaab in Somalia* (London: Hurst, 2013).

16. Institute for Economics and Peace, "Global Terrorism Index 2017," p. 28.

17. Østebø, "Islamic Militancy in Africa," 5.

18. Abdisaid Musse Ali-Koor, "Islamist Extremism in East Africa," *Africa Security Brief: A Publication of the Africa Center for Strategic Studies*, no. 32 (August 2016): 1, 4.

19. Oscar Gakuo Mwangi, "State Collapse, *Al-Shabaab*, Islamism, and Legitimacy in Somalia," *Politics, Religion, and Ideology* 13, no. 4 (December 2012): 513.

20. Institute for Economics and Peace, "Global Terrorism Index 2017," p. 28.

21. Anderson, "Peacekeepers Fighting a Counterinsurgency Campaign," 943.

22. UN Security Council, "Resolution 1744 (2007)," February 20, 2007, pp. 1–4, available at http://www.un.org/en/ga/search/view_doc.asp?symbol=S/RES/1744(2007) (accessed March 24, 2018).

23. Thomas G. Weiss and Martin Welz, "The UN and the African Union in Mali and Beyond: A Shotgun Wedding?" *International Affairs* 90, no 4 (July 2014): 901.

24. Ali-Koor, "Islamist Extremism in East Africa," 1.

25. "Don't Tinker with Somalia," *Star*, July 14, 2010.

26. Anderson, "Peacekeepers Fighting a Counterinsurgency Campaign," 936.

27. Paul D. Williams, "After Westgate: Opportunities and Challenges in the War against Al-Shabaab," *International Affairs* 90, no. 4 (July 2014): 910.

28. UN Security Council, "Resolution 2102 (2013)," May 2, 2013, pp. 1–4, available at http://www.un.org/en/ga/search/view_doc.asp?symbol=S/RES/2102(2013) (accessed January 15, 2018).

29. Guy Alexander, "Dozens Die as Islamic Militants Attack Kenyan Shopping Mall," *Guardian*, September 21, 2013.

30. Williams, "After Westgate," 908.

31. "Operation Indian Ocean Starts in Galgadud," All Africa, September 1, 2014.

32. Peter Leftie, "Al-Shabaab Leader behind Westgate Attack Believed Killed in U.S. Military Attack," *Daily Nation, Kenya (Nairobi, Kenya)*, September 3, 2014.

33. Institute for Economics and Peace, "Global Terrorism Index 2017," p. 28.

34. "Interior CS [Cabinet Secretary] Joseph Nkaissery Says Garissa Attack Caught Government by 'Surprise,'" *Daily Nation, Kenya (Nairobi, Kenya)*, April 3, 2015.

35. "People Encouraged to Support Major Gains by AMISOM and the Somali National Army," All Africa, August 17, 2015.

36. Mwangi, "State Collapse, *Al-Shabaab*, Islamism, and Legitimacy in Somalia," 520.

37. "General Says Ethiopia Still Controls Al-Shabaab Fight," *Capital (Addis Ababa, Ethiopia)*, November 29, 2016.

38. Institute for Economics and Peace, "Global Terrorism Index 2017," p. 28.

39. Africa Center for Strategic Studies, "More Activity but Fewer Fatalities Linked to African Militant Islamist Groups in 2017," p. 2.

40. "AU Commission Chairperson Congratulates Somalia's President-Elect and Somalis for Democratic and Credible Elections," African Press Organization, February 9, 2017.

41. "With So Much Goodwill, New Somali Leader Should Be Better," *Daily Nation, Kenya (Nairobi, Kenya)*, February 13, 2017.

42. African Union Commission Peace and Security Department, Peace Support Operations Division, "Report of the Ten-Year AMISOM Lessons Learned Conference," March 9–10, 2017, pp. 1–20, available at http://www.peaceau.org/uploads/ll-eng-1.pdf (accessed February 24, 2018).

43. Kevin J. Kelley, "Al-Shabaab Ranked as Africa's Deadliest Militant Group," *Daily Nation, Kenya (Nairobi, Kenya)*, May 1, 2018.

44. On the Biafran War, see Lasse Heerten, *The Biafran War and Postcolonial Humanitarianism: Spectacles of Suffering* (Cambridge: University of Cambridge Press, 2017); R.T. Howard, "Biafra 50 Years On: The Civil War That Resulted from the Division of Nigeria Was a Major Human Disaster That Should Not Be Forgotten," *History Today* 67, no. 6 (June 2017): 36–41; Benjamin Maiangwa, "Revisiting the Nigeria-Biafra War: The Intangibles of Post-War Reconciliation," *International Journal of World Peace* 33, no. 4 (December 2016): 39–67; Marie-Luce Desgrandchamps, "Dealing with 'Genocide': The ICRC and the UN during the Nigeria-Biafra War, 1967–1970," *Journal of Genocide Research* 16, no. 2/3 (July 2014): 281–297; Michael Gould, *The Biafran War: The Struggle for Modern Nigeria* (London: I.B.Tauris, 2013).

45. John Paden, "Religion and Conflict in Nigeria: Countdown to the 2015 Elections," U.S. Institute of Peace Special Report 359, February 2015, p. 2, available at https://www.usip.org/sites/default/files/SR359-Religion-and-Conflict-in-Nigeria.pdf (accessed February 5, 2018).

46. Sophie McBain, "After the Brics, the Mints," *New Statesman* 143, no. 5193 (January 17–23, 2014): 30–31. Jim O'Neill, former chief economist at Goldman Sachs, first used in 2001 the term "BRICS." Although Fidelity Investments coined the term "MINT," O'Neill played a major role in making it widely discussed in economics.

47. Paden, "Religion and Conflict in Nigeria," p. 1.

48. Arnim Langer, Abdul Raufu Mustapha, and Frances Stewart, "Diversity and Discord: Ethnicity, Horizontal Inequalities and Conflict in Ghana and Nigeria," *Journal of International Development* 21, no. 4 (May 2009): 477–482.

49. Central Intelligence Agency, "Nigeria," in *The World Factbook* (Washington, DC: Central Intelligence Agency, 2018), available at https://www.cia.gov/library/publications/the-world-factbook/ (accessed May 9, 2018).

50. Institute for Economics and Peace, "Global Terrorism Index 2017," p. 24. Examples have included the Movement for the Emancipation of the Niger Delta (MEND), as well as Fulani and Ijaw extremists. On Fulani extremism, see p. 76.

51. Ibid., 74.

52. Eeben Barlow, "The Rise and Fall—And Rise Again of Boko Haram," *Harvard International Review* 37, no. 4 (Summer 2016): 16.

53. Oluwakemi Okenyodo, "Governance, Accountability, and Security in Nigeria," *Africa Security Brief: A Publication of the Africa Center for Strategic Studies*, no. 31 (June 2016): 6.

54. William Ehwarieme and Nathaniel Umukoro, "Civil Society and Terrorism in Nigeria: A Study of the Boko Haram Crisis," *International Journal on World Peace* 32, no. 3 (September 2015): 25–26.

55. Marc-Antoine Pérouse de Montclos, "Nigeria's Interminable Insurgency? Addressing the Boko Haram Crisis," Chatham House Research Paper, September 2014, p. 7, available at https://www.chathamhouse.org/sites/files/chatham house/field/field_document/20140901BokoHaramPerousedeMontclos_0.pdf (accessed February 6, 2018).

56. Amnesty International, "Nigeria: Trapped in the Cycle of Violence," November 1, 2012, pp. 18–33, available at https://www.amnesty.org/en/docu ments/afr44/043/2012/en/ (accessed February 7, 2018).

57. Okenyodo, "Governance, Accountability, and Security in Nigeria," 1.

58. Patrick Nanadozie Udefuna, Magnus Emeka Madu, Chiedo Akalefu, and Fadila Jumare, "Effective Community Policing: A Panacea to Inefficiency and Impunity in Nigerian Police," *International Journal of Humanities and Social Science* 4, no. 4 (February 2014): 260–267.

59. Human Rights Watch, "Spiraling Violence: Boko Haram Attacks and Security Force Abuses in Nigeria," October 2012, p. 10, available at https://www.hrw .org/sites/default/files/reports/nigeria1012webwcover_0.pdf (accessed February 7, 2018).

60. Michael Olufemi Sodipo, "Mitigating Radicalism in Northern Nigeria," *Africa Security Brief: A Publication of the Africa Center for Strategic Studies*, no. 26 (August 2013): 1.

61. Ibid.

62. "National Human Rights Commission in Nigeria Gains Independence," States News Service, June 23, 2011. Ghana's Commission for Human Rights and Administrative Justice has achieved some success in this regard.

63. Ehwarieme and Umukoro, "Civil Society and Terrorism in Nigeria," 33.

64. "Hollande Suspects Boko Haram Kidnapped French Tourists," Africa News Service, February 20, 2013.

65. Ronald Mutum, "Senate Approves Emergency Rule after Deliberation," Africa News Service, May 22, 2013.

66. Okenyodo, "Governance, Accountability, and Security in Nigeria," 5; Nina Strochlic, "Nigeria's Do-It-Yourself Boko Haram Busters," *Daily Beast*, May 16, 2014.

67. Human Rights Watch, "Those Terrible Weeks in Their Camp: Boko Haram Violence against Women and Girls in Northeast Nigeria," October 2014, p. 10, available at https://www.hrw.org/sites/default/files/reports/nigeria1014web.pdf (accessed February 7, 2018).

68. U.S. Department of State, "Terrorist Designations of Boko Haram and Ansaru," November 13, 2013, p. 1, available at https://www.state.gov/j/ct/rls/other/des/266565.htm (accessed February 15, 2018). For the complete listing of terrorist organizations, see U.S. Department of State, "Foreign Terrorist Organizations," 2018, https://www.state.gov/j/ct/rls/other/des/123085.htm (accessed May 28, 2018).

69. International Coalition for the Responsibility to Protect, "The Crisis in Nigeria," 2014, p. 1, available at http://www.responsibilitytoprotect.org/index.php/crises/crisis-in-nigeria (accessed on January 24, 2018).

70. "#BringBackOurGirls—World Rises against Boko Haram," Africa News Service, May 9, 2014. On the campaign, see Bring Back Our Girls, "A Call to Action," 2018, pp. 1–2, available at http://www.bringbackourgirls.ng/?page_id=1613 (accessed May 22, 2018).

71. Human Rights Watch, "Those Terrible Weeks in Their Camp," p. 2.

72. "Boko Haram Insurgency and the Blame Game," All Africa, April 15, 2014.

73. "Villagers Killed, Houses Razed as Militants Strike," *Mercury (South Africa)*, May 22, 2014.

74. "Suicide Blast, Second Bomb at Market Kill 82 in Nigeria," *Cape Times (South Africa)*, July 24, 2014.

75. "Nigeria's Jihadists: The Other Caliphate," *Economist*, September 6, 2014.

76. Mohammed Sambo Dasuki, "Challenges of Governance in Era of Insurgency," *People's Daily (Abuja, Nigeria)*, August 11, 2014, pp. 1–6, available at http://www.peoplesdailyng.com/challenges-of-governance-in-era-of-insurgency/ (accessed May 2, 2018).

77. "Out of Control Boko Haram Kills Dozens in Kano Mosque," All Africa, November 29, 2014.

78. Paden, "Religion and Conflict in Nigeria," p. 4.

79. On the impact of Boko Haram and the Nigerian government's response on civil society, see Ehwarieme and Umukoro, "Civil Society and Terrorism in Nigeria," 25–48.

80. Institute for Economics and Peace, "Global Terrorism Index 2015: Measuring and Understanding the Impact of Terrorism," November 2015, p. 4, available at http://visionofhumanity.org/app/uploads/2017/04/2015-Global-Terrorism-Index-Report.pdf (accessed May 3, 2018).

81. Marius Pricopi, "Tactics Used by the Terrorist Organisation Boko Haram," *Scientific Bulletin* 21, no. 1 (June 2016): 40–41.

82. Ibid., 41.

83. Paden, "Religion and Conflict in Nigeria," p. 3.

84. "Boko Haram Claims Baga Attack, Threatens Nigeria Neighbours," *NewsPoint (New Delhi, India)*, January 21, 2015.

85. Central Intelligence Agency, "Nigeria."

86. UN High Commissioner for Refugees, the UN Refugee Agency, "Nigeria Emergency," December 31, 2017, p. 1, available at http://www.unhcr.org/en-us/nigeria-emergency.html?query=boko%20haram (accessed March 6, 2018).

87. Institute for Economics and Peace, "Global Terrorism Index 2017," p. 74.

88. Pérouse de Montclos, "Nigeria's Interminable Insurgency?" p. 5.

89. Kingsley Omonobi and Joseph Erunke, "We're Tired of Senseless Killings, Say Boko Haram Leaders," Africa News Service, August 28, 2017.

90. "Cameroon Targeted by Boko Haram," *Cape Times (South Africa)*, July 28, 2014.

91. Institute for Economics and Peace, "Global Terrorism Index 2017," p. 24.

92. Africa Center for Strategic Studies, "More Activity but Fewer Fatalities Linked to African Militant Islamist Groups in 2017," p. 2.

93. On ISIS-West Africa, see Emmanuel Mayah, "18 New Armed Groups Spring Up in Nigeria," Africa News Service, October 19, 2016.

94. "Boko Haram Insurgency Not Over Yet—UN," All Africa, January 12, 2018.

95. Transparency International, "Corruption Perceptions Index 2016," January 25, 2017, available at https://www.transparency.org/whatwedo/publication/corruption_perceptions_index_2016 (accessed January 22, 2018).

96. "Boko Haram Kills 2,295 Teachers in North-East—Minister," All Africa, May 3, 2018.

97. "Final Desperate Efforts to Crush Boko Haram," All Africa, April 23, 2018.

98. Institute for Economics and Peace, "Global Terrorism Index 2017," pp. 10–13, 16, 19, 43, 46.

99. Africa Center for Strategic Studies, "More Activity but Fewer Fatalities Linked to African Militant Islamist Groups in 2017," pp. 1–2.

100. Institute for Economics and Peace, "Global Terrorism Index 2017," p. 28.

101. Paden, "Religion and Conflict in Nigeria," p. 4.

102. Pricopi, "Tactics Used by the Terrorist Organisation Boko Haram," 40–41; Central Intelligence Agency, "Nigeria."

103. Africa Center for Strategic Studies, "More Activity but Fewer Fatalities Linked to African Militant Islamist Groups in 2017," p. 2.

CHAPTER 6

1. Council on Foreign Relations, "The Global Oceans Regime: Report by International Institutions and Global Governance Program," June 19, 2013, pp. 1–14, available at https://www.cfr.org/report/global-oceans-regime (accessed May 2, 2018).

2. Francois Vreÿ, "Four Hubs of Maritime Insecurity off Africa: From Anti-Piracy to Anti-Crime?" *Acta Criminologica: Southern African Journal of Criminology* 29, no. 2 (2016): 156–171.

3. African Union, "Agenda 2063: The Africa We Want," final ed., April 2015, p. 3, available at http://www.un.org/en/africa/osaa/pdf/au/agenda2063.pdf (accessed February 4, 2018).

4. On piracy in Africa, see Jennifer Lofkrantz and Olatunji Ojo, eds., *Ransoming, Captivity and Piracy in Africa and the Mediterranean* (Trenton, NJ: Africa World Press, 2016).

5. Francois Vreÿ, "African Maritime Security: A Time for Good Order at Sea," *Australian Journal of Maritime and Ocean Affairs* 2, no. 4 (2010): 121.

6. On piracy and maritime security generally, see Maximo Q. Mejia Jr., Chie Kojima, and Mark Sawyer, eds., *Piracy at Sea* (Heidelberg: Springer, 2013); Robert Haywood and Roberta Spivak, *Maritime Piracy* (Abingdon: Routledge, 2012); James Kraska, *Contemporary Maritime Piracy: International Law, Strategy, and Diplomacy at Sea* (Santa Barbara, CA: Praeger, 2011).

7. United Nations, "Convention on the Law of the Sea," December 10, 1982, available at http://www.un.org/depts/los/convention_agreements/texts/unclos/unclos_e.pdf (accessed January 21, 2018).

8. On IMO, see International Maritime Organization, "IMO: What It Is," 2018, available at http://www.imo.org/en/About/Documents/What%20it%20is%20Oct%202013_Web.pdf (accessed May 22, 2018).

9. Ali Kamal-Deen, "The Anatomy of Gulf of Guinea Piracy," *Naval War College Review* 68, no. 1 (Winter 2015): 94.

10. On legal frameworks, see Robin Geiß and Anna Petrig, *Piracy and Armed Robbery at Sea: The Legal Framework for Counter-Piracy Operations in Somalia and the Gulf of Aden* (Oxford: Oxford University Press, 2011).

11. Lisa Otto, "Westward Ho! The Evolution of Maritime Piracy in Nigeria," *Portuguese Journal of Social Science* 13, no. 3 (September 2014): 314.

12. Neil Winn and Alexandra Lewis, "European Union Anti-Piracy Initiatives in the Horn of Africa: Linking Land-Based Counter-Piracy with Maritime Security and Regional Development," *Third World Quarterly* 38, no. 9 (September 2017): 2113–2128.

13. "Nigeria Arms Seizure Causes Alarm," *UPI Security and Terrorism*, October 29, 2010.

14. Gary E. Weir, "Fish, Family, and Profit: Piracy and the Horn of Africa," *Naval War College Review* 62, no. 3 (Summer 2009): 15–30.

15. Jeffrey Gettleman, "Somali Pirates Tell Their Side: They Want Only Money," *New York Times*, October 1, 2008.

16. "UN Agency Launches Assessment of Oil-Contaminated Region in Nigeria," UN News, November 30, 2009, available at https://news.un.org/en/story/2009/11/322792-un-agency-launches-assessment-oil-contaminated-region-nigeria (accessed March 6, 2018).

17. Donna Nincic, "Maritime Piracy in Africa: The Humanitarian Dimension," *African Security Review* 18, no. 3 (September 2009): 2–16.

18. Justin V. Hastings and Sarah G. Phillips, "Maritime Piracy Business Networks and Institutions in Africa," *African Affairs* 114, no. 457 (October 2015): 570.

19. Otto, "Westward Ho!" 316.

20. "Africa: Cutlass Express Military Exercise 2018; Criminal Activities Pose a Big Threat to the Security of Africa's Maritime Environment," African Press Organization, February 2, 2018.

21. "Navy's Frigates and the Somali Pirates," Africa News Service, December 13, 2010.

22. United Nations, "Convention on the Law of the Sea," p. 40.

23. Organization of African Unity, "African Maritime Transport Charter," July 26, 1994, pp. 1–16, available at https://au.int/sites/default/files/treaties/7776-treaty-0017_-_african_maritime_transport_charter_e.pdf (accessed March 7, 2018).

24. African Union, "Revised African Maritime Transport Charter," July 26, 2010, pp. 1–26, available at https://au.int/sites/default/files/treaties/7797-treaty-0041_-_revised_african_maritime_transport_charter_e.pdf (accessed March 7, 2018); "New African Maritime Charter," Algeria Press Service, October 22, 2009.

25. Chatham House, "Maritime Security in the Gulf of Guinea," March 2013, p. 5, available at https://www.chathamhouse.org/sites/files/chathamhouse/public/Research/Africa/0312confreport_maritimesecurity.pdf (accessed January 23, 2018).

26. International Maritime Organization, "Piracy and Armed Robbery against Ships: Maritime Safety Committee 98/15," April 4, 2017, p. 1.

27. Ibid., 2.

28. Francois Vreÿ, "Bad Order at Sea: From the Gulf of Aden to the Gulf of Guinea," *African Security Review* 18, no. 3 (September 2009): 17–30. On piracy and Somalia, see Zoltán Glück, "Piracy and the Production of Security Space," *Environment and Planning D: Society and Space* 33, no. 4 (August 2015): 642–659; Peter Woodward, *Crisis in the Horn of Africa: Politics, Piracy, and the Threat of Terror* (London: I.B.Tauris, 2013); Peter Eichstaedt, *Pirate State: Inside Somalia's Terrorism at Sea* (Chicago: Lawrence Hill, 2010); Martin N. Murphy, *Somalia, the New Barbary? Piracy and Islam in the Horn of Africa* (London: Hurst, 2010).

29. Hastings and Phillips, "Maritime Piracy Business Networks and Institutions in Africa," 555.

30. Lauren Ploch, Chistopher M. Blanchard, Ronald O'Rourke, R. Chuck Mason, and Rawle O. King, "Piracy Off the Horn of Africa," Congressional Research Service Report Prepared for Members and Committees of Congress, April 27, 2011, p. 1.

31. On transnational reactions to piracy in the Gulf of Aden, see Bibi van Ginkel and Frans-Paul van der Putten, eds., *The International Response to Somali Piracy: Challenges and Opportunities* (Leiden: Martinus Nijhoff, 2010).

32. Simon Goodley, "Piracy Is Growing Threat to Trade on the High Seas," *London Evening Standard*, February 11, 2010; "Maersk Alabama Repels Second Pirate Attack: Private Guards Used to Thwart Latest Incident," *Houston Chronicle*, November 19, 2009.

33. "U.S. Navy Holds Six Pirates after Battle," *Daily Post (Lahore, Pakistan)*, April 11, 2010.

34. "Somali Pirates Hijack Yacht with Four Americans on Board," AlArabiya.net, February 18, 2011.

35. Dan McDougall, "There's Treasure in Those Waters," *Sunday Times*, October 9, 2011.

36. UN Security Council, "Resolution 1816 (2008)," June 2, 2008, pp. 1–4, available at http://www.un.org/en/ga/search/view_doc.asp?symbol=S/RES/1816(2008) (accessed February 2, 2018).

37. Christian Kaunert and Kamil Zwolski, "Somalia versus Captain 'Hook': Assessing the EU's Security Actorness in Countering Piracy Off the Horn of Africa," *Cambridge Review of International Affairs* 27, no. 3 (September 2014): 593–612.

38. Carmen Gebhard and Simon J. Smith, "The Two Faces of EU-NATO Cooperation: Counter-Piracy Operations off the Somali Coast," *Cooperation and Conflict* 50, no. 1 (March 2015): 107.

39. On China's engagement in Africa generally, see Chapter 8 of this volume.

40. Andrew S. Erickson and Austin M. Strange, "China's Blue Soft Power: Antipiracy, Engagement, and Image Enhancement," *Naval War College Review* 68, no. 1 (Winter 2015): 74.

41. Chris Rowan, "The China-Africa Partnership: Working for Whom?" *Contemporary Review* 291, no. 1692 (Spring 2009): 63.

42. Marc Lanteigne, "Fire over Water: China's Strategic Engagement of Somalia and the Gulf of Aden Crisis," *Pacific Review* 26, no. 3 (July 2013): 291.

43. Erickson and Strange, "China's Blue Soft Power," 75.

44. Susanne Kamerling and Frans-Paul van der Putten, "An Overseas Naval Presence without Overseas Bases: China's Counter-Piracy Operation in the Gulf of Aden," *Journal of Current Chinese Affairs* 40, no. 4 (2011): 128.

45. Ibid., 138.

46. Erickson and Strange, "China's Blue Soft Power," 71–72.

47. Christopher P. Cavas, "The Chinese Navy Saves the Day!" *U.S. Naval Institute Proceedings* 144, no. 3 (March 2018): 1–2, available at https://www.usni.org/maga zines/proceedings/2018-03/chinese-navy-saves-day (accessed June 16, 2018).

48. International Maritime Organization, "Piracy and Armed Robbery against Ships," p. 3.

49. Ibid., 3–4. The 12 signatories were Comoros, Djibouti, Ethiopia, Jordan, Madagascar, Maldives, Mozambique, Saudi Arabia, Seychelles, United Arab Emirates, United Republic of Tanzania, and Yemen.

50. "Somali Pirates Strike Again," *Mercury (South Africa)*, February 28, 2018.

51. Adeniyi Adejimi Osinowo, "Combating Piracy in the Gulf of Guinea," *Africa Security Brief: A Publication of the Africa Center for Strategic Studies*, no. 30 (February 2015): 1.

52. Marc-Antoine Pérouse de Montclos, "Maritime Piracy in Nigeria: Old Wine in New Bottles?" *Studies in Conflict and Terrorism* 35, no. 7/8 (July/August 2012): 531–541.

53. Osinowo, "Combating Piracy in the Gulf of Guinea," 1.

54. Vreÿ, "African Maritime Security," 123.

55. Nigerian National Petroleum Corporation, "Oil Production," 2018, p. 1, available at http://nnpcgroup.com/NNPCBusiness/UpstreamVentures/OilPro duction.aspx (accessed March 9, 2018).

56. Hastings and Phillips, "Maritime Piracy Business Networks and Institutions in Africa," 555.

57. Osinowo, "Combating Piracy in the Gulf of Guinea," 2.

58. Council of the European Union, "EU Strategy on the Gulf of Guinea," March 17, 2014, p. 4. In 2013, the International Maritime Bureau reported 234 global maritime incidents, 30 of which occurred off the coast of Nigeria; therefore, the actual percentage was 12.82.

59. Osinowo, "Combating Piracy in the Gulf of Guinea," 3.

60. UN Office on Drugs and Crime, "Transnational Organized Crime in West Africa: A Threat Assessment," February 2013, pp. 1–62, available at http://www .unodc.org/documents/data-and-analysis/tocta/West_Africa_TOCTA_2013_ EN.pdf (accessed January 21, 2018).

61. Sayed M. Hasan and Daud Hassan, "Current Arrangements to Combat Piracy in the Gulf of Guinea Region: An Evaluation," *Journal of Maritime Law and Commerce* 47, no. 2 (April 2016): 171–217.

62. Gulf of Guinea Commission, "Treaty Establishing the Gulf of Guinea Commission," July 3, 2001, pp. 1–17, available at http://cggrps.org/wp-content/up loads/Tratado-EN1.pdf (accessed February 2, 2018).

63. On the commission, see "The Gulf of Guinea Commission," 2018, p. 1, available at http://cggrps.org/en/the-gulf-of-guinea-commission/ (accessed May 16, 2018).

64. Emmanuel Kendemeh, "Fosters Bonds of Integration in Kinshasa," *Cameroon Tribune (Yaounde, Cameroon)*, October 27, 2009.

65. UN Security Council, "Resolution 2018 (2011)," October 31, 2011, pp. 1–3, available at http://www.un.org/en/ga/search/view_doc.asp?symbol=S/RES/2018 (2011) (accessed February 2, 2018).

66. UN Security Council, "Report of the United Nations Assessment Mission on Piracy in the Gulf of Guinea," January 19, 2012, p. 3, available at http:// www.securitycouncilreport.org/atf/cf/%7B65BFCF9B-6D27-4E9C-8CD3-CF6E4FF96FF9%7D/AUUN%20S%202012%2045.pdf (accessed January 25, 2018).

67. UN Security Council, "Resolution 2039 (2012)," February 29, 2012, pp. 1–3, available at http://www.un.org/en/ga/search/view_doc.asp?symbol=S/RES/ 2039(2012) (accessed February 2, 2018).

68. Timothy Walker, "Maritime Security in West Africa," *African Security Review* 22, no. 2 (June 2013): 85–91.

69. "Angola Hosts Conference on Gulf of Guinea Peace and Security," *Malaysian Government News*, November 30, 2012; Gulf of Guinea Commission, "Luanda Declaration on Peace and Security in the Gulf of Guinea Region," November 29, 2012, pp. 1–7, available at http://cggrps.org/wp-content/uploads/ DeclaracaodeLuanda-29NOV2012EN.pdf (accessed February 2, 2018).

70. Gulf of Guinea Commission, "Declaration of the Heads of State and Government of Central and West African States on Maritime Safety and Security in Their Common Maritime Domain," June 25, 2013, pp. 1–7, available at http:// cggrps.org/wp-content/uploads/DECLARACAO-DE-YAOUNDE-EN.pdf (accessed February 2, 2018).

71. "President Underlines Importance of Gulf of Guinea Commission," Angola Press Agency (Luanda, Angola), August 10, 2013.

72. Alastair Craig, "Keeping Peace on the Piracy-Hit Seas," *Journal*, June 6, 2012.

73. Peter Clottey, "West African Leaders to Meet in Ivory Coast," Africa News Service, March 28, 2014.

74. Council of the European Union, "EU Strategy on the Gulf of Guinea," p. 2.

75. On the MTISC-GOG, see NATO Allied Maritime Command, "The Maritime Trade Information Sharing Centre-Gulf of Guinea (MTISC-GOG)," June 20, 2016, p. 1, available at https://www.shipping.nato.int/nsc/operations/news/2016/ the-maritime-trade-information-sharing-centre-gulf-of-guinea-mtiscgog.aspx (accessed March 9, 2018). In June 2016, the Maritime Domain Awareness for Trade-Gulf of Guinea (MDAT-GOG) replaced the MTISC-GOG.

76. International Maritime Organization, "Piracy and Armed Robbery against Ships," pp. 1–2. The South China Sea was the other major body of water menaced, recording 68 incidents in 2016.

77. "NIMASA Charges ECOWAS to Eradicate Maritime Piracy," *Nigerian Tribune (Oyo State, Nigeria)*, November 24, 2016.

78. Africa Research Bulletin, "Gulf of Guinea Anti-Piracy Network," *Political, Social, and Cultural Series* 54, no. 6 (July 2017): 21457–21458.

79. On drug and human trafficking in the Gulf of Guinea, see UN Office for West Africa and the Sahel, "Drug Trafficking and Organised Crime," p. 1, available at https://unowas.unmissions.org/drug-trafficking-and-organised-crime (accessed March 9, 2018).

80. Muhammad Bello, "Piracy on the Rise in the Gulf of Guinea," Africa News Service, April 16, 2018. During the first three months of 2018, pirates fired on 11 ships worldwide, of which 8 vessels were off the coast of Nigeria.

81. Nincic, "Maritime Piracy in Africa," 7.

82. Sean Patrick Mahard, "Blackwater's New Battlefield: Toward a Regulatory Regime in the United States for Privately Armed Contractors Operating at Sea," *Vanderbilt Journal of Transnational Law* 47, no. 1 (January 2014): 331–369.

83. Oceans beyond Piracy, "The State of Maritime Piracy 2014," June 8, 2015, p. 41, available at http://oceansbeyondpiracy.org/sites/default/files/attach ments/StateofMaritimePiracy2014.pdf (accessed January 21, 2018).

84. Fund for Peace, "Fragile States Index 2017—Annual Report," May 14, 2017, p. 37, available at http://fundforpeace.org/fsi/2017/05/14/fragile-states-index-2017-annual-report/ (accessed January 24, 2018). Only South Sudan ranked worse, with a score of 113.9.

85. Ibid., 38–41.

86. UN Development Programme, "Human Development Report 2016: Human Development for Everyone," 2016, pp. 200, 204, 271, available at http://hdr .undp.org/sites/default/files/2016_human_development_report.pdf (accessed March 17, 2018).

87. Transparency International, "Corruption Perceptions Index 2017," February 15, 2018, p. 5, available at https://www.transparency.org/whatwedo/publi cation/corruption_perceptions_index_2017 (accessed March 15, 2018).

88. Fund for Peace, "Fragile States Index 2017—Annual Report," pp. 40–41.

89. Council on Foreign Relations, "The Global Oceans Regime," pp. 1–14.

90. International Maritime Organization, "Piracy and Armed Robbery against Ships," pp. 1–2.

CHAPTER 7

1. Food and Agriculture Organization, International Fund for Agricultural Development, UNICEF, World Food Programme, and World Health Organization, "The State of Food Security and Nutrition in the World: Building Resilience for Peace and Security," 2017, p. ii, available at http://www.fao.org/3/a-I7695E.pdf (accessed May 7, 2018).

2. Ibid.

3. O. P. Godwin, "Embracing the Challenges for Africa," *Environment* 44, no. 4 (May 2002): 10.

4. Food and Agriculture Organization, "Definitions and Classification of Commodities: Pulses and Derived Products," 2015, p. 1, available at http://www .fao.org/es/faodef/fdef04e.htm (assessed January 24, 2018).

5. Food and Agriculture Organization, "Crop Prospects and Food Situation: Quarterly Global Report," December 2017, p. 4, available at http://www.fao .org/3/a-i8278e.pdf (accessed January 6, 2018).

6. Steven Haggblade, "Unscrambling Africa: Regional Requirements for Achieving Food Security," *Development Policy Review* 31, no. 2 (March 2013): 149–176.

7. Godwin, "Embracing the Challenges for Africa," 13.

8. Food and Agriculture Organization, International Fund for Agricultural Development, UNICEF, World Food Programme, and World Health Organization, "The State of Food Security and Nutrition in the World: Building Resilience for Peace and Security," p. 7.

9. J.R. McNeill, *Something New under the Sun: An Environmental History of the Twentieth-Century World* (New York: W. W. Norton, 2000), 283–286.

10. UN Department of Economic and Social Affairs, Population Division, "World Urbanization Prospects: The 2014 Revision," 2015, p. 11, available at https://esa.un.org/unpd/wup/Publications/Files/WUP2014-Report.pdf (accessed January 23, 2018).

11. World Health Organization, "Millennium Development Goals (MDGs)," 2018, p. 1, available at http://www.who.int/topics/millennium_development_goals/about/en/ (accessed March 17, 2018).

12. United Nations, "The Millennium Development Goals Report," 2015, p. 20, available at http://www.un.org/millenniumgoals/2015_MDG_Report/pdf/MDG%202015%20rev%20(July%201).pdf (accessed March 26, 2018).

13. Food and Agriculture Organization, "Regional Overview of Food Insecurity, Africa: African Food Security Prospects Brighter Than Ever," 2015, p. 1.

14. Ibid.

15. Ibid., 1–2.

16. ReGina Jane Jere, "How Africa Can Feed Itself: Beyond Food Aid and Corporate Greed," *New African*, no. 537 (March 2014): 8–9.

17. Africa Center for Strategic Studies, "Conflict and Famine in South Sudan," March 20, 2017, pp. 1–2, available at https://africacenter.org/spotlight/conflict-and-famine-in-south-sudan/ (accessed February 9, 2018).

18. Food and Agriculture Organization, "Malawi Country Programme Framework, 2014–2017," April 28, 2014, p. 7, available at http://www.fao.org/3/a-bp619e.pdf (accessed February 9, 2018).

19. On CAADP, see Charles Nhemachena, Greenwell Matchaya, and Sibusiso Nhlengethwa, "Strengthening Mutual Accountability and Performance in Agriculture in Southern Africa," *South African Journal of Science* 113, no. 5/6 (May/June 2017): 50–56.

20. Jere, "How Africa Can Feed Itself," 10.

21. Nouman Keith, "Global Food Crisis Response Program: A World Bank Initiative for Food Security and Hunger Fight," *Scholedge International Journal of Multidisciplinary and Allied Studies* 2, no. 10 (October 2015): 5–10.

22. "Washington: New Alliance for Food Security and Nutrition," *U.S. Official News*, May 24, 2012.

23. African Union, "Food Security," 2018, p. 1, available at https://www.au.int/web/en/auc/priorities/food-security (accessed May 16, 2018).

24. Nature Conservancy, "Sub-Saharan Africa's Urban Water Blueprint: Securing Water through Water Funds and Other Investments in Ecological Infrastructure," August 2016, pp. 1–19, available at https://thought-leadership-production.s3.amazonaws.com/2016/08/24/20/30/36/9c3def4a-36d5-42f3-a844-a3df1f0e6d01/Urban_Water_Blueprint_Region_Africa_Aug2016.pdf (accessed May 7, 2018).

25. African Union, "Food Security," p. 1.

26. Ibid., 3.

27. Lisa F. Clark, "Implementing Multilevel Food and Nutrition Security Frameworks in Sub-Saharan Africa: Challenges and Opportunities for Scaling Up Pulses in Ethiopia," *Journal of Rural Social Sciences* 32, no. 1 (2017): 56.

28. Food and Agriculture Organization, "FAO Calls for Renewed Commitment to Get Africa Back on Track to Eliminate Hunger," January 27, 2018, p. 1, available at http://www.fao.org/news/story/en/item/1099215/icode/ (accessed February 15, 2018).

29. On the Italian occupation, see G. Bruce Strang, *Collision of Empires: Italy's Invasion of Ethiopia and Its International Impact* (Farnham: Ashgate, 2013).

30. Jeffrey Meyers, "Abyssinia out of the Shadows," *History Today* 65, no. 11 (November 2015): 49–54.

31. Central Intelligence Agency, "Ethiopia," in *The World Factbook* (Washington, DC: Central Intelligence Agency, 2018), available at https://www.cia.gov/library/publications/the-world-factbook/ (accessed May 9, 2018).

32. World Bank, "Ethiopia Country Overview," October 30, 2017, pp. 1–2, available at http://www.worldbank.org/en/country/ethiopia/overview (accessed February 16, 2018). Ethiopia's per capita income has been approximately $660 per year.

33. Food and Agriculture Organization, "Ethiopia and FAO: Partnering to Achieve Sustainable Agricultural Growth and Food Security," 2016, p. 1, available at http://www.fao.org/3/a-au242e.pdf (accessed February 15, 2018).

34. On the famine, see Peter Gill, *A Year in the Death of Africa: Politics, Bureaucracy, and the Famine* (London: Picador, 1986). On events since the famine, see Peter Gill, *Famine and Foreigners: Ethiopia since Live Aid* (Oxford: University of Oxford Press, 2010).

35. World Bank, "Ethiopia Country Overview," pp. 1–2. The regional average has been 5.4 percent.

36. Food and Agriculture Organization Food and Agriculture Policy Decision Analysis, "Country Fact Sheet on Food and Agriculture Policy Trends, Ethiopia," October 2014, p. 1, available at http://www.fao.org/3/a-i4181e.pdf (accessed February 16, 2018).

37. Intergovernmental Authority on Development Center for Pastoral Areas and Livestock Development, "The Contribution of Livestock to the Ethiopian Economy," 2013, pp. 1–4, available at https://igad.int/attachments/714_ETHIOPIA%20BRIEF%20(1).pdf (accessed February 16, 2018).

38. Food and Agriculture Organization Representation in Ethiopia and Government of Ethiopia, "Country Programming Framework for Ethiopia, 2016–2020," 2017, p. 4, available at http://www.fao.org/3/a-i7527e.pdf (accessed February 16, 2018). On maize, see Food and Agriculture Organization, "Analysis of Price Incentives for Maize in Ethiopia for the Time Period 2005–2012," February 2015, pp. i–vi, 1–48, available at http://www.fao.org/3/a-i4527e.pdf (accessed February 16, 2018).

39. Jere, "How Africa Can Feed Itself," 13.

40. Figure 1.1, "Growth of Real Per Capita GDP in Malawi and Selected Benchmark Countries in Sub-Saharan Africa, 1990–2015," in Richard Record, Praveen Kumar, and Priscilla Kandoole, "From Falling Behind to Catching Up: A Country

Economic Memorandum for Malawi," World Bank Directions in Development, 2018, p. 2, available at https://openknowledge.worldbank.org/bitstream/han dle/10986/28683/9781464811944.pdf?sequence=2&isAllowed=y (accessed February 17, 2018).

41. Food and Agriculture Organization Food and Agriculture Policy Decision Analysis, "Country Fact Sheet on Food and Agriculture Policy Trends, Ethiopia," p. 1. On underweight, stunting, and wasting indicators, see World Health Organization, "Nutrition Landscape Information System (NLIS) Country Profile Indicators Interpretation Guide," 2010, pp. 1–3, available at http://www.who.int/ nutrition/nlis_interpretation_guide.pdf (accessed February 16, 2018).

42. World Bank, "Ethiopia Country Overview," pp. 1–2.

43. Ibrahim Worku Hassen, Mekdim Dereje, Bart Minten, and Kalle Hirvonen, "Diet Transformation in Africa: The Case of Ethiopia," *Agricultural Economics* 48, no. 1 (November 2017): 84.

44. L. Hammond and D. Maxwell, "The Ethiopian Crisis of 1999–2000: Lessons Learned, Questions Unanswered," *Disasters* 26, no. 3 (September 2002): 262–279.

45. World Bank, "Improving Food Security in Ethiopia," February 3, 2016, p. 1, available at http://www.worldbank.org/en/news/video/2016/02/03/ improving-food-security-in-ethiopia (accessed February 16, 2018). Those Ethiopians unable to work have received direct support.

46. On the PIF, see Mafa Chipeta, Bezabih Emana, and Demese Chanyalew, "Ethiopia's Agriculture Sector Policy and Investment Framework (2010–2020) External Mid-Term Review," October 2015, available at http://www.agri-learning-ethiopia.org/wp-content/uploads/2015/10/Agriculture-Policy-MTR_FINAL. pdf (accessed March 26, 2018).

47. Food and Agriculture Organization Representation in Ethiopia and Government of Ethiopia, "Country Programming Framework for Ethiopia, 2016–2020," p. 2.

48. Federal Democratic Republic of Ethiopia, Ministry of Labour and Social Affairs, "National Social Protection Policy of Ethiopia, Final Draft," March 26, 2012, pp. 1–24, available at http://phe-ethiopia.org/resadmin/uploads/attach ment-188-Ethiopia_National_Social_Protection.pdf (accessed February 16, 2018).

49. "African Leaders Set 2025 Target to End Hunger," *South African Official News (Pretoria, South Africa)*, July 2, 2013. On the Lula Institute, see Lula Institute, "What Is the Lula Institute and What Does It Do," July 14, 2016, pp. 1–4, available at http://www.institutolula.org/what-is-the-lula-institute-and-what-does-it-do (accessed March 18, 2018).

50. Food and Agriculture Organization, "Ethiopia and FAO," p. 1.

51. African Union, "Malabo Declaration on Accelerated Agricultural Growth and Transformation for Shared Prosperity and Improved Livelihoods," June 26–27, 2014, pp. 3–4, available at https://au.int/sites/default/files/ documents/31006-doc-malabo_declaration_2014_11_26-.pdf (accessed February 15, 2018).

52. Ibid., 4.

53. Food and Agriculture Organization Representation in Ethiopia and Government of Ethiopia, "Country Programming Framework for Ethiopia, 2016–2020," p. 3.

54. Ibid., 4.

55. Ibid., 5.

56. Food and Agriculture Organization, "Crop Prospects and Food Situation," p. 5.

57. Boaz Blackie Keizire, "What Does Africa Need?" *African Business*, no. 400 (August/September 2013): 39.

58. Food and Agriculture Organization Food and Agriculture Policy Decision Analysis, "Country Fact Sheet on Food and Agriculture Policy Trends, Ethiopia," p. 3.

59. Clark, "Implementing Multilevel Food and Nutrition Security Frameworks in Sub-Saharan Africa," 70.

60. Hassen, Dereje, Minten, and Hirvonen, "Diet Transformation in Africa," 84.

61. Food and Agriculture Organization, "Ethiopia and FAO," p. 2.

62. Food and Agriculture Organization Representation in Ethiopia and Government of Ethiopia, "Country Programming Framework for Ethiopia, 2016–2020," p. vii.

63. African Union, "Statement of the Chairperson of the Commission of the African Union on the Situation in Ethiopia," February 21, 2018, p. 1, available at http://www.peaceau.org/uploads/statement-of-the-chairperson-on-the-situation-in-ethiopia.pdf (accessed February 24, 2018).

64. Food and Agriculture Organization Food and Agriculture Policy Decision Analysis, "Country Fact Sheet on Food and Agriculture Policy Trends, Ethiopia," p. 1.

65. UN Development Programme, "Human Development Report 2016: Human Development for Everyone," 2016, pp. 200–201, available at http://hdr.undp.org/sites/default/files/2016_human_development_report.pdf (accessed March 17, 2018).

66. International Food Policy Research Institute, "Global Hunger Index 2017: The Inequalities of Hunger," October 2017, p. 13, available at http://ebrary.ifpri.org/utils/getfile/collection/p15738coll2/id/131422/filename/131628.pdf (accessed March 17, 2018).

67. "Growing Unrest in Ethiopia and What It Means for Gulf Food Security," AlArabiya.net, February 26, 2018.

68. "Ethiopia Says Nearly 7.9 Million People Need Emergency Food Aid," Xinhua News Agency, March 13, 2018.

69. UN Development Programme, "Human Development Report 2016," pp. 204, 271.

70. Food and Agriculture Organization, "Malawi Country Programme Framework, 2014–2017," p. 7.

71. Record, Kumar, and Kandoole, "From Falling Behind to Catching Up," pp. 8–9.

72. World Bank, "Malawi Country Profile," 2016, p. 1, available at http://databank.worldbank.org/data/views/reports/reportwidget.aspx?Report_Name=CountryProfile&Id=b450fd57&tbar=y&dd=y&inf=n&zm=n&country=MWI (accessed March 26, 2018).

73. Transparency International, "Corruption Perceptions Index 2017," February 15, 2018, pp. 4–5, available at https://www.transparency.org/whatwedo/publication/corruption_perceptions_index_2017 (accessed March 18, 2018).

74. Food and Agriculture Organization, "Malawi Country Programme Framework, 2014–2017," p. 4.

75. Andrew Dorward and Jonathan Kydd, "The Malawi 2002 Food Crisis: The Rural Development Challenge," *Journal of Modern African Studies* 42, no. 3 (September 2004): 358–359.

76. Paul Justice Kamlongera, "Making the Poor 'Poorer' or Alleviating Poverty? Artisanal Mining Livelihoods in Rural Malawi," *Journal of International Development* 23, no. 8 (November 2011): 1131–1132.

77. Dorward and Kydd, "The Malawi 2002 Food Crisis," 347.

78. Central Intelligence Agency, "Malawi," in *The World Factbook* (Washington, DC: Central Intelligence Agency, 2018), available at https://www.cia.gov/library/publications/the-world-factbook/ (accessed May 9, 2018). On Cashgate, see Jimmy Kainja, "Malawi: Will 'Cashgate' Sink Joyce Banda?" *New African*, no. 538 (April 2014): 54–55.

79. Liam Riley, "Operation Dongosolo and the Geographies of Urban Poverty in Malawi," *Journal of Southern African Studies* 40, no. 3 (May 2014): 444.

80. Ibid.

81. "Mining and Energy," *Foreign Affairs* 94, no. 2 (March 2015): 12–13.

82. Human Rights Watch, "They Destroyed Everything: Mining and Human Rights in Malawi," September 2016, p. 5, available at https://www.hrw.org/sites/default/files/report_pdf/malawi0916_web.pdf (accessed February 7, 2018).

83. Ibid., 12.

84. Extractive Industries Transparency Initiative, "Malawi," 2018, available at https://eiti.org/malawi (accessed May 22, 2018).

85. Kamlongera, "Making the Poor 'Poorer' or Alleviating Poverty?" 1131.

86. Food and Agriculture Organization Representation in Malawi and the Government of the Republic of Malawi, "National Medium-Term Priority Framework (NMTPF), 2010–2015," April 2010, available at http://www.fao.org/3/a-bp620e.pdf (accessed February 10, 2018).

87. Food and Agriculture Organization, "Malawi Country Programme Framework, 2014–2017," p. 4.

88. Ciugu Mwagiru, "Mutharika's Triumph Ended Convoluted Charade," *Daily Nation, Kenya (Nairobi, Kenya)*, May 31, 2014. The exact percentage was 36.4.

89. Anna Cox, "SA [South African] Lifeline for Flood-Hit Malawi; Mad Dash to Help 200,000 Displaced, More Rain Expected," *Star (South Africa)*, January 20, 2015.

90. World Bank, "Malawi Country Profile," p. 1.

91. World Bank, "Malawi Country Overview," October 10, 2017, pp. 1–2, available at http://www.worldbank.org/en/country/malawi/overview (accessed February 17, 2018).

92. Record, Kumar, and Kandoole, "From Falling Behind to Catching Up," p. 1. See especially Figure 1.1, "Growth of Real Per Capita GDP in Malawi and Selected Benchmark Countries in Sub-Saharan Africa, 1990–2015."

93. World Bank, "Malawi Country Overview," pp. 1–2.

94. World Bank, "How to Harness the Benefits of Urbanization for More Economic Growth Overall," June 1, 2017, pp. 1–2, available at http://www.worldbank.org/en/country/malawi/publication/malawi-economic-monitor-how-to-harness-the-benefits-of-urbanization-for-more-economic-growth-overall (accessed February 17, 2018).

95. Record, Kumar, and Kandoole, "From Falling Behind to Catching Up," pp. 14–20. See especially Figure 2.8, "Inflation Rate in Malawi, 1980–2015," p. 15.

96. "Hunger Rates Remain High amid Conflict, Climate Shocks, Warns UN Food Security Report," *Premium Official News*, March 6, 2018. The FAO highlighted 37 total countries worldwide; 29 of them were in Africa, including Ethiopia and Malawi.

97. "Poor Rains, Fall Armyworm Leaves Southern Africa Vulnerable; Early Action Crucial to Avert Crisis," African Press Organization, February 12, 2018.

98. "No One Will Die of Hunger in the Country—Chilima," All Africa, April 11, 2018.

99. Food and Agriculture Organization, International Fund for Agricultural Development, UNICEF, World Food Programme, and World Health Organization, "The State of Food Security and Nutrition in the World: Building Resilience for Peace and Security," p. ii.

100. Food and Agriculture Organization, "Crop Prospects and Food Situation," p. 4.

101. Food and Agriculture Organization, International Fund for Agricultural Development, UNICEF, World Food Programme, and World Health Organization, "The State of Food Security and Nutrition in the World: Building Resilience for Peace and Security," pp. ii, 2, 7.

102. World Bank, "Ethiopia Country Overview," pp. 1–2.

103. Jere, "How Africa Can Feed Itself," 13.

104. UN Development Programme, "Human Development Report 2016," pp. 204, 271; Food and Agriculture Organization, "Malawi Country Programme Framework, 2014–2017," p. 7.

CHAPTER 8

1. On Africa's increased prominence in international relations, see John W. Harbeson and Donald Rothchild, eds., *Africa in World Politics: Constructing Political and Economic Order*, 6th ed. (Boulder, CO: Westview Press, 2017); William Brown and Sophie Harman, eds., *African Agency in International Politics* (Abingdon: Routledge, 2013).

2. World Economic Forum, "These Will Be Africa's Fastest Growing Economies in 2018," January 16, 2018, pp. 1–2, available at https://www.weforum.org/agenda/2018/01/what-does-2018-hold-for-african-economies (accessed February 25, 2018). The other four countries were India (7.3 percent), Cambodia (6.9 percent), Bhutan (6.9 percent), and the Philippines (6.7 percent).

3. Michael Asiedu, "Turkey as a Development Partner in Africa," Global Political Trends Center Policy Brief no. 44, October 2016, p. 3.

4. Isaac Fokuo, "Fresh Opportunities for Africa in a Multipolar World," *African Business* 51, no. 442 (June 2017): 42.

5. World Bank, "Doing Business 2018: Reforming to Create Jobs, Comparing Business Regulation for Domestic Firms in 190 Economies," A World Bank Group Flagship Report, 15th ed., 2018, pp. 1–3, available at http://www.doingbusiness.org/~/media/WBG/DoingBusiness/Documents/Annual-Reports/English/DB2018-Full-Report.pdf (accessed February 26, 2018). See especially Figure 1.1, "What Is Measured in *Doing Business*?" p. 2. Labor market regulation was not included in the ease of doing business ranking. On methodology, see pp. 11–21.

6. World Economic Forum, "African Nations Are Powering Up the Business Rankings: What Lessons Can We Learn from Them?" November 14, 2017, p. 1, available at https://www.weforum.org/agenda/2017/11/african-countries-power-up-the-world-banks-business-rankings/ (accessed February 26, 2018).

7. Jim O'Neill, "The MINT Countries: Next Economic Giants?" BBC News, January 6, 2014.

8. Scarlett Cornelissen, "Awkward Embraces: Emerging and Established Powers and the Shifting Fortunes of Africa's International Relations in the Twenty-First Century," *Politikon* 36, no. 1 (April 2009): 5–26.

9. World Economic Forum, "African Nations Are Powering Up the Business Rankings," p. 3.

10. Paul D. Williams, "Thinking about Security in Africa," *International Affairs* 83, no. 6 (November 2007): 1025.

11. World Economic Forum, "These Will Be Africa's Fastest Growing Economies in 2018," p. 2.

12. World Bank, "Doing Business 2018: Reforming to Create Jobs, Comparing Business Regulation for Domestic Firms in 190 Economies," p. 1.

13. David Thomas, "We See Africa as a Bright Spot," *African Business* 50, no. 433 (August/September 2016): 16.

14. Nicholas J. White, "The Settlement of Decolonization and Post-Colonial Economic Development: Indonesia, Malaysia, and Singapore Compared," *Journal of the Humanities and Social Sciences of Southeast Asia and Oceania* 173, no. 2 (April 2017): 208–241.

15. Thomas, "We See Africa as a Bright Spot," 16–17. Only 212,500 Singaporeans worked abroad in 2015.

16. "Brazil–Africa Relations: Bridging the Atlantic Gap," *African Business* 48, no. 412 (October 2014): 90. On Lula, see Richard Bourne, *Lula of Brazil: The Story So Far* (Berkeley: University of California Press, 2008).

17. "Brazil–Africa Relations," 90.

18. Baffour Ankomah, "Turkey and Africa Pledge Co-Operation," *New African*, no. 567 (December 2016): 76–78.

19. Asiedu, "Turkey as a Development Partner in Africa," p. 1.

20. "President Erdogan's Africa Visit," *Turkish Government News*, November 18, 2014.

21. Asiedu, "Turkey as a Development Partner in Africa," p. 2. Turkey has maintained an additional 26 commercial consulates on the continent.

22. Grant T. Harris, "Why Africa Matters to US National Security," Atlantic Council Africa Center and OCP Policy Center, May 2017, p. 25, available at http://www.atlanticcouncil.org/images/publications/Why_Africa_Matters_to_US_National_Security_0524_web.pdf (accessed May 7, 2018).

23. José de Arimatéia Da Cruz and Laura K. Stephens, "The U.S. Africa Command (AFRICOM): Building Partnership or Neo-Colonialism of U.S.–Africa Relations?" *Journal of Third World Studies* 27, no. 2 (Fall 2010): 194. On U.S. foreign policy in Africa, see Adebayo Oyebade, ed., *The United States' Foreign Policy in Africa in the 21st Century: Issues and Perspectives* (Durham, NC: Carolina Academic, 2014).

24. Fokuo, "Fresh Opportunities for Africa in a Multipolar World," 42.

25. Lina Benabdallah, "China's Peace and Security Strategies in Africa: Building Capacity Is Building Peace?" *African Studies Quarterly* 16, no. 3/4 (December 2016): 17–34; Chuka Enuka, "China's Military Presence in Africa: Implications for Africa's Woobling Peace," *Journal of Asia Pacific Studies* 2, no. 1 (May 2011): 97–118.

26. Sophie Harman and William Brown, "In from the Margins? The Changing Place of Africa in International Relations," *International Affairs* 89, no. 1
(January 2013): 80.

27. On the United States and security in Africa, see Robert J. Griffiths, *U.S. Security Cooperation with Africa: Political and Policy Challenges* (Abingdon: Routledge,
2016).

28. Robert Albro, "Anthropology and the Military: AFRICOM, 'Culture' and
Future of Human Terrain Analysis," *Anthropology Today* 26, no. 1 (February 2010):
22–24.

29. Carla E. Humud, "Al Qaeda and U.S. Policy: Middle East and Africa," Congressional Research Service Report Prepared for Members and Committees of
Congress, August 11, 2016, pp. 1–25.

30. John P. Banks, George Ingram, Mwangi Kimenyi, Steven Rocker, Witney
Schneidman, Yun Sun, and Lesley Anne Warner, "Top Five Reasons Why Africa
Should Be a Priority for the United States," Africa Growth Initiative at Brookings,
March 2013, pp. 1–16, available at https://www.brookings.edu/wp-content/up
loads/2016/06/04_africa_priority_united_states.pdf (accessed May 2, 2018).

31. Thomas Lum, Hannah Fischer, Julissa Gomez-Granger, and Anne Leland,
"China's Foreign Aid Activities in Africa, Latin America, and Southeast Asia,"
Congressional Research Service Report Prepared for Members and Committees of
Congress, February 25, 2009, pp. 1–25.

32. U.S. Africa Command, "United States Africa Command 2017 Posture
Statement," March 9, 2017, p. 2, available at http://www.africom.mil/Tags/
annual-posture-statement (accessed February 12, 2018).

33. Robert Gates, "Defense Secretary Gates Announces Creation of U.S.
Africa Command," February 6, 2007, p. 1, available at http://www.africom
.mil/media-room/transcript/7804/transcript-defense-secretary-gates-announ
ces-creat (accessed May 2, 2018). There are nine U.S. Combatant Commands, including six geographic ones and three functional ones. The geographic combatant
commands are Africa Command (AFRICOM), Central Command (CENTCOM),
European Command (EUCOM), Northern Command (NORTHCOM), Pacific
Command (PACOM), and Southern Command (SOUTHCOM). The functional
combatant commands are Special Operations Command (SOCOM), Transportation Command (TRANSCOM), and Strategic Command (STRATCOM). On combatant commands, see Cynthia Watson, *Combatant Commands: Origins, Structure,
and Engagements* (Santa Barbara, CA: Praeger, 2010).

34. U.S. Africa Command, "African Union, USAID, State Department Officials Speak at U.S. Africa Command Establishment Ceremony," October 17, 2008,
pp. 1–8, available at http://www.africom.mil/media-room/transcript/6340/
transcript-african-union-usaid-state-department-of (accessed May 2, 2018).

35. William E. Ward, "Engaging AFRICOM," *Military Technology* 33, no. 1
(January 2009): 298. U.S. Marine Corps general Thomas D. Waldhauser assumed
command on July 18, 2016; U.S. Army general David M. Rodriguez oversaw AF-
RICOM from April 5, 2013, to July 18, 2016; U.S. Army general Carter F. Ham directed the command from March 9, 2011, to April 5, 2013; and Ward led AFRICOM
from October 1, 2007, to March 9, 2011.

36. Michael G. Kamas, David W. Pope, and Ryan N. Propst, "Exploring a New
System of Command and Control: The Case for Africa Command," *Joint Force
Quarterly*, no. 87 (October 2017): 83.

37. Brian J. Dunn, "The AFRICOM Queen," *Military Review* 96, no. 3 (May–June 2016): 51.

38. Ward, "Engaging AFRICOM," 299.

39. Dunn, "The AFRICOM Queen," 56–57.

40. Michael E. Hess, "Testimony before the United States Senate Committee on Foreign Relations," August 1, 2007, pp. 1–6, available at https://www.foreign.sen ate.gov/imo/media/doc/HessTestimony070801.pdf (accessed May 2, 2018).

41. Peter A. Dumbuya, "AFRICOM in US Transformational Diplomacy," *Journal of Global South Studies* 33, no. 1 (Spring 2016): 128. The various phases include Phase 0 (Shape), Phase I (Deter), Phase II (Seize Initiative), Phase III (Dominate), Phase IV (Stabilize), and Phase V (Enable Civil Authority). On Phase 0, see Joint Chiefs of Staff, "Joint Publication 3–0: Joint Operations," January 17, 2017, V-12–V-15, available at http://www.jcs.mil/Portals/36/Documents/Doctrine/pubs/jp3_0_20170117.pdf (accessed May 2, 2018).

42. Costas M. Constantinou and Sam Okoth Opondo, "Engaging the 'Ungoverned': The Merging of Diplomacy, Defence and Development," *Cooperation and Conflict* 51, no. 3 (September 2016): 318.

43. Sabelo J. Ndlovu-Gatsheni and Victor Ojakorotu, "Surveillance over a Zone of Conflict: Africom and the Politics of Securitisation of Africa," *Journal of Pan African Studies* 3, no. 6 (March 2010): 94–110; Gilbert L. Taguem Fah, "Dealing with Africom: The Political Economy of Anger and Protest," *Journal of Pan African Studies* 3, no. 6 (March 2010): 81–93.

44. Constantinou and Opondo, "Engaging the 'Ungoverned,'" 319.

45. U.S. White House Office of the Press Secretary, "Fact Sheet: Security Governance Initiative," August 6, 2014, pp. 1–2, available at https://obamawhitehouse. archives.gov/the-press-office/2014/08/06/fact-sheet-security-governance-initia tive (accessed May 2, 2018).

46. Roger Kaplan, "Losing Mali: The Administration Will Not Avoid Further Involvement in an African Tribal War," *American Spectator* 45, no. 10 (December 2012/January 2013): 34.

47. Ward, "Engaging AFRICOM," 299.

48. Jahi Issa and Salim Faraji, "The Obama Administration: Revisiting and Reconsidering AFRICOM," *Journal of Pan African Studies* 2, no. 9 (March 2009): 261.

49. Kamas, Pope, and Propst, "Exploring a New System of Command and Control," 84.

50. Patrick Dedham, "AFRICOM: Enabling African Partners," *Army Communicator* 40, no. 1 (Spring 2015): 21–23.

51. U.S. Africa Command, "United States Africa Command 2017 Posture Statement," pp. 4–5. AFRICOM has characterized its theater strategy as outlining the next five to twenty years.

52. Saeed Shabazz, "US in Niger: They Call It AFRICOM," *New York Amsterdam News*, November 2, 2017.

53. On debate over AFRICOM, see David J. Francis, ed., *U.S. Strategy in Africa: AFRICOM, Terrorism, and Security Challenges* (Abingdon: Routledge, 2010).

54. Da Cruz and Stephens, "The U.S. Africa Command (AFRICOM)," 198.

55. On SOFA and Article 98, see Attila Bogdan, "The United States and the International Criminal Court: Avoiding Jurisdiction through Bilateral Agreements in Reliance on Article 98," *International Criminal Law Review* 8, no. 1/2 (January 2008): 1–54.

56. Constantinou and Opondo, "Engaging the 'Ungoverned,'" 312.

57. U.S. Africa Command, "United States Africa Command 2017 Posture Statement," p. 3.

58. Ibid., 1.

59. "Washington: Africom Continues Efforts for Stable, Secure Continent," *U.S. Official News*, March 7, 2018.

60. Agnes Ngoma Leslie, "Introduction China–Africa Relations: Political and Economic Engagement and Media Strategies," *African Studies Quarterly* 16, no. 3/4 (December 2016): 1.

61. Chris Rowan, "The China–Africa Partnership: Working for Whom?" *Contemporary Review* 291, no. 1692 (Spring 2009): 57.

62. On the PRC and Africa, see Bruce D. Larkin, *China and Africa, 1949–1970: The Foreign Policy of the People's Republic of China* (Oakland: University of California Press, 1973).

63. On the Five Principles of Peaceful Coexistence and their contemporary relevance, see Wen Jiabao, "Carrying Forward the Five Principles of Peaceful Coexistence in the Promotion of Peace and Development," *Chinese Journal of International Law* 3, no. 2 (2004): 363–368.

64. Donovan C. Chau, *Exploiting Africa: The Influence of Maoist China in Algeria, Ghana, and Tanzania* (Annapolis, MD: Naval Institute, 2014).

65. On China's recent presence in Africa, see Courage Mlambo, Audrey Kushamba, and More Blessing Simawu, "China–Africa Relations: What Lies Beneath?" *Chinese Economy* 49, no. 4 (2016): 257–276; Deborah Brautigam, *Will Africa Feed China?* (Oxford: Oxford University Press, 2015); Sven Grimm, "China–Africa Cooperation: Promises, Practice and Prospects," *Journal of Contemporary China* 23, no. 90 (November 2014): 993–1011; Martyn Davies, Peter Draper, and Hannah Edinger, "Changing China, Changing Africa: Future Contours of an Emerging Relationship," *Asian Economic Policy Review* 9, no. 2 (July 2014): 180–197; Saferworld, "China's Growing Role in African Peace and Security," January 2011, available at https://www.saferworld.org.uk/resources/publications/500-chinas-growing-role-in-african-peace-and-security (accessed March 27, 2018); Pádraig Carmody, *The New Scramble for Africa* (Cambridge: Polity, 2011); Deborah Brautigam, *The Dragon's Gift: The Real Story of China in Africa* (Oxford: Oxford University Press, 2009); Robert I. Rotberg, ed., *China into Africa: Trade, Aid, and Influence* (Baltimore, MD: Brookings Institution Press, 2008); Chris Alden, *China in Africa* (London: Zed, 2007); Ian Taylor, *China and Africa: Engagement and Compromise* (Abingdon: Routledge, 2006).

66. Emmanuel Obuah, "Trade between China and Africa: Trends, Changes, and Challenges," *International Journal of China Marketing* 2, no. 2 (2012): 74.

67. On these countries' involvement in Africa, see Yu Lintao, "Bigger BRICS, Larger Role," *Beijing Review* 60, no. 37 (September 14, 2017), available at http://www.bjreview.com/Current_Issue/Editor_Choice/201709/t20170911_800104364.html (accessed February 18, 2018).

68. On Tiananmen Square, see Louisa Lim, *The People's Republic of Amnesia: Tiananmen Revisited* (Oxford: Oxford University Press, 2014); Randolph Kluver, "Rhetorical Trajectories of Tiananmen Square," *Diplomatic History* 34, no. 1 (January 2010): 71–94; Guo-Qiang Zhang and Sidney Kraus, "Constructing Public Opinion and Manipulating Symbols: China's Press Coverage of the Student Movement in 1989," *Journalism and Mass Communication Quarterly* 72, no. 2

(Summer 1995): 412–425; Craig Calhoun, "Revolution and Repression in Tiananmen Square," *Society* 26, no. 6 (September/October 1989): 21–38.

69. Rowan, "The China–Africa Partnership," 56.

70. On soft power, see Joseph S. Nye Jr., *Soft Power: The Means to Success in World Politics* (New York: PublicAffairs, 2004). On China's soft power, see Yejoo Kim, "China's Soft Power Expansion in Africa through Industrialisation: Opportunities and Challenges," *Africa Insight* 44, no. 4 (March 2015): 1–13; William A. Callahan and Elena Barabantseva, eds., *China Orders the World: Normative Soft Power and Foreign Policy* (Baltimore, MD: Johns Hopkins University Press, 2012); Wei Liang, "China's Soft Power in Africa: Is Economic Power Sufficient?" *Asian Perspective* 36, no. 4 (2012): 667–692; Michael D. Swaine and Ashley J. Tellis, *Interpreting China's Grand Strategy: Past, Present, and Future* (Santa Monica, CA: RAND, 2000).

71. Michael Leslie, "The Dragon Shapes Its Image: A Study of Chinese Media Influence Strategies in Africa," *African Studies Quarterly* 16, no. 3/4 (December 2016): 161–174.

72. Marc Lanteigne, "Fire over Water: China's Strategic Engagement of Somalia and the Gulf of Aden Crisis," *Pacific Review* 26, no. 3 (July 2013): 289.

73. On "no strings attached," see Boutros Boutros-Ghali, "The Five Principles," *Chinese Journal of International Law* 3, no. 2 (2004): 373–377.

74. Harman and Brown, "In from the Margins?" 79.

75. Forum on China-Africa Cooperation, "About FOCAC," p. 1, available at http://www.focac.org/eng/ltjj_3/ltjz/ (accessed August 25, 2018); Chuka Enuka, "The Forum on China-Africa Cooperation (FOCAC): A Framework for China's Re Engagement with Africa in the 21st Century," *Pakistan Journal of Social Sciences* 30, no. 2 (December 2010): 209–218.

76. Rowan, "The China–Africa Partnership," 60.

77. "SGR [Standard Gauge Railway] Workers Protest Denial of Equal Pay," Africa News Service, July 22, 2015; Janet Otieno, Johnstone Ole Turana, and Saudah Mayanja, "Africa-Chinese Labour Ties Turn Increasingly Icy," Africa News Service, October 22, 2010.

78. Marcus Power, "Angola 2025: The Future of the 'World's Richest Poor Country' as Seen through a Chinese Rear-View Mirror," *Antipode* 44, no. 3 (June 2012): 993.

79. Nelson Santos António and Shaozhuang Ma, "China's Special Economic Zone in Africa: Context, Motivations and Progress," *Euro Asia Journal of Management* 25, no. 1/2 (December 2015): 79–103.

80. "Forum on Partnership with Africa Ends in Bonn," Africa News Service, November 7, 2005.

81. Forum on China-Africa Cooperation, "China's African Policy," January 2006, pp. 1–5, available at http://www.fmprc.gov.cn/zflt/eng/zt/zgdfzzcwj/t230479.htm (accessed August 25, 2018).

82. "China's Africa Policy Addresses Poverty," Africa News Service, December 29, 2016.

83. Jakkie Cilliers, Barry Hughes, and Jonathan Moyer, "African Futures 2050," Institute for Security Studies Monograph 175, January 2011, pp. 4–5.

84. Bruce Guenther, "The Asian Drivers and the Resource Curse in Sub-Saharan Africa: The Potential Impacts of Rising Commodity Prices for Conflict and Governance in the DRC," *European Journal of Development Research* 20, no. 2 (June 2008): 357.

85. "Angola/China: An Example of South-South Cooperation," Africa News Service, March 25, 2004.

86. "China, Africa Enjoy Bright Prospect of Mutual Investment," Xinhua News Agency, January 12, 2006.

87. Todd A. Hofstedt, "China in Africa: An AFRICOM Response," *Naval War College Review* 62, no. 3 (Summer 2009): 81.

88. Obuah, "Trade between China and Africa," 74.

89. "China, Congo Agree to Further Economic, Trade Cooperation," Xinhua News Agency, March 21, 2005.

90. Hofstedt, "China in Africa," 81.

91. Howard W. French, *China's Second Continent: How a Million Migrants Are Building a New Empire in Africa* (New York: Alfred A. Knopf, 2014), 5.

92. Ngari Gituku, "New Dawn for China in Africa," *Diplomat East Africa* (February 2015): 22.

93. "Sudan Welcomes China's Decision to Appoint Special Envoy for Africa," Xinhua News Agency, May 13, 2007.

94. "China Approves China-Africa Development Fund," Xinhua News Agency, May 13, 2007.

95. Damilola Oyedele, "China Seeks End to Darfur Crises," Africa News Service, September 26, 2007.

96. Tang Xiaoyang, "Models of Chinese Engagement in Africa's Extractive Sectors and Their Implications," *Environment* 56, no. 2 (March/April 2014): 27.

97. Jonathan Holslag, "China's Evolving Behaviour in Africa and the Options of Cooperation with Europe," *Journal of Current Chinese Affairs* 40, no. 4 (2011): 5.

98. Renato Aguilar and Andrea Goldstein, "The Chinisation of Africa: The Case of Angola," *World Economy* 32, no. 11 (November 2009): 1559.

99. Ibid., 1560.

100. "Defying China Is No Longer a Viable Option," *African Business* 51, no. 438 (February 2017): 66.

101. Gituku, "New Dawn for China in Africa," 23.

102. Forum on China-Africa Cooperation, "Xi Announces 10 Major China-Africa Cooperation Plans for Coming Three Years," December 8, 2015, p. 1, available at http://www.xinhuanet.com/english/2015-12/04/c_134886420.htm (accessed August 25, 2018).

103. Ibid.

104. Seifudein Adem, "Sino-Optimism in Africa," *African Studies Quarterly* 16, no. 3/4 (December 2016): 7–16.

105. Holslag, "China's Evolving Behaviour in Africa and the Options of Cooperation with Europe," 6.

106. Saferworld, "China's Growing Role in African Peace and Security," pp. 72–82. See especially Figure 3, "China's Increasing Contributions to United Nations Peacekeeping Missions," p. 73.

107. Andrew S. Erickson and Austin M. Strange, "China's Blue Soft Power: Antipiracy, Engagement, and Image Enhancement," *Naval War College Review* 68, no. 1 (Winter 2015): 72.

108. For example, see Susanne Kamerling and Frans-Paul van der Putten, "An Overseas Naval Presence without Overseas Bases: China's Counter-Piracy

Operation in the Gulf of Aden," *Journal of Current Chinese Affairs* 40, no. 4 (2011): 119–146.

109. Erickson and Strange, "China's Blue Soft Power," 76.

110. Celia W. Dugger, "Zimbabwe Arms Shipped by China Spark an Uproar," *New York Times*, April 19, 2008.

111. Forum on China-Africa Cooperation, "Xi Announces 10 Major China-Africa Cooperation Plans for Coming Three Years," p. 1.

112. "What China's President Xi's Extended Tenure Means for Africa," All Africa, April 10, 2018.

113. "Defying China Is No Longer a Viable Option," 66.

114. World Economic Forum, "These Will Be Africa's Fastest Growing Economies in 2018," pp. 1–2.

115. Cilliers, Hughes, and Moyer, "African Futures 2050," pp. 4–5.

116. China-Africa Research Initiative, "China-Africa Trade," December 2017, p. 1, available at http://www.sais-cari.org/data-china-africa-trade/ (accessed March 27, 2018).

117. Yiagadeesen Samy, "China's Aid Policies in Africa: Opportunities and Challenges," Round Table 99, no. 406 (February 2010): 75–90.

118. Dumbuya, "AFRICOM in US Transformational Diplomacy," 129.

119. Issa and Faraji, "The Obama Administration," 263.

CHAPTER 9

1. Fund for Peace, "Fragile States Index 2017: Annual Report," May 14, 2017, pp. 6–7, available at http://fundforpeace.org/fsi/2017/05/14/fragile-states-index-2017-annual-report/ (accessed March 28, 2018).

2. Ibrahim Elbadawi and Nicholas Sambanis, "Why Are There So Many Civil Wars in Africa? Understanding and Preventing Violent Conflict," *Journal of African Economies* 9, no. 3 (October 2000): 244–269.

3. Food and Agriculture Organization, "Crop Prospects and Food Situation: Quarterly Global Report," December 2017, p. 4, available at http://www.fao.org/3/a-i8278e.pdf (accessed January 6, 2018).

4. African Union, "Agenda 2063: The Africa We Want," final ed., April 2015, p. 11, available at http://www.un.org/en/africa/osaa/pdf/au/agenda2063.pdf (accessed February 4, 2018).

5. Ibid., 2.

6. Clement Mweyang Aapengnuo, "Misinterpreting Ethnic Conflicts in Africa," *Africa Security Brief: A Publication of the Africa Center for Strategic Studies*, no. 4 (April 2010): 2.

7. François Heisbourg, "A Surprising Little War: First Lessons of Mali," *Survival* 55, no. 2 (April–May 2013): 14.

8. Oluwakemi Okenyodo, "Governance, Accountability, and Security in Nigeria," *Africa Security Brief: A Publication of the Africa Center for Strategic Studies*, no. 31 (June 2016): 2.

9. Adama Dieng, "Protecting Vulnerable Populations from Genocide," *UN Chronicle* 53, no. 4 (December 2016): 12.

10. Africa Center for Strategic Studies, "South Sudan Conflict Drives Massive Population Movement," October 31, 2017, pp. 1–2, available at https://africacen ter.org/spotlight/south-sudan-conflict-drives-massive-population-movement/ (accessed February 6, 2018).

11. Kate Almquist Knopf, "Ending South Sudan's Civil War," Council on Foreign Relations Special Report no. 77, November 2016, p. 3, available at https:// cfrd8-files.cfr.org/sites/default/files/pdf/2016/11/CSR77_Knopf_South%20 Sudan.pdf (accessed February 8, 2018).

12. Institute for Economics and Peace, "Global Terrorism Index 2017: Measuring and Understanding the Impact of Terrorism," November 2017, p. 46, available at http://visionofhumanity.org/app/uploads/2017/11/Global-Terro rism-Index-2017.pdf (accessed February 6, 2018).

13. Africa Center for Strategic Studies, "South Sudan Conflict Drives Massive Population Movement," pp. 1–2.

14. Jeffrey Herbst, *States and Power in Africa: Comparative Lessons in Authority and Control*, 2nd ed. (Princeton, NJ: Princeton University Press, 2014).

15. Tore Wig, "Peace from the Past: Pre-Colonial Political Institutions and Civil Wars in Africa," *Journal of Peace Research* 53, no. 4 (July 2016): 512. On the connection between land and conflict in Africa, see Catherine Boone, *Property and Political Order in Africa: Land Rights and the Structure of Politics* (Cambridge: Cambridge University Press, 2014).

16. Paul D. Williams, "Thinking about Security in Africa," *International Affairs* 83, no. 6 (November 2007): 1024.

17. Rafael Marques de Morais, "The New Imperialism: China in Angola," *World Affairs* 173, no. 6 (March/April 2011): 69.

18. U.S. Africa Command, "United States Africa Command 2017 Posture Statement," March 9, 2017, p. 7, available at http://www.africom.mil/Tags/ annual-posture-statement (accessed February 12, 2018).

19. Chris Kwaja, "Nigeria's Pernicious Drivers of Ethno-Religious Conflict," *Africa Security Brief: A Publication of the Africa Center for Strategic Studies*, no. 14 (July 2011): 4.

20. Fund for Peace, "Fragile States Index 2017: Annual Report," pp. 6–7. On Boko Haram's impact, see Fund for Peace, "Fragile States Index 2016," June 27, 2016, pp. 16–17, available at http://fundforpeace.org/fsi/2016/06/27/ fragile-states-index-2016-annual-report/ (accessed March 28, 2018).

21. Andrew S. Erickson and Austin M. Strange, "China's Blue Soft Power: Antipiracy, Engagement, and Image Enhancement," *Naval War College Review* 68, no. 1 (Winter 2015): 72.

22. On Rim of the Pacific, see "Chinese Fleet Director Hails Successful RIMPAC Debut," Xinhua News Agency, August 2, 2014; Andrew S. Erickson and Austin M. Strange, "China's RIMPAC Debut: What's in It for America?" *National Interest*, July 3, 2014, available at http://nationalinterest.org/feature/ china%E2%80%99s-rimpac-debut-what%E2%80%99s-it-america-10801 (accessed January 22, 2018).

23. Ben Werner, "China's Past Participation in RIMPAC Didn't Yield Intended Benefits of Easing Tensions," *U.S. Naval Institute News*, May 24, 2018, available at https://news.usni.org/2018/05/24/33834 (accessed May 25, 2018);

Megan Eckstein, "China Disinvited from Participating in 2018 RIMPAC Exercise," *U.S. Naval Institute News*, May 23, 2018, available at https://news.usni.org/2018/05/23/china-disinvited-participating-2018-rimpac-exercise (accessed May 24, 2018).

24. Food and Agriculture Organization, "FAO Calls for Renewed Commitment to Get Africa Back on Track to Eliminate Hunger," January 27, 2018, p. 1, available at http://www.fao.org/news/story/en/item/1099215/icode/ (accessed February 15, 2018).

25. Food and Agriculture Organization, "Crop Prospects and Food Situation: Quarterly Global Report," p. 4.

26. U.S. Agency for International Development, "Nigeria—Complex Emergency," July 23, 2015, pp. 1–8, available at https://www.usaid.gov/sites/default/files/documents/1866/nigeria_ce_fs02_07-23-2015.pdf (accessed May 2, 2018).

27. Food and Agriculture Organization, "Crop Prospects and Food Situation: Quarterly Global Report," p. 14.

28. U.S. Agency for International Development, "Mali-Complex Emergency Fact Sheet #1," September 14, 2017, available at https://www.usaid.gov/sites/default/files/documents/1866/mali_ce_fs01_09-14-2017.pdf (accessed January 12, 2018).

29. U.S. Agency for International Development, "Sahel—Food Insecurity and Complex Emergency, Fact Sheet #1," November 6, 2012, available at https://reliefweb.int/sites/reliefweb.int/files/resources/11.06.12%20-%20USAID-DCHA%20Sahel%20Food%20Insecurity%20and%20Complex%20Emergency%20Fact%20Sheet%20%231.pdf (accessed January 12, 2018).

30. Africa Center for Strategic Studies, "Humanitarian Costs of South Sudan Conflict Continue to Escalate," January 29, 2018, p. 1, available at https://africacenter.org/wp-content/uploads/2018/01/Food-Insecurity-in-South-Sudan-2013-v-Feb-May-2018-.pdf (accessed February 5, 2018).

31. Africa Center for Strategic Studies, "South Sudan Conflict Drives Massive Population Movement," pp. 1–2.

32. Richard Record, Praveen Kumar, and Priscilla Kandoole, "From Falling Behind to Catching Up: A Country Economic Memorandum for Malawi," World Bank Directions in Development, 2018, pp. 1–2, available at https://openknowledge.worldbank.org/bitstream/handle/10986/28683/9781464811944.pdf?sequence=2&isAllowed=y (accessed February 17, 2018).

33. M.J. Morgan, "Making the Most of Africa's Resources," *African Business*, no. 382 (January 2012): 32.

34. Isaac Fokuo, "Fresh Opportunities for Africa in a Multipolar World," *African Business* 51, no. 442 (June 2017): 43.

35. U.S. Africa Command, "United States Africa Command 2017 Posture Statement," p. 3.

36. Jakkie Cilliers, Barry Hughes, and Jonathan Moyer, "African Futures 2050," Institute for Security Studies Monograph 175, January 2011, pp. 12–13. See especially Figure 2.1, "African Population in Global Context," p. 12.

37. UNICEF Division of Data, Research, and Policy, "Generation 2030: Africa," August 2014, p. 5, available at https://www.unicef.org/publications/files/Generation_2030_Africa.pdf (accessed May 7, 2018).

38. Cilliers, Hughes, and Moyer, "African Futures 2050," p. xii.

39. Alex de Waal, ed., *Demilitarizing the Mind: African Agendas for Peace and Security* (Trenton, NJ: Africa World Press, 2002), 93–114.

40. Cilliers, Hughes, and Moyer, "African Futures 2050," p. 16. See especially Figure 2.5, "Urban Population as a Share of the Total, Africa in Global Context."

41. UN Environment Programme, "Responding to Climate Change," 2018, pp. 1–2, available at https://www.unenvironment.org/regions/africa/regional-initiatives/responding-climate-change (accessed May 28, 2018).

42. African Union, "Agenda 2063," p. 1.

43. Ibid., 17.

44. Louis Gnagbe, "Enhancing UN-AU-RECs [Regional Economic Communities] Cooperation towards Silencing the Guns by 2020 in the Context of the First 10-Year Implementation Plan of Agenda 2063," October 12, 2015, pp. 1–3, available at http://www.un.org/en/africa/osaa/pdf/events/20151012/statements/gnagbe20151012pm.pdf (accessed May 3, 2018).

45. African Union, "Agenda 2063," p. 9.

Selected Bibliography

INTERNATIONAL INSTITUTIONS, REGIONAL ORGANIZATIONS, AND GOVERNMENT DOCUMENTS

Africa Center for Strategic Studies. "Conflict and Famine in South Sudan." March 20, 2017. Available at https://africacenter.org/spotlight/conflict-and-famine-in-south-sudan/ (accessed February 9, 2018).

Africa Center for Strategic Studies. "Humanitarian Costs of South Sudan Conflict Continue to Escalate." January 29, 2018. Available at https://africacenter.org/wp-content/uploads/2018/01/Food-Insecurity-in-South-Sudan-2013-v-Feb-May-2018-.pdf (accessed February 5, 2018).

Africa Center for Strategic Studies. "More Activity but Fewer Fatalities Linked to African Militant Islamist Groups in 2017." January 26, 2018. Available at https://africacenter.org/spotlight/activity-fewer-fatalities-linked-african-militant-islamist-groups-2017/ (accessed February 5, 2018).

Africa Center for Strategic Studies. "South Sudan Conflict Drives Massive Population Movement." October 31, 2017. Available at https://africacenter.org/spotlight/south-sudan-conflict-drives-massive-population-movement/ (accessed February 6, 2018).

African Union. "The African Union Appoints a New Special Envoy for the Issue of the Lord's Resistance Army." July 10, 2014. Available at http://www.peaceau.org/uploads/auc-com-lra-10-07-2014.pdf (accessed February 24, 2018).

African Union. "Agenda 2063: The Africa We Want." Final ed. April 2015. Available at http://www.un.org/en/africa/osaa/pdf/au/agenda2063.pdf (accessed February 4, 2018).

African Union. "Food Security." 2018. Available at https://www.au.int/web/en/auc/priorities/food-security (accessed May 16, 2018).

African Union. "Joint Communiqué by Federica Mogherini, EU High Representative and Vice-President; Neven Mimica, EU Commissioner for International Cooperation and Development; and Smail Chergui, AU Commissioner for Peace and Security." August 1, 2016. Available at http://www.peaceau .org/uploads/joint-communique-eng.pdf (accessed February 24, 2018).

African Union. "Malabo Declaration on Accelerated Agricultural Growth and Transformation for Shared Prosperity and Improved Livelihoods." June 26–27, 2014. Available at https://au.int/sites/default/files/documents/31006-doc-malabo_declaration_2014_11_26-.pdf (accessed February 15, 2018).

African Union. "Revised African Maritime Transport Charter." July 26, 2010. Available at https://au.int/sites/default/files/treaties/7797-treaty-0041_-_revised_african_maritime_transport_charter_e.pdf (accessed March 7, 2018).

African Union. "Statement of the Chairperson of the Commission of the African Union on the Situation in Ethiopia." February 21, 2018. Available at http://www.peaceau.org/uploads/statement-of-the-chairperson-on-the-situation-in-ethiopia.pdf (accessed February 24, 2018).

African Union Commission Peace and Security Department, Peace Support Operations Division. "Report of the Ten-Year AMISOM Lessons Learned Conference." March 9–10, 2017. Available at http://www.peaceau.org/uploads /ll-eng-1.pdf (accessed February 24, 2018).

African Union Peace and Security Council. "Report of the Chairperson of the Commission on the Implementation of the African Union-Led Regional Cooperation Initiative for the Elimination of the Lord's Resistance Army." June 17, 2013. Available at http://www.peaceau.org/uploads/psc-rpt-lra-380-17-06-2013-2-.pdf (accessed February 24, 2018).

African Union Peace and Security Council. "Report on Mali and the Sahel and the Activities of the African Union Mission for Mali and the Sahel." August 11, 2014. Available at http://www.peaceau.org/uploads/psc.rpt.449.mali-sahel .11.08.2014.pdf (accessed February 24, 2018).

Arieff, Alexis. "Crisis in Mali." Congressional Research Service Report Prepared for Members and Committees of Congress. January 14, 2013.

Arieff, Alexis, Rhoda Margesson, Marjorie Ann Browne, and Matthew C. Weed. "International Criminal Court Cases in Africa: Status and Policy Issues." Congressional Research Service Report Prepared for Members and Committees of Congress. July 22, 2011.

Arieff, Alexis, and Lauren Ploch. "The Lord's Resistance Army: The U.S. Response." Congressional Research Service Report Prepared for Members and Committees of Congress. April 11, 2012.

Calles, Teodardo. "The International Year of Pulses: What Are They and Why Are They Important?" Food and Agriculture Organization of the United Nations Article 7. Available at http://www.fao.org/3/a-bl797e.pdf (accessed January 15, 2018).

Central Intelligence Agency. The World Factbook. Washington, DC: Central Intelligence Agency, 2018. Available at https://www.cia.gov/library/publications/the-world-factbook/ (accessed May 9, 2018).

Chipeta, Mafa, Bezabih Emana, and Demese Chanyalew. "Ethiopia's Agriculture Sector Policy and Investment Framework (2010–2020) External Mid-Term

Review." October 2015. Available at http://www.agri-learning-ethiopia. org/wp-content/uploads/2015/10/Agriculture-Policy-MTR_FINAL.pdf (accessed March 26, 2018).

Cook, Nicolas. "Conflict Minerals in Central Africa: U.S. and International Responses." Congressional Research Service Report Prepared for Members and Committees of Congress. July 20, 2012.

Council of the European Union. "EU Strategy on the Gulf of Guinea." March 17, 2014.

Dieng, Adama. "Protecting Vulnerable Populations from Genocide." *UN Chronicle* 53, no. 4 (December 2016): 9–12.

Economic Community of West African States. "History." 2018. Available at http:// www.ecowas.int/about-ecowas/history/ (accessed May 17, 2018).

Energy Information Administration. "Country Analysis Brief: Angola." May 18, 2016. Available at https://www.eia.gov/beta/international/analysis_ includes/countries_long/Angola/angola.pdf (accessed February 8, 2018).

Federal Democratic Republic of Ethiopia, Ministry of Labour and Social Affairs. "National Social Protection Policy of Ethiopia, Final Draft." March 26, 2012. Available at http://phe-ethiopia.org/resadmin/uploads/attachment-188-Ethiopia_National_Social_Protection.pdf (accessed February 16, 2018).

Food and Agriculture Organization. "Analysis of Price Incentives for Maize in Ethiopia for the Time Period 2005–2012." February 2015. Available at http://www.fao.org/3/a-i4527e.pdf (accessed February 16, 2018).

Food and Agriculture Organization. "Crop Prospects and Food Situation: Quarterly Global Report." December 2017. Available at http://www.fao .org/3/a-i8278e.pdf (accessed January 6, 2018).

Food and Agriculture Organization. "Definitions and Classification of Commodities: Pulses and Derived Products." 2015. Available at http://www.fao .org/es/faodef/fdef04e.htm (assessed January 23, 2018).

Food and Agriculture Organization. "Ethiopia and FAO: Partnering to Achieve Sustainable Agricultural Growth and Food Security." 2016. Available at http://www.fao.org/3/a-au242e.pdf (accessed February 15, 2018).

Food and Agriculture Organization. "FAO Calls for Renewed Commitment to Get Africa Back on Track to Eliminate Hunger." January 27, 2018. Available at http://www.fao.org/news/story/en/item/1099215/icode/ (accessed February 15, 2018).

Food and Agriculture Organization. "Global Forest Resources Assessment 2015: How Are the World's Forests Changing?" 2nd ed. 2016. Available at http:// www.fao.org/3/a-i4793e.pdf (accessed March 25, 2018).

Food and Agriculture Organization. "Increasing Agricultural Production in Angola." July 2014. Available at http://www.fao.org/3/a-bt830e.pdf (accessed January 6, 2018).

Food and Agriculture Organization. "Malawi Country Programme Framework, 2014–2017." April 28, 2014. Available at http://www.fao.org/3/a-bp619e. pdf (accessed February 9, 2018).

Food and Agriculture Organization. "Regional Overview of Food Insecurity, Africa: African Food Security Prospects Brighter Than Ever." Accra: Food and Agriculture Organization of the United Nations, 2015.

Food and Agriculture Organization Food and Agriculture Policy Decision Analy-
sis. "Country Fact Sheet on Food and Agriculture Policy Trends, Ethiopia."
October 2014. Available at http://www.fao.org/3/a-i4181e.pdf (accessed
February 16, 2018).

Food and Agriculture Organization, International Fund for Agricultural Development, UNICEF, World Food Programme, and World Health Organization.
"The State of Food Security and Nutrition in the World: Building Resilience
for Peace and Security." 2017. Available at http://www.fao.org/3/a-I7695E
.pdf (accessed May 7, 2018).

Food and Agriculture Organization Representation in Ethiopia and Government
of Ethiopia. "Country Programming Framework for Ethiopia, 2016–2020."
2017. Available at http://www.fao.org/3/a-i7527e.pdf (accessed February 16, 2018).

Food and Agriculture Organization Representation in Malawi and the Government of the Republic of Malawi. "National Medium-Term Priority Framework (NMTPF), 2010–2015." April 2010. Available at http://www.fao
.org/3/a-bp620e.pdf (accessed February 10, 2018).

Forum on China-Africa Cooperation. "About FOCAC." Available at http://www
.focac.org/eng/ltjj_3/ltjz/ (accessed August 25, 2018).

Forum on China-Africa Cooperation. "China's African Policy." January 2006.
Available at http://www.fmprc.gov.cn/zflt/eng/zt/zgdfzzcwj/t230479
.htm (accessed August 25, 2018).

Forum on China-Africa Cooperation. "Xi Announces 10 Major China-Africa Cooperation Plans for Coming Three Years." December 8, 2015. Available at
http://www.xinhuanet.com/english/2015-12/04/c_134886420.htm (accessed
August 25, 2018).

Gates, Robert. "Defense Secretary Gates Announces Creation of U.S. Africa Command." February 6, 2007. Available at http://www.africom.mil/media-room
/transcript/7804/transcript-defense-secretary-gates-announces-creat (accessed
May 2, 2018).

Gnagbe, Louis. "Enhancing UN-AU-RECs [Regional Economic Communities]
Cooperation towards Silencing the Guns by 2020 in the Context of the First
10-Year Implementation Plan of Agenda 2063." October 12, 2015. Available at http://www.un.org/en/africa/osaa/pdf/events/20151012/state
ments/gnagbe20151012pm.pdf (accessed May 3, 2018).

Gulf of Guinea Commission. "Declaration of the Heads of State and Government of Central and West African States on Maritime Safety and Security
in Their Common Maritime Domain." June 25, 2013. Available at http://
cggrps.org/wp-content/uploads/DECLARACAO-DE-YAOUNDE-EN
.pdf (accessed February 2, 2018).

Gulf of Guinea Commission. "The Gulf of Guinea Commission." 2018. Available at
http://cggrps.org/en/the-gulf-of-guinea-commission/ (accessed May 16,
2018).

Gulf of Guinea Commission. "Luanda Declaration on Peace and Security in the
Gulf of Guinea Region." November 29, 2012. Available at http://cggrps
.org/wp-content/uploads/DeclaracaodeLuanda-29NOV2012EN.pdf
(accessed February 2, 2018).

Gulf of Guinea Commission. "Treaty Establishing the Gulf of Guinea Commission." July 3, 2001. Available at http://cggrps.org/wp-content/uploads/Tratado-EN1.pdf (accessed February 2, 2018).

Hess, Michael E. "Testimony before the United States Senate Committee on Foreign Relations." August 1, 2007. Available at https://www.foreign.senate.gov/imo/media/doc/HessTestimony070801.pdf (accessed May 2, 2018).

Humud, Carla E. "Al Qaeda and U.S. Policy: Middle East and Africa." Congressional Research Service Report Prepared for Members and Committees of Congress. August 11, 2016.

Intergovernmental Authority on Development Center for Pastoral Areas and Livestock Development. "The Contribution of Livestock to the Ethiopian Economy." 2013. Available at https://igad.int/attachments/714_ETHIOPIA%20BRIEF%20(1).pdf (accessed February 16, 2018).

International Monetary Fund. "Standing with the Central African Republic." January 25, 2017. Available at https://www.imf.org/en/News/Articles/2017/01/25/SP012517-Standing-with-Central-African-Republic (accessed January 14, 2018).

Joint Chiefs of Staff. "Joint Publication 3–0: Joint Operations." January 17, 2017. Available at http://www.jcs.mil/Portals/36/Documents/Doctrine/pubs/jp3_0_20170117.pdf (accessed May 2, 2018).

Lum, Thomas, Hannah Fischer, Julissa Gomez-Granger, and Anne Leland. "China's Foreign Aid Activities in Africa, Latin America, and Southeast Asia." Congressional Research Service Report Prepared for Members and Committees of Congress. February 25, 2009.

Murray, Elizabeth, and Fiona Mangan. "The 2015–2016 CAR Elections, A Look Back: Peaceful Process Belies Serious Risks." U.S. Institute of Peace Special Report 403. May 2017. Available at https://www.usip.org/sites/default/files/2017-05/sr403-2015-2016-car-elections-a-look-back-peaceful-process-belies-serious-risks.pdf (accessed January 15, 2018).

Nigerian National Petroleum Corporation. "Oil Production." 2018. Available at http://nnpcgroup.com/NNPCBusiness/UpstreamVentures/OilProduction.aspx (accessed March 9, 2018).

North Atlantic Treaty Organization Allied Maritime Command. "The Maritime Trade Information Sharing Centre-Gulf of Guinea (MTISC-GOG)." June 20, 2016. Available at https://www.shipping.nato.int/nsc/operations/news/2016/the-maritime-trade-information-sharing-centre-gulf-of-guinea-mtiscgog.aspx (accessed March 9, 2018).

Organisation for Economic Co-Operation and Development. "Angola." 2007. Available at https://www.oecd.org/countries/angola/38561655.pdf (accessed May 2, 2018).

Organisation for Economic Co-Operation and Development. "Due Diligence Guidance for Responsible Supply Chains of Minerals from Conflict-Affected and High-Risk Areas." 2016. Available at http://www.oecd.org/daf/inv/mne/OECD-Due-Diligence-Guidance-Minerals-Edition3.pdf (accessed March 13, 2018).

Organisation for Economic Co-Operation and Development. "History." 2018. Available at http://www.oecd.org/about/ (accessed March 13, 2018).

Organization of African Unity. "African Maritime Transport Charter." July 26,
    1994. Available at https://au.int/sites/default/files/treaties/7776-treaty-
    0017_-_african_maritime_transport_charter_e.pdf (accessed March 7, 2018).
Paden, John. "Religion and Conflict in Nigeria: Countdown to the 2015 Elections."
    U.S. Institute of Peace Special Report 359. February 2015. Available at
    https://www.usip.org/sites/default/files/SR359-Religion-and-Conflict-
    in-Nigeria.pdf (accessed February 5, 2018).
Ploch, Lauren, Christopher M. Blanchard, Ronald O'Rourke, R. Chuck Mason, and
    Rawle O. King. "Piracy off the Horn of Africa." Congressional Research
    Service Report Prepared for Members and Committees of Congress.
    April 27, 2011.
Record, Richard, Praveen Kumar, and Priscilla Kandoole. "From Falling Behind
    to Catching Up: A Country Economic Memorandum for Malawi." World
    Bank Directions in Development. 2018. Available at https://openknowl
    edge.worldbank.org/bitstream/handle/10986/28683/9781464811944
    .pdf?sequence=2&isAllowed=y (accessed February 17, 2018).
UN Department of Economic and Social Affairs, Population Division. "World
    Urbanization Prospects: The 2014 Revision." 2015. Available at https://esa
    .un.org/unpd/wup/Publications/Files/WUP2014-Report.pdf (accessed
    January 23, 2018).
UN Development Programme. "Human Development Report 2016: Human
    Development for Everyone." 2016. Available at http://hdr.undp.org/sites
    /default/files/2016_human_development_report.pdf (accessed March 17,
    2018).
UN Environment Programme. "Responding to Climate Change." 2018. Available
    at   https://www.unenvironment.org/regions/africa/regional-initiatives
    /responding-climate-change (accessed May 28, 2018).
UN High Commissioner for Refugees, the UN Refugee Agency. "Nigeria Emer-
    gency." December 31, 2017. Available at http://www.unhcr.org/en-us
    /nigeria-emergency.html?query=boko%20haram (accessed March 6, 2018).
UNICEF Division of Data, Research, and Policy. "Generation 2030: Africa."
    August 2014. Available at https://www.unicef.org/publications/files
    /Generation_2030_Africa.pdf (accessed May 7, 2018).
United Nations. "Convention on the Law of the Sea." December 10, 1982. Available
    at   http://www.un.org/Depts/los/convention_agreements/texts/unclos
    /unclos_e.pdf (accessed January 21, 2018).
United Nations. "Convention on the Prevention and Punishment of the Crime
    of Genocide." December 9, 1948. Available at https://treaties.un.org/doc
    /publication/unts/volume%2078/volume-78-i-1021-english.pdf (accessed
    February 28, 2018).
United Nations. "The Millennium Development Goals Report." 2015. Avail-
    able   at   http://www.un.org/millenniumgoals/2015_MDG_Report/pdf
    /MDG%202015%20rev%20(July%201).pdf (accessed March 26, 2018).
United Nations. "MONUC Background." 2018. Available at https://peacekeeping
    .un.org/en/mission/past/monuc/background.shtml (accessed May 22,
    2018).
United Nations. "MONUSCO Fact Sheet." 2018. Available at https://peacekeep
    ing.un.org/en/mission/monusco (accessed May 22, 2018).

United Nations. "Republic of the Congo-ONUC Background." 2018. Available at https://peacekeeping.un.org/en/mission/past/onucB.htm (accessed May 22, 2018).

United Nations. "UNAMID: African Union/United Nations Hybrid Operation in Darfur." 2018. Available at https://peacekeeping.un.org/en/mission/unamid (accessed June 1, 2018).

United Nations. "United Nations Convention to Combat Desertification." 1994. Available at http://www2.unccd.int/sites/default/files/relevant-links/2017-01/UNCCD_Convention_ENG_0.pdf (accessed November 14, 2017).

UN Mechanism for International Criminal Tribunals. "The ICTR in Brief." 2018. Available at http://unictr.unmict.org/en/tribunal (accessed May 22, 2018).

UN Office for West Africa and the Sahel. "Drug Trafficking and Organised Crime." 2018. Available at https://unowas.unmissions.org/drug-trafficking-and-organised-crime (accessed May 22, 2018).

UN Office on Drugs and Crime. "Transnational Organized Crime in West Africa: A Threat Assessment." February 2013. Available at http://www.unodc.org/documents/data-and-analysis/tocta/West_Africa_TOCTA_2013_EN.pdf (accessed January 21, 2018).

UN Peacekeeping. "MINUSMA Fact Sheet." 2018. Available at https://peacekeeping.un.org/en/mission/minusma (accessed May 22, 2018).

UN Peacekeeping. "MONUC: United Nations Organization Mission in the Democratic Republic of the Congo." 2018. Available at http://peacekeeping.un.org/sites/default/files/past/monuc/index.shtml (accessed May 22, 2018).

UN Secretariat. "Convention to Combat Desertification: Update on Ratification of the UNCCD." December 21, 2016. Available at http://www2.unccd.int/sites/default/files/relevant-links/2017-07/Ratification%20list%20Dec2016.pdf (accessed November 14, 2017).

UN Secretary-General. "Action Plan to Prevent Genocide." April 7, 2004. Available at http://www.un.org/en/genocideprevention/documents/about-us/Doc.2_Press%20Release_SG%20Plan%20of%20Action.pdf (accessed March 25, 2018).

UN Security Council. "Central African Republic: Monthly Forecast." November 2017. Available at http://www.securitycouncilreport.org/monthly-forecast/2017-11/central_african_republic_23.php (accessed January 15, 2018).

UN Security Council. "Report of the Secretary-General on the Situation in Mali." June 11, 2015. Available at http://www.un.org/en/ga/search/view_doc.asp?symbol=S/2015/426 (accessed March 11, 2018).

UN Security Council. "Report of the United Nations Assessment Mission on Piracy in the Gulf of Guinea." January 19, 2012. Available at http://www.securitycouncilreport.org/atf/cf/%7B65BFCF9B-6D27-4E9C-8CD3-CF6E4FF96FF9%7D/AUUN%20S%202012%2045.pdf (accessed January 25, 2018).

UN Security Council. "Resolution 143 (1960)." July 14, 1960. Available at http://www.un.org/en/ga/search/view_doc.asp?symbol=S/RES/143(1960) (accessed March 24, 2018).

UN Security Council. "Resolution 955 (1994)." November 8, 1994. Available at http://www.unmict.org/specials/ictr-remembers/docs/res955-1994_en.pdf?q=ictr-remembers/docs/res955-1994_en.pdf (accessed March 25, 2018).

UN Security Council. "Resolution 1279 (1999)." November 30, 1999. Available at
    http://www.un.org/en/ga/search/view_doc.asp?symbol=S/RES/1279
    (1999) (accessed March 24, 2018).
UN Security Council. "Resolution 1698 (2006)." July 31, 2006. Available at http://
    www.un.org/en/ga/search/view_doc.asp?symbol=S/RES/1698(2006)
    (accessed November 20, 2017).
UN Security Council. "Resolution 1744 (2007)." February 20, 2007. Available at
    http://www.un.org/en/ga/search/view_doc.asp?symbol=S/RES/1744
    (2007) (accessed March 24, 2018).
UN Security Council. "Resolution 1816 (2008)." June 2, 2008. Available at http://
    www.un.org/en/ga/search/view_doc.asp?symbol=S/RES/1816(2008)
    (accessed February 2, 2018).
UN Security Council. "Resolution 1925 (2010)." May 28, 2010. Available at http://
    www.un.org/en/ga/search/view_doc.asp?symbol=S/RES/1925(2010)
    (accessed March 24, 2018).
UN Security Council. "Resolution 1973 (2011)." March 17, 2011. Available at http://
    www.un.org/en/ga/search/view_doc.asp?symbol=S/RES/1973(2011)
    (accessed March 24, 2018).
UN Security Council. "Resolution 2018 (2011)." October 31, 2011. Available
    at http://www.un.org/en/ga/search/view_doc.asp?symbol=S/RES/2018
    (2011) (accessed February 2, 2018).
UN Security Council. "Resolution 2039 (2012)." February 29, 2012. Available at
    http://www.un.org/en/ga/search/view_doc.asp?symbol=S/RES/2039
    (2012) (accessed February 2, 2018).
UN Security Council. "Resolution 2056 (2012)." July 5, 2012. Available at http://
    www.un.org/en/ga/search/view_doc.asp?symbol=S/RES/2056(2012)
    (accessed January 15, 2018).
UN Security Council. "Resolution 2071 (2012)." October 12, 2012. Available
    at http://www.un.org/en/ga/search/view_doc.asp?symbol=S/RES/20
    71(2012) (accessed January 15, 2018).
UN Security Council. "Resolution 2085 (2012)." December 20, 2012. Available
    at http://www.un.org/en/ga/search/view_doc.asp?symbol=S/RES/2085
    (2012) (accessed March 24, 2018).
UN Security Council. "Resolution 2100 (2013)." April 25, 2013. Available at http://
    www.un.org/en/ga/search/view_doc.asp?symbol=S/RES/2100(2013)
    (accessed March 24, 2018).
UN Security Council. "Resolution 2102 (2013)." May 2, 2013. Available at http://
    www.un.org/en/ga/search/view_doc.asp?symbol=S/RES/2102(2013)
    (accessed January 15, 2018).
UN Security Council. "Resolution 2127 (2013)." December 5, 2013. Available at
    http://www.un.org/en/ga/search/view_doc.asp?symbol=S/RES/2127
    (2013) (accessed January 15, 2018).
UN Security Council. "Resolution 2339 (2017)." January 27, 2017. Available at
    http://www.un.org/en/ga/search/view_doc.asp?symbol=S/RES/2339
    (2017) (accessed January 15, 2018).
UN Security Council. "Resolution 2372 (2017)." August 30, 2017. Available at
    http://www.un.org/en/ga/search/view_doc.asp?symbol=S/RES/2372
    (2017) (accessed February 13, 2018).

UN Security Council. "Resolution 2387 (2017)." November 15, 2017. Available at http://www.un.org/en/ga/search/view_doc.asp?symbol=S/RES/2387 (2017) (accessed February 7, 2018).

U.S. Africa Command. "African Union, USAID, State Department Officials Speak at U.S. Africa Command Establishment Ceremony." October 17, 2008. Available at http://www.africom.mil/media-room/transcript/6340/transcript-african-union-usaid-state-department-of (accessed May 2, 2018).

U.S. Africa Command. "United States Africa Command 2017 Posture Statement." March 9, 2017. Available at http://www.africom.mil/Tags/annual-posture-statement (accessed February 12, 2018).

U.S. Agency for International Development. "Mali-Complex Emergency Fact Sheet #1." September 14, 2017. Available at https://www.usaid.gov/sites/default/files/documents/1866/mali_ce_fs01_09-14-2017.pdf (accessed January 12, 2018).

U.S. Agency for International Development. "Nigeria—Complex Emergency." July 23, 2015. Available at https://www.usaid.gov/sites/default/files/documents/1866/nigeria_ce_fs02_07-23-2015.pdf (accessed May 2, 2018).

U.S. Agency for International Development. "Sahel—Food Insecurity and Complex Emergency, Fact Sheet #1." November 6, 2012. Available at https://reliefweb.int/sites/reliefweb.int/files/resources/11.06.12%20-%20USAID-DCHA%20Sahel%20Food%20Insecurity%20and%20Complex%20Emergency%20Fact%20Sheet%20%231.pdf (accessed January 12, 2018).

U.S. Congress. "Public Law 111–172, Lord's Resistance Army Disarmament and Northern Uganda Recovery Act of 2009." May 24, 2010. Available at https://www.congress.gov/111/plaws/publ172/PLAW-111publ172.pdf (accessed January 29, 2018).

U.S. Department of State. "Foreign Terrorist Organizations." 2018. Available at https://www.state.gov/j/ct/rls/other/des/123085.htm (accessed May 28, 2018).

U.S. Department of State. "Terrorist Designations of Boko Haram and Ansaru." November 13, 2013. Available at https://www.state.gov/j/ct/rls/other/des/266565.htm (accessed February 15, 2018).

U.S. White House Office of the Press Secretary. "Fact Sheet: Security Governance Initiative." August 6, 2014. Available at https://obamawhitehouse.archives.gov/the-press-office/2014/08/06/fact-sheet-security-governance-initiative (accessed May 2, 2018).

World Bank. "Doing Business 2018: Reforming to Create Jobs, Comparing Business Regulation for Domestic Firms in 190 Economies." A World Bank Group Flagship Report. 15th ed. 2018. Available at http://www.doingbusiness.org/~/media/WBG/DoingBusiness/Documents/Annual-Reports/English/DB2018-Full-Report.pdf (accessed February 26, 2018).

World Bank. "Ethiopia Country Overview." October 30, 2017. Available at http://www.worldbank.org/en/country/ethiopia/overview (accessed February 16, 2018).

World Bank. "How to Harness the Benefits of Urbanization for More Economic Growth Overall." June 1, 2017. Available at http://www.worldbank.org/en/country/malawi/publication/malawi-economic-monitor-how-to-harness-the-benefits-of-urbanization-for-more-economic-growth-overall (accessed February 17, 2018).

World Bank. "Improving Food Security in Ethiopia." February 3, 2016. Available at http://www.worldbank.org/en/news/video/2016/02/03/impro ving-food-security-in-ethiopia (accessed February 16, 2018).

World Bank. "Malawi Country Overview." October 10, 2017. Available at http://www .worldbank.org/en/country/malawi/overview (accessed February 17, 2018).

World Bank. "Malawi Country Profile." 2016. Available at http://databank. worldbank.org/data/views/reports/reportwidget.aspx?Report_Name=C ountryProfile&Id=b450fd57&tbar=y&dd=y&inf=n&zm=n&country=MWI (accessed March 26, 2018).

World Health Organization. "Millennium Development Goals (MDGs)." 2018. Available at http://www.who.int/topics/millennium_development_goals /about/en/ (accessed March 17, 2018).

World Health Organization. "Nutrition Landscape Information System (NLIS) Country Profile Indicators Interpretation Guide." 2010. Available at http:// www.who.int/nutrition/nlis_interpretation_guide.pdf (accessed February 16, 2018).

NONGOVERNMENTAL ORGANIZATION DOCUMENTS

Africa Research Bulletin. "Gulf of Guinea Anti-Piracy Network." *Political, Social, and Cultural Series* 54, no. 6 (July 2017): 21457–21458.

Amnesty International. "The Central African Republic's Human Rights Crisis." April 9, 2014. Available at https://www.amnesty.org/en/latest /news/2014/04/qa-central-african-republic-s-human-rights-crisis / (accessed January 14, 2018).

Amnesty International. "Ethnic Cleansing and Sectarian Killings in the Central African Republic." February 12, 2014. Available at https://s3-eu-west-1. amazonaws.com/alfrescotemporary/AI_CAR+report_Feb2014.pdf (accessed January 14, 2018).

Amnesty International. "Nigeria: Trapped in the Cycle of Violence." November 1, 2012. Available at https://www.amnesty.org/en/documents/afr44 /043/2012/en/ (accessed February 7, 2018).

Asiedu, Michael. "Turkey as a Development Partner in Africa." Global Political Trends Center Policy Brief no. 44. October 2016.

Banks, John P., George Ingram, Mwangi Kimenyi, Steven Rocker, Witney Schneidman, Yun Sun, and Lesley Anne Warner. "Top Five Reasons Why Africa Should Be a Priority for the United States." Africa Growth Initiative at Brookings. March 2013. Available at https://www.brookings.edu/wp-content /uploads/2016/06/04_africa_priority_united_states.pdf (accessed May 2, 2018).

Bring Back Our Girls. "A Call to Action." 2018. Available at http://www.bring backourgirls.ng/?page_id=1613 (accessed May 22, 2018).

Bruton, Bronwyn. "Somalia: A New Approach." Council on Foreign Relations Center for Preventative Action Council Special Report No. 52. March 2010.

Chatham House. "Maritime Security in the Gulf of Guinea." March 2013. Available at https://www.chathamhouse.org/sites/files/chathamhouse/public /Research/Africa/0312confreport_maritimesecurity.pdf (accessed January 23, 2018).

China-Africa Research Initiative. "China-Africa Trade." December 2017. Available at http://www.sais-cari.org/data-china-africa-trade/ (accessed March 27, 2018).

Cilliers, Jakkie, Barry Hughes, and Jonathan Moyer. "African Futures 2050." Institute for Security Studies Monograph 175. January 2011.

Conciliation Resources. "Analysis of Conflict and Peacebuilding in the Central African Republic." London: Conciliation Resources, 2015.

Council on Foreign Relations. "The Global Oceans Regime: Report by International Institutions and Global Governance Program." June 19, 2013. Available at https://www.cfr.org/report/global-oceans-regime (accessed May 2, 2018).

Eckstein, Megan. "China Disinvited from Participating in 2018 RIMPAC Exercise." *U.S. Naval Institute News*. May 23, 2018. Available at https://news.usni.org/2018/05/23/china-disinvited-participating-2018-rimpac-exercise (accessed May 24, 2018).

Extractive Industries Transparency Initiative. "Malawi." 2018. Available at https://eiti.org/malawi (accessed May 22, 2018).

Freedom House. "Freedom in the World 2018: Democracy in Crisis." 2018. Available at https://freedomhouse.org/sites/default/files/FH_FITW_Report_2018_Final_SinglePage.pdf (accessed March 3, 2018).

Fund for Peace. "Fragile States Index 2016: Annual Report." June 27, 2016. Available at http://fundforpeace.org/fsi/2016/06/27/fragile-states-index-2016-annual-report/ (accessed March 28, 2018).

Fund for Peace. "Fragile States Index 2017: Annual Report." May 14, 2017. Available at http://fundforpeace.org/fsi/2017/05/14/fragile-states-index-2017-annual-report/ (accessed March 28, 2018).

Harris, Grant T. "Why Africa Matters to US National Security." Atlantic Council Africa Center and OCP Policy Center. May 2017. Available at http://www.atlanticcouncil.org/images/publications/Why_Africa_Matters_to_US_National_Security_0524_web.pdf (accessed May 7, 2018).

Higazi, Adam. "The Jos Crisis: A Recurrent Nigerian Tragedy." Friedrich-Ebert-Stiftung (FES) Nigeria Discussion Paper no. 2. January 2011. Available at http://library.fes.de/pdf-files/bueros/nigeria/07812.pdf (accessed March 1, 2018).

Human Rights Watch. "Central African Republic: Muslims Forced to Flee." February 12, 2014. Available at https://www.hrw.org/news/2014/02/12/central-african-republic-muslims-forced-flee (accessed January 14, 2018).

Human Rights Watch. "DR Congo: Human Rights Watch Submission to the African Commission on Human and Peoples' Rights." November 1, 2017. Available at https://www.hrw.org/print/310992 (accessed January 16, 2018).

Human Rights Watch. " 'Even a "Big Man" Must Face Justice': Lessons from the Trial of Charles Taylor." July 2012. Available at https://www.hrw.org/sites/default/files/reports/sierraLeone0712ForUpload_0.pdf (accessed March 25, 2018).

Human Rights Watch. "Spiraling Violence: Boko Haram Attacks and Security Force Abuses in Nigeria." October 2012. Available at https://www.hrw.org/sites/default/files/reports/nigeria1012webwcover_0.pdf (accessed February 7, 2018).

Human Rights Watch. "They Burned It All: Destruction of Villages, Killings, and Sexual Violence in Unity State, South Sudan." July 2015. Available at

https://www.hrw.org/sites/default/files/report_pdf/southsudan0715_
web_0.pdf (accessed January 14, 2018).

Human Rights Watch. "They Destroyed Everything: Mining and Human Rights
in Malawi." September 2016. Available at https://www.hrw.org/sites
/default/files/report_pdf/malawi0916_web.pdf (accessed February 7,
2018).

Human Rights Watch. "'They Do Not Own This Place': Government Discrimination against 'Non-Indigenes' in Nigeria." April 2006. Available at https://
www.hrw.org/sites/default/files/reports/nigeria0406webwcover.pdf
(accessed March 1, 2018).

Human Rights Watch. "Those Terrible Weeks in Their Camp: Boko Haram Violence
against Women and Girls in Northeast Nigeria." October 2014. Available
at https://www.hrw.org/sites/default/files/reports/nigeria1014web.pdf
(accessed February 7, 2018).

Institute for Economics and Peace. "Global Terrorism Index 2015: Measuring and
Understanding the Impact of Terrorism." November 2015. Available at
http://visionofhumanity.org/app/uploads/2017/04/2015-Global-Terror
ism-Index-Report.pdf (accessed May 3, 2018).

Institute for Economics and Peace. "Global Terrorism Index 2017: Measuring and
Understanding the Impact of Terrorism." November 2017. Available at
http://visionofhumanity.org/app/uploads/2017/11/Global-Terrorism-
Index-2017.pdf (accessed March 18, 2018).

Institute for Justice and Reconciliation. "Central African Republic: A Conflict
Misunderstood." Occasional Paper 22. May 12, 2017. Available at http://
www.ijr.org.za/home/wp-content/uploads/2012/07/CAR-Report-.pdf
(accessed May 4, 2018).

International Coalition for the Responsibility to Protect. "The Crisis in Nigeria."
2014. Available at http://www.responsibilitytoprotect.org/index.php/cri
ses/crisis-in-nigeria (accessed January 24, 2018).

International Food Policy Research Institute. "Global Hunger Index 2017: The
Inequalities of Hunger." October 2017. Available at http://ebrary.ifpri
.org/utils/getfile/collection/p15738coll2/id/131422/filename/131628.
pdf (accessed March 17, 2018).

International Maritime Organization. "IMO: What It Is." 2018. Available at http://
www.imo.org/en/About/Documents/What%20it%20is%20Oct%202013_
Web.pdf (accessed May 22, 2018).

International Maritime Organization. "Piracy and Armed Robbery against Ships:
Maritime Safety Committee 98/15." April 4, 2017.

International Rescue Committee. "Mortality in the Democratic Republic of Congo:
An Ongoing Crisis." May 1, 2007. Available at https://www.rescue.org
/sites/default/files/document/661/2006-7congomortalitysurvey.pdf
(accessed March 25, 2018).

Johannessen, Cathrine. "Kingship in Uganda: The Role of the Buganda Kingdom in Ugandan Politics." Christian Michelsen Institute (CMI) Working Paper no. 8. 2006. Available at https://www.cmi.no/publications
/file/2176-kingship-in-uganda.pdf (accessed March 2, 2018).

Knopf, Kate Almquist. "Ending South Sudan's Civil War." Council on Foreign Relations Special Report no. 77. November 2016. Available at https://cfrd8-files

.cfr.org/sites/default/files/pdf/2016/11/CSR77_Knopf_South%20Sudan
.pdf (accessed February 8, 2018).

Kraus, Kimber. "Poverty in Angola: Causes, Updates and Statistics." Borgen Project. February 19, 2016. Available at https://borgenproject.org
/poverty-angola-causes-updates-statistics/ (accessed March 13, 2018).

Krause, Jana. "A Deadly Cycle: Ethno-Religious Conflict in Jos, Plateau State,
Nigeria." Geneva Declaration Secretariat Working Paper. 2011. Available
at https://reliefweb.int/sites/reliefweb.int/files/resources/GD-WP-Jos-
deadly-cycle.pdf (accessed March 25, 2018).

Lula Institute. "What Is the Lula Institute and What Does It Do." July 14, 2016.
Available at http://www.institutolula.org/what-is-the-lula-institute-and-
what-does-it-do (accessed March 18, 2018).

Nature Conservancy. "Sub-Saharan Africa's Urban Water Blueprint: Securing
Water through Water Funds and Other Investments in Ecological Infrastructure." August 2016. Available at https://thought-leadership-production
.s3.amazonaws.com/2016/08/24/20/30/36/9c3def4a-36d5-42f3-a844-
a3df1f0e6d01/Urban_Water_Blueprint Region_Africa_Aug2016.pdf
(accessed May 7, 2018).

Oceans beyond Piracy. "The State of Maritime Piracy 2014." June 8, 2015. Available at http://oceansbeyondpiracy.org/sites/default/files/attachments
/StateofMaritimePiracy2014.pdf (accessed January 21, 2018).

Pérouse de Montclos, Marc-Antoine. "Nigeria's Interminable Insurgency?
Addressing the Boko Haram Crisis." Chatham House Research Paper.
September 2014. Available at https://www.chathamhouse.org/sites/files
/chathamhouse/field/field_document/20140901BokoHaramPerousedeM
ontclos_0.pdf (accessed February 6, 2018).

Saferworld. "China's Growing Role in African Peace and Security." January 2011.
Available at https://www.saferworld.org.uk/resources/publications/500-
chinas-growing-role-in-african-peace-and-security (accessed March 27,
2018).

Trading Economics. "Crude Oil Production: Africa." March 2018. Available at
https://tradingeconomics.com/country-list/crude-oil-production?conti
nent=africa (accessed May 2, 2018).

Transparency International. "Corruption Perceptions Index 2016." January 25,
2017. Available at https://www.transparency.org/whatwedo/publication
/corruption_perceptions_index_2016 (accessed January 22, 2018).

Transparency International. "Corruption Perceptions Index 2017." February 15,
2018. Available at https://www.transparency.org/whatwedo/publication
/corruption_perceptions_index_2017 (accessed March 18, 2018).

Transparency International. "Our Organisation." 2018. Available at https://www
.transparency.org/whoweare/organisation (accessed May 16, 2018).

Transparency International. "What Are the Costs of Corruption." 2018. Available
at https://www.transparency.org/what-is-corruption#costs-of-corruption
(accessed May 16, 2018).

Uppsala University Uppsala Conflict Data Program. "Armed Conflict by Region,
1946–2016." 2017. Available at http://www.pcr.uu.se/digitalAssets/667/c_
667494-l_1-k_armed-conflict-by-region--1946-2016.pdf (accessed March 4,
2018).

Uppsala University Uppsala Conflict Data Program. "Definitions." 2018. Available at http://www.pcr.uu.se/research/ucdp/definitions/ (accessed March 4, 2018).

Uppsala University Uppsala Conflict Data Program. "UCDP Conflict Encyclopedia." 2018. Available at http://ucdp.uu.se/?id=1 (accessed March 4, 2018).

Werner, Ben. "China's Past Participation in RIMPAC Didn't Yield Intended Benefits of Easing Tensions." *U.S. Naval Institute News*. May 24, 2018. Available at https://news.usni.org/2018/05/24/33834 (accessed May 25, 2018).

World Economic Forum. "African Nations Are Powering Up the Business Rankings: What Lessons Can We Learn from Them?" November 14, 2017. Available at https://www.weforum.org/agenda/2017/11/african-countries-power-up-the-world-banks-business-rankings/ (accessed February 26, 2018).

World Economic Forum. "These Will Be Africa's Fastest Growing Economies in 2018." January 16, 2018. Available at https://www.weforum.org/agenda/2018/01/what-does-2018-hold-for-african-economies (accessed February 25, 2018).

MAGAZINES, NEWSPAPERS, AND NEWSWIRES

African Business

Africa News

Africa News Service

African Press Organization

Africa Research Bulletin

Agency Tunis Afrique Presse

AlArabiya.net

Algeria Press Service

All Africa

Angola Press Agency (Luanda, Angola)

BBC News

Beijing Review

Cameroon Tribune (Yaounde, Cameroon)

Cape Times (South Africa)

Capital (Addis Ababa, Ethiopia)

Daily Beast

Daily Monitor, Uganda (Kampala, Uganda)

Daily Nation, Kenya (Nairobi, Kenya)

Daily News Egypt

Daily Post (Lahore, Pakistan)

Daily Trust (Abuja, Nigeria)

Diplomat East Africa

East African

Economist

Financial Times

Foreign Affairs

France 24

Guardian

Gulf News (United Arab Emirates)

Houston Chronicle

Journal

London Evening Standard

Malaysian Government News

Mercury (South Africa)

Morocco World News

National (Abu Dhabi, United Arab Emirates)

National Geographic

National Interest

New African

NewsPoint (New Delhi, India)

New Statesman

New York Amsterdam News

New York Times

Nigerian Tribune (Oyo State, Nigeria)

People's Daily (Abuja, Nigeria)

Premium Official News

Quartz Africa

South African Official News (Pretoria, South Africa)

Star (South Africa)

States News Service

Sudan Tribune

Sunday Age

Sunday Times

Targeted News Service

Turkish Government News

UN News

UPI Security and Terrorism

U.S. Official News

Weekend Argus (South Africa)

Xinhua News Agency

BOOKS

Abegunrin, Olayiwola, ed. *Africa in the New World Order: Peace and Security Challenges in the Twenty-First Century*. Plymouth: Lexington Books, 2014.

Alden, Chris. *China in Africa*. London: Zed, 2007.

Allen, Tim, and Koen Vlassenroot, eds. *The Lord's Resistance Army: Myth and Reality*. London: Zed, 2010.

Amony, Evelyn. *I Am Evelyn Amony: Reclaiming My Life from the Lord's Resistance Army*. Edited with an Introduction by Erin Baines. Madison: University of Wisconsin Press, 2015.

Austen, Ralph A. *Trans-Saharan Africa in World History*. Oxford: Oxford University Press, 2010.

Auty, Richard M. *Sustaining Development in Mineral Economies: The Resource Curse Thesis*. Abingdon: Routledge, 1993.

Bayat, Asef. *Revolution without Revolutionaries: Making Sense of the Arab Spring*. Stanford, CA: Stanford University Press, 2017.

Boone, Catherine. *Property and Political Order in Africa: Land Rights and the Structure of Politics*. Cambridge: Cambridge University Press, 2014.

Bourne, Richard. *Lula of Brazil: The Story So Far*. Berkeley: University of California Press, 2008.

Branch, Adam. *Displacing Human Rights: War and Intervention in Northern Uganda*. Oxford: Oxford University Press, 2011.

Brautigam, Deborah. *The Dragon's Gift: The Real Story of China in Africa*. Oxford: Oxford University Press, 2009.

Brautigam, Deborah. *Will Africa Feed China?* Oxford: Oxford University Press, 2015.

Brown, William, and Sophie Harman, eds. *African Agency in International Politics*. Abingdon: Routledge, 2013.

Brownlee, Jason, Tarek Masoud, and Andrew Reynolds. *The Arab Spring: Pathways of Repression and Reform*. Oxford: Oxford University Press, 2015.

Cakaj, Ledio. *When the Walking Defeats You: One Man's Journey as Joseph Kony's Bodyguard*. London: Zed, 2016.

Callahan, William A., and Elena Barabantseva, eds. *China Orders the World: Normative Soft Power and Foreign Policy*. Baltimore, MD: Johns Hopkins University Press, 2012.

Campbell, Greg. *Blood Diamonds: Tracing the Deadly Path of the World's Most Precious Stones*. New York: Basic Books, 2004.

Carmody, Pádraig. *The New Scramble for Africa*. Cambridge: Polity, 2011.

Chau, Donovan C. *Exploiting Africa: The Influence of Maoist China in Algeria, Ghana, and Tanzania*. Annapolis, MD: Naval Institute, 2014.

Cheadle, Don, and John Prendergast. *Not on Our Watch: The Mission to End Genocide in Darfur and Beyond*. New York: Hyperion, 2007.

Chivvis, Christopher S. *The French War on Al Qa'ida in Africa*. Cambridge: Cambridge University Press, 2016.

Chorin, Ethan. *Exit the Colonel: The Hidden History of the Libyan Revolution*. New York: PublicAffairs, 2012.

Clarke, Walter, and Jeffrey Herbst, eds. *Learning from Somalia: The Lessons of Armed Humanitarian Intervention*. Boulder, CO: Westview Press, 1997.

Cline, Lawrence E. *The Lord's Resistance Army*. Santa Barbara, CA: Praeger, 2013.

Dallaire, Roméo. *Shake Hands with the Devil: The Failure of Humanity in Rwanda.* New York: Carroll & Graf, 2003.

Dau, John Bul with Michael S. Sweeney. *God Grew Tired of Us.* Washington, DC: National Geographic, 2007.

Decker, Alicia C. *In Idi Amin's Shadow: Women, Gender, and Militarism in Uganda.* Athens: Ohio University Press, 2014.

Deng, Alephonsion, Benson Deng, and Benjamin Ajak with Judy A. Bernstein. *They Poured Fire on Us from the Sky: The True Story of Three Lost Boys from Sudan.* New York: PublicAffairs, 2005.

De Waal, Alex, ed. *Demilitarizing the Mind: African Agendas for Peace and Security.* Trenton, NJ: Africa World Press, 2002.

Dolnik, Adam, and Herman Butime. *Understanding the Lord's Resistance Army Insurgency.* Hackensack, NJ: World Scientific, 2017.

Eichstaedt, Peter. *First Kill Your Family: Child Soldiers of Uganda and the Lord's Resistance Army.* Chicago: Lawrence Hill, 2009.

Eichstaedt, Peter. *Pirate State: Inside Somalia's Terrorism at Sea.* Chicago: Lawrence Hill, 2010.

Falola, Toyin, ed. *The Dark Webs: Perspectives on Colonialism in Africa.* Durham, NC: Carolina Academic, 2005.

Falola, Toyin, and Adebayo O. Oyebade. *Hot Spot: Sub-Saharan Africa.* Santa Barbara, CA: Greenwood, 2010.

Fergusson, James. *The World's Most Dangerous Place: Inside the Outlaw State of Somalia.* Boston, MA: Da Capo Press, 2013.

Finnström, Sverker. *Living with Bad Surroundings: War, History and Everyday Moments in Northern Uganda.* Durham, NC: Duke University Press, 2008.

Francis, David J., ed. *U.S. Strategy in Africa: AFRICOM, Terrorism, and Security Challenges.* Abingdon: Routledge, 2010.

French, Howard W. *China's Second Continent: How a Million Migrants Are Building a New Empire in Africa.* New York: Alfred A. Knopf, 2014.

Furnish, Timothy R. *Holiest Wars: Islamic Mahdis, Their Jihads, and Osama bin Laden.* Westport, CT: Praeger, 2005.

Geiß, Robin, and Anna Petrig. *Piracy and Armed Robbery at Sea: The Legal Framework for Counter-Piracy Operations in Somalia and the Gulf of Aden.* Oxford: Oxford University Press, 2011.

Gill, Peter. *Famine and Foreigners: Ethiopia since Live Aid.* Oxford: Oxford University Press, 2010.

Gill, Peter. *A Year in the Death of Africa: Politics, Bureaucracy, and the Famine.* London: Picador, 1986.

Gould, Michael. *The Biafran War: The Struggle for Modern Nigeria.* London: I.B.Tauris, 2013.

Gourevitch, Philip. *We Wish to Inform You That Tomorrow We Will Be Killed with Our Families: Stories from Rwanda.* London: Picador, 1998.

Green, Dominic. *Three Empires on the Nile: The Victorian Jihad, 1869–1899.* New York: Free Press, 2007.

Griffiths, Robert J. *U.S. Security Cooperation with Africa: Political and Policy Challenges.* Abingdon: Routledge, 2016.

Haas, Mark L., and David W. Lesch, eds. *The Arab Spring: The Hope and Reality of the Uprisings.* Boulder, CO: Westview Press, 2017.

Hansen, Stig Jarle. *Al-Shabaab in Somalia*. London: Hurst, 2013.

Harbeson, John W., and Donald Rothchild, eds. *Africa in World Politics: Constructing Political and Economic Order*. 6th ed. Boulder, CO: Westview Press, 2017.

Harding, Andrew. *The Mayor of Mogadishu: A Story of Chaos and Redemption in the Ruins of Somalia*. New York: St. Martin's Press, 2016.

Harrison, Graham, ed. *Global Encounters: International Political Economy, Development and Globalization*. London: Palgrave Macmillan, 2005.

Hatzfeld, Jean. *Machete Season: The Killers in Rwanda Speak*. New York: Farrar, Straus and Giroux, 2005.

Haywood, Robert, and Roberta Spivak. *Maritime Piracy*. Abingdon: Routledge, 2012.

Heerten, Lasse. *The Biafran War and Postcolonial Humanitarianism: Spectacles of Suffering*. Cambridge: University of Cambridge Press, 2017.

Hentz, James J., ed. *Routledge Handbook of African Security*. Abingdon: Routledge, 2014.

Herbst, Jeffrey. *States and Power in Africa: Comparative Lessons in Authority and Control*. 2nd ed. Princeton, NJ: Princeton University Press, 2014.

Hochschild, Adam. *King Leopold's Ghost: A Story of Greed, Terror, and Heroism in Colonial Africa*. New York: Houghton Mifflin Harcourt, 1998.

Horowitz, Donald L. *Ethnic Groups in Conflict*. 2nd ed. Berkeley: University of California Press, 2000.

James, Lawrence. *Empires in the Sun: The Struggle for the Mastery of Africa*. New York: Pegasus, 2017.

Kapteijns, Lidwien. *Clan Cleansing in Somalia: The Ruinous Legacy of 1991*. Philadelphia: University of Pennsylvania Press, 2013.

Keen, David. *Useful Enemies: When Waging Wars Is More Important Than Winning Them*. New Haven, CT: Yale University Press, 2012.

Kraska, James. *Contemporary Maritime Piracy: International Law, Strategy, and Diplomacy at Sea*. Santa Barbara, CA: Praeger, 2011.

Larkin, Bruce D. *China and Africa, 1949–1970: The Foreign Policy of the People's Republic of China*. Oakland: University of California Press, 1973.

Lim, Louisa. *The People's Republic of Amnesia: Tiananmen Revisited*. Oxford: Oxford University Press, 2014.

Lofkrantz, Jennifer, and Olatunji Ojo, eds. *Ransoming, Captivity and Piracy in Africa and the Mediterranean*. Trenton, NJ: Africa World Press, 2016.

Mamdani, Mahmood. *Citizen and Subject: Contemporary Africa and the Legacy of Late Colonialism*. Princeton, NJ: Princeton University Press, 1996.

Mazov, Sergey. *A Distant Front in the Cold War: The USSR in West Africa and the Congo, 1956–1964*. Stanford, CA: Stanford University Press, 2010.

McNeill, J.R. *Something New under the Sun: An Environmental History of the Twentieth-Century World*. New York: W. W. Norton, 2000.

Mejia, Maximo Q., Jr., Chie Kojima, and Mark Sawyer, eds. *Piracy at Sea*. Heidelberg: Springer, 2013.

Meredith, Martin. *The Fate of Africa: A History of the Continent since Independence*. New York: PublicAffairs, 2005.

Meredith, Martin. *The Fortunes of Africa: A 5000-Year History of Wealth, Greed, and Endeavour*. New York: PublicAffairs, 2014.

Murphy, Martin N. *Somalia, the New Barbary? Piracy and Islam in the Horn of Africa*. London: Hurst, 2010.

Namikas, Lise. *Battleground Africa: Cold War in the Congo, 1960–1965*. Stanford, CA: Stanford University Press, 2013.

Netto, Andrei. *Bringing Down Gaddafi: On the Ground with the Libyan Rebels*. Translated by Michael Marsden. New York: St. Martin's Press, 2014.

Nye, Joseph S., Jr. *Soft Power: The Means to Success in World Politics*. New York: PublicAffairs, 2004.

Nzongola-Ntalaja, Georges. *The Congo: From Leopold to Kabila, A People's History*. London: Zed, 2002.

Oloya, Opiyo. *Child to Soldier: Stories from Joseph Kony's Lord's Resistance Army*. Toronto: University of Toronto Press, 2013.

Oyebade, Adebayo, ed. *The United States' Foreign Policy in Africa in the 21st Century: Issues and Perspectives*. Durham, NC: Carolina Academic, 2014.

Posner, Daniel N. *Institutions and Ethnic Politics in Africa*. Cambridge: Cambridge University Press, 2005.

Prunier, Gérard. *Darfur: A 21st Century Genocide*. Ithaca, NY: Cornell University Press, 2005.

Reno, William. *Corruption and State Politics in Sierra Leone*. Cambridge: Cambridge University Press, 1995.

Reveron, Derek S., and Kathleen A. Mahoney-Norris. *Human Security in a Borderless World*. Boulder, CO: Westview Press, 2011.

Rice, Andrew. *The Teeth May Smile but the Heart Does Not Forget*. New York: Metropolitan, 2009.

Richards, Paul. *Fighting for the Rain Forest: War, Youth, and Resources in Sierra Leone*. Oxford: James Currey, 1996.

Roberts, Andrew, ed. *The Colonial Moment in Africa: Essays on the Movement of Minds and Materials, 1900–1940*. Cambridge: Cambridge University Press, 1990.

Rotberg, Robert I., ed. *China into Africa: Trade, Aid, and Influence*. Baltimore, MD: Brookings Institution Press, 2008.

Rotberg, Robert I., ed. *When States Fail: Causes and Consequences*. Princeton, NJ: Princeton University Press, 2004.

Russell, Alec. *Big Men, Little People: The Leaders Who Defined Africa*. New York: New York University Press, 2000.

Saad, Elias N. *Social History of Timbuktu: The Role of Muslim Scholars and Notables, 1400–1900*. Cambridge: Cambridge University Press, 1983.

Schmidt, Elizabeth. *Foreign Intervention in Africa: From the Cold War to the War on Terror*. Cambridge: Cambridge University Press, 2013.

Shaxson, Nicholas. *Poisoned Wells: The Dirty Politics of African Oil*. Basingstoke: Palgrave, 2007.

Strang, G. Bruce. *Collision of Empires: Italy's Invasion of Ethiopia and Its International Impact*. Farnham: Ashgate, 2013.

Swaine, Michael D., and Ashley J. Tellis. *Interpreting China's Grand Strategy: Past, Present, and Future*. Santa Monica, CA: RAND, 2000.

Taylor, Ian. *China and Africa: Engagement and Compromise*. Abingdon: Routledge, 2006.

Thomas-Hope, Elizabeth, ed. *Climate Change and Food Security: Africa and the Caribbean*. Abingdon: Routledge, 2017.

Vandewalle, Dirk. *A History of Modern Libya*. 2nd ed. Cambridge: Cambridge University Press, 2012.

Van Ginkel, Bibi, and Frans-Paul van der Putten, eds. *The International Response to Somali Piracy: Challenges and Opportunities.* Leiden: Martinus Nijhoff, 2010.

Watson, Cynthia. *Combatant Commands: Origins, Structure, and Engagements.* Santa Barbara, CA: Praeger, 2010.

Williams, Paul D. *War and Conflict in Africa.* Cambridge: Polity, 2011.

Williams, Susan. *Who Killed Hammarskjöld? The UN, the Cold War and White Supremacy in Africa.* Oxford: Oxford University Press, 2014.

Woodward, Peter. *Crisis in the Horn of Africa: Politics, Piracy, and the Threat of Terror.* London: I.B.Tauris, 2013.

Wrong, Michela. *In the Footsteps of Mr. Kurtz: Living on the Brink of Disaster in Mobutu's Congo.* New York: HarperCollins, 2001.

JOURNAL ARTICLES

Aapengnuo, Clement Mweyang. "Misinterpreting Ethnic Conflicts in Africa." *Africa Security Brief: A Publication of the Africa Center for Strategic Studies,* no. 4 (April 2010): 1–6.

Achvarina, Vera, and Simon F. Reich. "No Place to Hide: Refugees, Displaced Persons, and the Recruitment of Child Soldiers." *International Security* 31, no. 1 (Summer 2006): 127–164.

Adem, Seifudein. "Sino-Optimism in Africa." *African Studies Quarterly* 16, no. 3/4 (December 2016): 7–16.

Aguilar, Renato, and Andrea Goldstein. "The Chinisation of Africa: The Case of Angola." *World Economy* 32, no. 11 (November 2009): 1543–1562.

Akanji, Olajide. "A Critical Analysis of the Security Crisis in Post-Gaddafi Libya." *Africa Insight* 45, no. 2 (September 2015): 11–26.

Albro, Robert. "Anthropology and the Military: AFRICOM, 'Culture' and Future of Human Terrain Analysis." *Anthropology Today* 26, no. 1 (February 2010): 22–24.

Alesbury, Andrew. "A Society in Motion: The Tuareg from the Pre-Colonial Era to Today." *Nomadic Peoples* 17, no. 1 (Summer 2013): 106–125.

Ali-Koor, Abdisaid Musse. "Islamist Extremism in East Africa." *Africa Security Brief: A Publication of the Africa Center for Strategic Studies,* no. 32 (August 2016): 1–8.

Anderson, Noel. "Peacekeepers Fighting a Counterinsurgency Campaign: A Net Assessment of the African Union Mission in Somalia." *Studies in Conflict and Terrorism* 37, no. 11 (November 2014): 936–958.

Angstrom, Jan. "The Sociology of Studies of Ethnic Conflict: Explaining the Causal Status of Development." *Civil Wars* 3, no. 3 (Autumn 2000): 23–44.

Ankomah, Baffour. "Turkey and Africa Pledge Co-Operation." *New African,* no. 567 (December 2016): 76–78.

António, Nelson Santos, and Shaozhuang Ma. "China's Special Economic Zone in Africa: Context, Motivations and Progress." *Euro Asia Journal of Management* 25, no. 1/2 (December 2015): 79–103.

Arcand, Jean-Louis, Aude-Sophie Rodella-Boitreaud, and Matthias Rieger. "The Impact of Land Mines on Child Health: Evidence from Angola." *Economic Development and Cultural Change* 63, no. 2 (January 2015): 249–279.

Badru, Pade. "Ethnic Conflict and State Formation in Post-Colonial Africa: A Comparative Study of Ethnic Genocide in the Congo, Liberia, Nigeria, and Rwanda-Burundi." *Journal of Third World Studies* 27, no. 2 (Fall 2010): 149–169.

Barlow, Eeben. "The Rise and Fall—and Rise Again of Boko Haram." *Harvard International Review* 37, no. 4 (Summer 2016): 16–20.

Benabdallah, Lina. "China's Peace and Security Strategies in Africa: Building Capacity Is Building Peace?" *African Studies Quarterly* 16, no. 3/4 (December 2016): 17–34.

Bevan, James. "The Myth of Madness: Cold Rationality and 'Resource' Plunder by the Lord's Resistance Army." *Civil Wars* 9, no. 4 (December 2007): 343–358.

Bøås, Morten, and Liv Elin Torheim. "The Trouble in Mali—Corruption, Collusion, Resistance," *Third World Quarterly* 34, no. 7 (2013): 1279–1292.

Bogdan, Attila. "The United States and the International Criminal Court: Avoiding Jurisdiction through Bilateral Agreements in Reliance on Article 98." *International Criminal Law Review* 8, no. 1/2 (January 2008): 1–54.

Boutros-Ghali, Boutros. "The Five Principles." *Chinese Journal of International Law* 3, no. 2 (2004): 373–377.

Bunte, Jonas B. "Wage Bargaining, Inequality, and the Dutch Disease." *International Studies Quarterly* 60, no. 4 (December 2016): 677–692.

Burgos, Sigfrido, and Sophal Ear. "China's Oil Hunger in Angola: History and Perspective." *Journal of Contemporary China* 21, no. 74 (March 2012): 351–367.

Calhoun, Craig. "Revolution and Repression in Tiananmen Square." *Society* 26, no. 6 (September/October 1989): 21–38.

Cavas, Christopher P. "The Chinese Navy Saves the Day!" *U.S. Naval Institute Proceedings* 144, no. 3 (March 2018): 1–2. Available at https://www.usni.org/magazines/proceedings/2018-03/chinese-navy-saves-day (accessed June 16, 2018).

Clark, Lisa F. "Implementing Multilevel Food and Nutrition Security Frameworks in Sub-Saharan Africa: Challenges and Opportunities for Scaling Up Pulses in Ethiopia." *Journal of Rural Social Sciences* 32, no. 1 (2017): 56–76.

Constantinou, Costas M., and Sam Okoth Opondo. "Engaging the 'Ungoverned': The Merging of Diplomacy, Defence and Development." *Cooperation and Conflict* 51, no. 3 (September 2016): 307–324.

Cornelissen, Scarlett. "Awkward Embraces: Emerging and Established Powers and the Shifting Fortunes of Africa's International Relations in the Twenty-First Century." *Politikon* 36, no. 1 (April 2009): 5–26.

Da Cruz, José de Arimatéia, and Laura K. Stephens. "The U.S. Africa Command (AFRICOM): Building Partnership or Neo-Colonialism of U.S.–Africa Relations?" *Journal of Third World Studies* 27, no. 2 (Fall 2010): 193–213.

Davies, Martyn, Peter Draper, and Hannah Edinger. "Changing China, Changing Africa: Future Contours of an Emerging Relationship." *Asian Economic Policy Review* 9, no. 2 (July 2014): 180–197.

Debos, Marielle. "Fluid Loyalties in a Regional Crisis: Chadian 'Ex-Liberators' in the Central African Republic." *African Affairs* 107, no. 427 (April 2008): 225–241.

Dedham, Patrick. "AFRICOM: Enabling African Partners." *Army Communicator* 40, no. 1 (Spring 2015): 21–23.

De Morais, Rafael Marques. "The New Imperialism: China in Angola." *World Affairs* 173, no. 6 (March/April 2011): 67–74.

Desgrandchamps, Marie-Luce. "Dealing with 'Genocide': The ICRC and the UN during the Nigeria-Biafra War, 1967–1970." *Journal of Genocide Research* 16, no. 2/3 (July 2014): 281–297.

Devlin-Foltz, Zachary. "Africa's Fragile States: Empowering Extremists, Exporting Terrorism." *Africa Security Brief: A Publication of the Africa Center for Strategic Studies*, no. 6 (August 2010): 1–8.

De Waal, Alex. "When Kleptocracy Becomes Insolvent: Brute Causes of the Civil War in South Sudan." *African Affairs* 113, no. 452 (July 2014): 347–369.

Dorward, Andrew, and Jonathan Kydd. "The Malawi 2002 Food Crisis: The Rural Development Challenge." *Journal of Modern African Studies* 42, no. 3 (September 2004): 343–361.

Dowden, Richard. "A Convenient War: Uganda's President Has Ensured That the West Is Dependent on Him." *Prospect*, no. 222 (September 2014): 44–47.

Dumbuya, Peter A. "AFRICOM in US Transformational Diplomacy." *Journal of Global South Studies* 33, no. 1 (Spring 2016): 115–146.

Dunn, Brian J. "The AFRICOM Queen." *Military Review* 96, no. 3 (May–June 2016): 50–61.

Ehwarieme, William, and Nathaniel Umukoro. "Civil Society and Terrorism in Nigeria: A Study of the Boko Haram Crisis." *International Journal on World Peace* 32, no. 3 (September 2015): 25–48.

Ekmen, Pelin. "From Riches to Rags—the Paradox of Plenty and Its Linkage to Violent Conflict." *Goettingen Journal of International Law* 3, no. 2 (2011): 473–493.

Elbadawi, Ibrahim, and Nicholas Sambanis. "Why Are There So Many Civil Wars in Africa? Understanding and Preventing Violent Conflict." *Journal of African Economies* 9, no. 3 (October 2000): 244–269.

Ellis, Stephen, and Gerrie ter Haar. "Religion and Politics: Taking African Epistemologies Seriously." *Journal of Modern African Studies* 45, no. 3 (September 2007): 385–401.

Enuka, Chuka. "China's Military Presence in Africa: Implications for Africa's Woobling Peace." *Journal of Asia Pacific Studies* 2, no. 1 (May 2011): 97–118.

Enuka, Chuka. "The Forum on China-Africa Cooperation (FOCAC): A Framework for China's Re Engagement with Africa in the 21st Century." *Pakistan Journal of Social Sciences* 30, no. 2 (December 2010): 209–218.

Erickson, Andrew S., and Austin M. Strange. "China's Blue Soft Power: Antipiracy, Engagement, and Image Enhancement." *Naval War College Review* 68, no. 1 (Winter 2015): 71–91.

Fasanya, Ismail O., Adegbemi B. O. Onakoya, and Misbaudeen A. Adabanija. "Oil Discovery and Sectoral Performance in Nigeria: An Appraisal of the Dutch Disease." *IUP Journal of Applied Economics* 12, no. 2 (April 2013): 25–40.

Fokuo, Isaac. "Fresh Opportunities for Africa in a Multipolar World." *African Business* 51, no. 442 (June 2017): 42–43.

Frahm, Ole. "Making Borders and Identities in South Sudan." *Journal of Contemporary African Studies* 33, no. 2 (April 2015): 251–267.

Frynas, Jedrzej George, and Geoffrey Wood. "Patrimonialism and Petro-Diamond Capitalism: Peace, Geopolitics and the Economics of War in Angola." *Review of African Political Economy* 28, no. 90 (December 2001): 587–606.

Gebhard, Carmen, and Simon J. Smith. "The Two Faces of EU-NATO Cooperation: Counter-Piracy Operations off the Somali Coast." *Cooperation and Conflict* 50, no. 1 (March 2015): 107–127.

Glennerster, Rachel, Edward Miguel, and Alexander D. Rothenberg. "Collective Action in Diverse Sierra Leone Communities." *Economic Journal* 123, no. 568 (May 2013): 285–316.

Glück, Zoltán. "Piracy and the Production of Security Space." *Environment and Planning D: Society and Space* 33, no. 4 (August 2015): 642–659.

Godwin, O. P. "Embracing the Challenges for Africa." *Environment* 44, no. 4 (May 2002): 8–19.

Grimm, Sven. "China–Africa Cooperation: Promises, Practice and Prospects." *Journal of Contemporary China* 23, no. 90 (November 2014): 993–1011.

Guenther, Bruce. "The Asian Drivers and the Resource Curse in Sub-Saharan Africa: The Potential Impacts of Rising Commodity Prices for Conflict and Governance in the DRC." *European Journal of Development Research* 20, no. 2 (June 2008): 347–363.

Gwin, Peter. "The Burning Heart of Africa." *National Geographic* 231, no. 5 (May 2017): 56–77.

Haggblade, Steven. "Unscrambling Africa: Regional Requirements for Achieving Food Security." *Development Policy Review* 31, no. 2 (March 2013): 149–176.

Hammond, L., and D. Maxwell, "The Ethiopian Crisis of 1999–2000: Lessons Learned, Questions Unanswered," *Disasters* 26, no. 3 (September 2002): 262–279.

Harkin, James. "The Stillborn State: The Creation of South Sudan Has Brought War Not Peace—Those Who Would Divide Syria Should Take Note." *Prospect*, no. 246 (September 2016): 58–62.

Harman, Sophie, and William Brown. "In from the Margins? The Changing Place of Africa in International Relations." *International Affairs* 89, no. 1 (January 2013): 69–87.

Hasan, Sayed M., and Daud Hassan. "Current Arrangements to Combat Piracy in the Gulf of Guinea Region: An Evaluation." *Journal of Maritime Law and Commerce* 47, no. 2 (April 2016): 171–217.

Hassen, Ibrahim Worku, Mekdim Dereje, Bart Minten, and Kalle Hirvonen. "Diet Transformation in Africa: The Case of Ethiopia." *Agricultural Economics* 48, no. 1 (November 2017): 73–86.

Hastings, Justin V., and Sarah G. Phillips. "Maritime Piracy Business Networks and Institutions in Africa." *African Affairs* 114, no. 457 (October 2015): 555–576.

Heisbourg, François. "A Surprising Little War: First Lessons of Mali." *Survival* 55, no. 2 (April–May 2013): 7–18.

Hofstedt, Todd A. "China in Africa: An AFRICOM Response." *Naval War College Review* 62, no. 3 (Summer 2009): 79–100.

Holslag, Jonathan. "China's Evolving Behaviour in Africa and the Options of Cooperation with Europe." *Journal of Current Chinese Affairs* 40, no. 4 (2011): 3–16.

Howard, R. T. "Biafra 50 Years On: The Civil War That Resulted from the Division of Nigeria Was a Major Human Disaster That Should Not Be Forgotten." *History Today* 67, no. 6 (June 2017): 36–41.

Howe, Herbert M. "Private Security Forces and African Stability: The Case of Executive Outcomes." *Journal of Modern African Studies* 36, no. 2 (June 1998): 307–331.

Ikome, Francis Nguendi. "After Gaddafi and Mubarak: A New North African Role in the African Union." *Africa Insight* 42, no. 3 (December 2012): 68–90.

Ingiriis, Mohamed Haji. "How Somalia Works: Mimicry and the Making of Mohamed Siad Barre's Regime in Mogadishu." *Africa Today* 63, no. 1 (Fall 2016): 57–82.

Issa, Jahi, and Salim Faraji. "The Obama Administration: Revisiting and Reconsidering AFRICOM." *Journal of Pan African Studies* 2, no. 9 (March 2009): 260–263.

Jere, ReGina Jane. "How Africa Can Feed Itself: Beyond Food Aid and Corporate Greed." *New African*, no. 537 (March 2014): 8–16.

Jiabao, Wen. "Carrying Forward the Five Principles of Peaceful Coexistence in the Promotion of Peace and Development." *Chinese Journal of International Law* 3, no. 2 (2004): 363–368.

Kainja, Jimmy. "Malawi: Will 'Cashgate' Sink Joyce Banda?" *New African*, no. 538 (April 2014): 54–55.

Kamal-Deen, Ali. "The Anatomy of Gulf of Guinea Piracy." *Naval War College Review* 68, no. 1 (Winter 2015): 93–118.

Kamas, Michael G., David W. Pope, and Ryan N. Propst. "Exploring a New System of Command and Control: The Case for Africa Command." *Joint Force Quarterly*, no. 87 (October 2017): 82–87.

Kamerling, Susanne, and Frans-Paul van der Putten. "An Overseas Naval Presence without Overseas Bases: China's Counter-Piracy Operation in the Gulf of Aden." *Journal of Current Chinese Affairs* 40, no. 4 (2011): 119–146.

Kamlongera, Paul Justice. "Making the Poor 'Poorer' or Alleviating Poverty? Artisanal Mining Livelihoods in Rural Malawi." *Journal of International Development* 23, no. 8 (November 2011): 1128–1139.

Kaplan, Robert D. "The Coming Anarchy: How Scarcity, Crime, Overpopulation, Tribalism, and Disease Are Rapidly Destroying the Social Fabric of Our Planet." *Atlantic* 273, no. 2 (February 1994): 44–77.

Kaplan, Roger. "Losing Mali: The Administration Will Not Avoid Further Involvement in an African Tribal War." *American Spectator* 45, no. 10 (December 2012/January 2013): 32–42.

Kaunert, Christian, and Kamil Zwolski. "Somalia versus Captain 'Hook': Assessing the EU's Security Actorness in Countering Piracy off the Horn of Africa." *Cambridge Review of International Affairs* 27, no. 3 (September 2014): 593–612.

Kaye, Julie, and Daniel Béland. "The Politics of Ethnicity and Post-Conflict Reconstruction: The Case of Northern Ghana." *Journal of Contemporary African Studies* 27, no. 2 (April 2009): 177–200.

Keith, Nouman. "Global Food Crisis Response Program: A World Bank Initiative for Food Security and Hunger Fight." *Scholedge International Journal of Multidisciplinary and Allied Studies* 2, no. 10 (October 2015): 5–10.

Keizire, Boaz Blackie. "What Does Africa Need?" *African Business*, no. 400 (August/September 2013): 39–40.

Kim, Yejoo. "China's Soft Power Expansion in Africa through Industrialisation: Opportunities and Challenges." *Africa Insight* 44, no. 4 (March 2015): 1–13.

Kisangani, Emizet F. "Social Cleavages and Politics of Exclusion: Instability in the Central African Republic." *International Journal on World Peace* 32, no. 1 (March 2015): 33–59.

Kluver, Randolph. "Rhetorical Trajectories of Tiananmen Square." *Diplomatic History* 34, no. 1 (January 2010): 71–94.

Kopiński, Dominik, Andrzej Polus, and Wojciech Tycholiz. "Resource Curse or Resource Disease? Oil in Ghana." *African Affairs* 112, no. 449 (October 2013): 583–601.

Kwaja, Chris. "Nigeria's Pernicious Drivers of Ethno-Religious Conflict." *Africa Security Brief: A Publication of the Africa Center for Strategic Studies*, no. 14 (July 2011): 1–8.

Langer, Arnim, Abdul Raufu Mustapha, and Frances Stewart. "Diversity and Discord: Ethnicity, Horizontal Inequalities and Conflict in Ghana and Nigeria." *Journal of International Development* 21, no. 4 (May 2009): 477–482.

Lanteigne, Marc. "Fire over Water: China's Strategic Engagement of Somalia and the Gulf of Aden Crisis." *Pacific Review* 26, no. 3 (July 2013): 289–312.

Lartey, Emmanuel K. K. "Financial Openness and the Dutch Disease." *Review of Development Economics* 15, no. 3 (August 2011): 556–568.

Le Billon, Philippe. "Angola's Political Economy of War: The Role of Oil and Diamonds, 1975–2000." *African Affairs* 100, no. 398 (January 2001): 55–80.

Leslie, Agnes Ngoma. "Introduction China–Africa Relations: Political and Economic Engagement and Media Strategies." *African Studies Quarterly* 16, no. 3/4 (December 2016): 1–6.

Leslie, Michael. "The Dragon Shapes Its Image: A Study of Chinese Media Influence Strategies in Africa." *African Studies Quarterly* 16, no. 3/4 (December 2016): 161–174.

Liang, Wei. "China's Soft Power in Africa: Is Economic Power Sufficient?" *Asian Perspective* 36, no. 4 (2012): 667–692.

Lloyd, Robert B. "Ungoverned Spaces and Regional Insecurity: The Case of Mali." *School of Advanced International Studies Review of International Affairs* 36, no. 1 (Winter/Spring 2016): 133–141.

Lombard, Louisa, and Sylvain Batianga-Kinzi. "Violence, Popular Punishment, and War in the Central African Republic." *African Affairs* 114, no. 454 (January 2015): 52–71.

Mahard, Sean Patrick. "Blackwater's New Battlefield: Toward a Regulatory Regime in the United States for Privately Armed Contractors Operating at Sea." *Vanderbilt Journal of Transnational Law* 47, no. 1 (January 2014): 331–369.

Maiangwa, Benjamin. "Revisiting the Nigeria-Biafra War: The Intangibles of Post-War Reconciliation." *International Journal of World Peace* 33, no. 4 (December 2016): 39–67.

Marchal, Roland. "Briefing: Military (Mis)adventures in Mali." *African Affairs* 112, no. 448 (July 2013): 486–497.

Martins, Pedro M. G. "Do Large Capital Inflows Hinder Competitiveness? The Dutch Disease in Ethiopia." *Applied Economics* 45, no. 8 (March 2013): 1075–1088.

McBain, Sophie. "After the Brics, the Mints." *New Statesman* 143, no. 5193 (January 17–23, 2014): 30–31.

McFerson, Hazel M. "Extractive Industries and African Democracy: Can the 'Resource Curse' Be Exorcised?" *International Studies Perspectives* 11, no. 4 (November 2010): 335–353.

Menkhaus, Ken. "The Crisis in Somalia: Tragedy in Five Acts," *African Affairs* 106, no. 204 (July 2007): 357–390.

Meyers, Jeffrey. "Abyssinia Out of the Shadows." *History Today* 65, no. 11 (November 2015): 49–54.

Mlambo, Courage, Audrey Kushamba, and More Blessing Simawu. "China–Africa Relations: What Lies Beneath?" *Chinese Economy* 49, no. 4 (2016): 257–276.

Moody, Jessica. "Senegal's Gas Discoveries—Gift or Curse." *African Business* 51, no. 438 (February 2017): 62–63.

Morgan, M. J. "Making the Most of Africa's Resources." *African Business* 46, no. 382 (January 2012): 32–33.

Mullins, Christopher W., and Dawn L. Rothe. "Gold, Diamonds, and Blood: International State-Corporate Crime in the Democratic Republic of the Congo." *Contemporary Justice Review* 11, no. 2 (June 2008): 81–99.

Mwangi, Oscar Gakuo. "State Collapse, *Al-Shabaab*, Islamism, and Legitimacy in Somalia." *Politics, Religion, and Ideology* 13, no. 4 (December 2012): 513–527.

Ndlovu-Gatsheni, Sabelo J., and Victor Ojakorotu. "Surveillance over a Zone of Conflict: Africom and the Politics of Securitisation of Africa." *Journal of Pan African Studies* 3, no. 6 (March 2010): 94–110.

Neethling, Theo. "The Lord's Resistance Army in the DRC: The Problem of Ungoverned Spaces and Related Regional Insecurity." *Africa Insight* 43, no. 1 (June 2013): 32–44.

Nhemachena, Charles, Greenwell Matchaya, and Sibusiso Nhlengethwa. "Strengthening Mutual Accountability and Performance in Agriculture in Southern Africa." *South African Journal of Science* 113, no. 5/6 (May/June 2017): 50–56.

Nincic, Donna. "Maritime Piracy in Africa: The Humanitarian Dimension." *African Security Review* 18, no. 3 (September 2009): 2–16.

Obuah, Emmanuel. "Trade between China and Africa: Trends, Changes, and Challenges." *International Journal of China Marketing* 2, no. 2 (2012): 74–88.

Ojakorotu, Victor. "Nature's Gift, Man's Curse: Natural Resources and Civil Conflicts in the Niger Delta and Cabinda." *Africa Insight* 41, no. 3 (December 2011): 111–126.

Okenyodo, Oluwakemi. "Governance, Accountability, and Security in Nigeria." *Africa Security Brief: A Publication of the Africa Center for Strategic Studies*, no. 31 (June 2016): 1–8.

Omeje, Kenneth, and Nicodemus Minde. "The SPLM Government and the Challenges of Conflict Settlement, State-Building and Peace-Building in South Sudan." *Africa Insight* 45, no. 1 (June 2015): 52–67.

Osinowo, Adeniyi Adejimi. "Combating Piracy in the Gulf of Guinea." *Africa Security Brief: A Publication of the Africa Center for Strategic Studies*, no. 30 (February 2015): 1–8.

Østebø, Terje. "Islamic Militancy in Africa." *Africa Security Brief: A Publication of the Africa Center for Strategic Studies*, no. 23 (November 2012): 1–8.

Otto, Lisa. "Westward Ho! The Evolution of Maritime Piracy in Nigeria." *Portuguese Journal of Social Science* 13, no. 3 (September 2014): 313–329.

Owusu-Sekyere, Emmanuel, Reneé van Eyden, and Francis M. Kemegue. "Remittances and the Dutch Disease in Sub-Saharan Africa: A Dynamic Panel Approach." *Contemporary Economics* 8, no. 3 (September 2014): 289–298.

Pérouse de Montclos, Marc-Antoine. "Maritime Piracy in Nigeria: Old Wine in New Bottles?" *Studies in Conflict and Terrorism* 35, no. 7/8 (July/August 2012): 531–541.

Phayal, Anup, Prabin B. Khadka, and Clayton L. Thyne. "What Makes an Ex-Combatant Happy? A Micro-Analysis of Disarmament, Demobilization, and Reintegration in South Sudan." *International Studies Quarterly* 59, no. 4 (December 2015): 654–668.

Picciotto, Robert. "Conflict Prevention and Development Co-Operation in Africa: An Introduction." *Conflict, Security, and Development* 10, no. 1 (March 2010): 1–25.

Ping, Jean. "The Crisis in Mali: Outline the Course to Peace and Stability." *Harvard International Review* 35, no. 3 (Winter 2014): 22–25.

Power, Marcus. "Angola 2025: The Future of the 'World's Richest Poor Country' as Seen through a Chinese Rear-View Mirror." *Antipode* 44, no. 3 (June 2012): 993–1014.

Pricopi, Marius. "Tactics Used by the Terrorist Organisation Boko Haram." *Scientific Bulletin* 21, no. 1 (2016): 40–45.

Radon, Jenik, and Sarah Logan. "South Sudan: Governance Arrangements, War, and Peace." *Journal of International Affairs* 68, no. 1 (Fall/Winter 2014): 149–167.

Riley, Liam. "Operation Dongosolo and the Geographies of Urban Poverty in Malawi." *Journal of Southern African Studies* 40, no. 3 (May 2014): 443–458.

Rowan, Chris. "The China–Africa Partnership: Working for Whom?" *Contemporary Review* 291, no. 1692 (Spring 2009): 56–64.

Samset, Ingrid. "Conflict of Interests or Interests in Conflict? Diamonds and War in the DRC." *Review of African Political Economy* 29, no. 93/94 (September–December 2002): 463–480.

Samy, Yiagadeesen. "China's Aid Policies in Africa: Opportunities and Challenges." *Round Table* 99, no. 406 (February 2010): 75–90.

Sıradağ, Abjurrahim. "Explaining the Conflict in Central African Republic: Causes and Dynamics." *Epiphany: Journal of Transdisciplinary Studies* 9, no. 3 (2016): 86–103.

Sodipo, Michael Olufemi. "Mitigating Radicalism in Northern Nigeria." *Africa Security Brief: A Publication of the Africa Center for Strategic Studies*, no. 26 (August 2013): 1–8.

Sweeney, Michael S. "The Spoiling of the World: In South Sudan Decades of Civil War Led to Independence—And Yet More War." *Military History Quarterly: Quarterly Journal of Military History* 29, no. 1 (Autumn 2016): 76–84.

Taguem Fah, Gilbert L. "Dealing with Africom: The Political Economy of Anger and Protest." *Journal of Pan African Studies* 3, no. 6 (March 2010): 81–93.

Thomas, David. "We See Africa as a Bright Spot." *African Business* 50, no. 433 (August/September 2016): 16–17.

Thomas, Linda E. "South African Independent Churches, Syncretism, and Black Theology." *Journal of Religious Thought* 53, no. 2/1 (January 1997): 39–50.

Udefuna, Patrick Nanadozie, Magnus Emeka Madu, Chiedo Akalefu, and Fadila Jumare. "Effective Community Policing: A Panacea to Inefficiency and Impunity in Nigerian Police." *International Journal of Humanities and Social Science* 4, no. 4 (2014): 260–267.

Van Vliet, Martin. "Weak Legislatures, Failing MPs, and the Collapse of Democracy in Mali." *African Affairs* 113, no. 450 (January 2014): 45–66.

Venkatasawmy, Rama. "Ethnic Conflict in Africa: A Short Critical Discussion." *Transcience* 6, no. 2 (2015): 26–37.

Versi, Anver. "A Future Full of Light." *African Business* 49, no. 417 (March 2015): 77.

Vreÿ, Francois. "African Maritime Security: A Time for Good Order at Sea." *Australian Journal of Maritime and Ocean Affairs* 2, no. 4 (2010): 121–132.

Vreÿ, Francois. "Bad Order at Sea: From the Gulf of Aden to the Gulf of Guinea." *African Security Review* 18, no. 3 (September 2009): 17–30.

Vreÿ, Francois. "Four Hubs of Maritime Insecurity off Africa: From Anti-Piracy to Anti-Crime?" *Acta Criminologica: Southern African Journal of Criminology* 29, no. 2 (2016): 156–171.

Walker, Timothy. "Maritime Security in West Africa." *African Security Review* 22, no. 2 (June 2013): 85–91.

Ward, William E. "Engaging AFRICOM." *Military Technology* 33, no. 1 (January 2009): 298–300.

Weir, Gary E. "Fish, Family, and Profit: Piracy and the Horn of Africa." *Naval War College Review* 62, no. 3 (Summer 2009): 15–30.

Weiss, Thomas G., and Martin Welz. "The UN and the African Union in Mali and Beyond: A Shotgun Wedding?" *International Affairs* 90, no 4 (July 2014): 889–905.

Welz, Martin. "Briefing: Crisis in the Central African Republic and the International Response." *African Affairs* 113, no. 453 (October 2014): 601–610.

White, Nicholas J. "The Settlement of Decolonization and Post-Colonial Economic Development: Indonesia, Malaysia, and Singapore Compared." *Journal of the Humanities and Social Sciences of Southeast Asia and Oceania* 173, no. 2 (April 2017): 208–241.

Wig, Tore. "Peace from the Past: Pre-Colonial Political Institutions and Civil Wars in Africa." *Journal of Peace Research* 53, no. 4 (July 2016): 509–524.

Williams, Paul D. "After Westgate: Opportunities and Challenges in the War against Al-Shabaab." *International Affairs* 90, no. 4 (July 2014): 907–923.

Williams, Paul D. "The African Union's Peace Operations: A Comparative Analysis." *African Security* 2, no. 2/3 (November 2009): 97–118.

Williams, Paul D. "Thinking about Security in Africa." *International Affairs* 83, no. 6 (November 2007): 1021–1038.

Williams, Paul D., and Arthur Boutellis. "Partnership Peacekeeping: Challenges and Opportunities in the United Nations–African Union Relationship." *African Affairs* 113, no. 451 (April 2014): 254–278.

Winn, Neil, and Alexandra Lewis. "European Union Anti-Piracy Initiatives in the Horn of Africa: Linking Land-Based Counter-Piracy with Maritime Security and Regional Development." *Third World Quarterly* 38, no. 9 (September 2017): 2113–2128.

Xiaoyang, Tang. "Models of Chinese Engagement in Africa's Extractive Sectors and Their Implications." *Environment* 56, no. 2 (March/April 2014): 27–29.

Zhang, Guo-Qiang, and Sidney Kraus. "Constructing Public Opinion and Manipulating Symbols: China's Press Coverage of the Student Movement in 1989." *Journalism and Mass Communication Quarterly* 72, no. 2 (Summer 1995): 412–425.

Zulu, Leo Charles. "Neoliberalization, Decentralization and Community-Based Natural Resources Management in Malawi: The First Sixteen Years and Looking Ahead." *Progress in Development Studies* 12, no. 2/3 (April 2012): 193–212.

Index

About the Author

WILLIAM A. TAYLOR is an associate professor of security studies at Angelo State University in San Angelo, Texas. After graduating from the U.S. Naval Academy with honors and distinction, he participated in the navy's highly selective Voluntary Graduate Education Program, through which he earned an MA degree in history from the University of Maryland. He also completed an MA degree in security studies at Georgetown University, graduating with honors. He then earned MPhil and PhD degrees in history from George Washington University.

Taylor won grants from the Society for Military History / ABC-CLIO (2010), Harry S. Truman Library Institute (2013), and Angelo State University Faculty Research Enhancement Program (2013) and a George C. Marshall/Baruch Fellowship (2012) to research *Every Citizen a Soldier: The Campaign for Universal Military Training after World War II* (Texas A&M University Press, 2014), which won a 2015 Crader Family Book Prize Honorable Mention. Taylor won grants from the Dwight D. Eisenhower Foundation (2014), Gerald R. Ford Foundation (2014), Harry S. Truman Library Institute (2015), U.S. Army Military History Institute (2015), Lyndon B. Johnson Foundation (2016), and Angelo State University Faculty Research Enhancement Program (2014) and a University of North Texas Libraries Special Collections Fellowship (2015) to research *Military Service and American Democracy: From World War II to the Iraq and Afghanistan Wars* (University Press of Kansas, 2016). Taylor won the 2016 Angelo State University President's Award for Faculty Excellence in Research/Creative Endeavor and the 2016 Texas Tech University System Chancellor's Council Distinguished Research Award.

Taylor maintains research interests in contemporary security issues in Africa, civil–military relations, security studies, military history, grand strategy, and defense policy. He has contributed to 17 other books and has published more than 70 reference articles and book reviews. His books are housed in more than 900 libraries throughout the United States and in more than 35 countries around the world, including Armenia, Australia, Bulgaria, Canada, China, Colombia, Curaçao, Denmark, Ecuador, Egypt, France, Germany, Iraq, Ireland, Israel, Italy, Jamaica, Japan, Lebanon, Malaysia, Namibia, the Netherlands, New Zealand, Peru, Philippines, Qatar, Singapore, South Africa, Switzerland, Taiwan, Thailand, Trinidad and Tobago, Turkey, United Arab Emirates, and the United Kingdom. His work has appeared in *African Studies Quarterly, Human Rights Review, Strategic Studies Quarterly, Choice, Joint Force Quarterly, Journal of Military History, Naval War College Review, Army History, U.S. Naval Institute Proceedings, On Point: The Journal of Army History, Journal of American History, Maryland Historical Magazine, Marine Corps University Journal, Michigan War Studies Review, Journal of America's Military Past, North Dakota History: Journal of the Northern Plains, U.S. Military History Review,* and *H-Net Reviews,* among others.

In addition to his academic credentials, Taylor served as an officer in the U.S. Marine Corps for more than six years, holding posts in III Marine Expeditionary Force, Expeditionary Force Development Center, and Marine Corps Combat Development Command.

www.ingramcontent.com/pod-product-compliance
Lightning Source LLC
Chambersburg PA
CBHW071417290326
41932CB00046B/1908